The Curse of Souw

Kagoiano

ROY WAGNER

The Curse of Souw

Principles of Daribi Clan Definition and Alliance
in New Guinea

THE UNIVERSITY OF CHICAGO PRESS
Chicago and London

Library of Congress Catalog Card Number: 67-25524

THE UNIVERSITY OF CHICAGO PRESS, CHICAGO & LONDON
The University of Toronto Press, Toronto 5, Canada

to Kagoiano, son of Bapo,
of Kurube' (Weriai) Clan,
Karimui

Men black as birds perch
aslant the light
on the soaked grey platform house,
over them blows
a white gleam of rain,
their eyes tight with a fear
that needs no gods, with the merchandising
of death, they pull the sharp stink
of woodsmoke through their guts; being
men, they are not often brave, they kill
seldom and sloppily, but hold their lives firm
against the horror man makes
to try his own heart; beyond
the sprawling forms
vines and leaf-furze blot the late
afternoon, cloud boils
through the humped ranges
seeding the land with myths.

Foreword

The hallmark of anthropology is good field work; for, if anthropology is anything, it is the study of culture—its nature, its history, its forms, its processes and so on. Without good field work, there is only that knowledge of other cultures that expresses our concern for confirming our own special worth and anxieties— *we* are civilized, they are savage; *we* worship God, they worship demons and spirits; *our* wars are righteous and moral, theirs are barbaric.

There is only one way to learn another culture and that is to live it for some time. One must learn to speak it, to do it, to think it, to hear it, to taste it; and the good field worker learns to dream it and to talk it in his sleep as well. The problem is to find out what that other culture's parts are, in its own terms; how those parts relate as that culture formulates its relations; who its players are and whether they have players or not.

All too often the anthropologist goes into the field and, instead of *asking* the natives what their cultural categories consist in, he *tells* the natives what kinship and economics and politics are all about and glosses some native term with a good, well-established technical term and leave it at that.

But, Dr. Wagner's book is based on some very fine field work. In it he tells of Daribi culture, of what its parts are and of how they are linked. As one reads his live and lucid account, one has the feeling of knowing and understanding. In some of its features, Daribi culture is not unlike our own, and so understanding seems to come easily. But, in other ways, Daribi is so unlike anything that we know that the problem of understanding and of communicating might have become an insurmountable one.

It is at such points that good field work is just not enough. Legion are the stories of anthropologists who are such magnificent field workers that they actually went native, or should have, who could do the tribal dances but not describe them, who could become possessed by the native spirits but not discuss them. Such stories are no surprise, of course, since one of the fundamental fantasies of anthropology is that somewhere there must be a life really worth living.

The task of communicating what is barely understandable in another culture is but one side of the coin. The other is of building a workable theory of culture. For if we have a good enough theory of culture, then none of its various forms is incomprehensible, since the very essence of a good theory is that it makes the incomprehensible into that which is understood.

This is the strength of Dr. Wagner's book. He has engineered, and entirely without the use of a shotgun, a wedding of very fine field work and first-rate theory into an account of Daribi which is understandable, which explains and which has far wider and more general significance than just the explanation of Daribi itself.

He does this by concentrating on Daribi culture as a system of symbols, by undertaking to describe what those symbols consist in, their native definition and the implications of their definition. This he distinguishes clearly from what he calls the anthropologist's model of the system, and his distinction between the symbols of the culture and the anthropologist's model is a fundamental one.

But there is no need for me to guide the reader through this book, for the clarity of its exposition is remarkable. Dr. Wagner is not only a good anthropologist, he is a literate one.

DAVID M. SCHNEIDER

Center for Advanced Study in the
Behavioral Sciences

Preface

The purpose of this study is to describe and analyze the social structure of the Daribi people of east New Guinea as parsimoniously as possible within a theoretical framework applicable generally to societies characterized by large, multifunctional segments, and referring to the total social system as seen in the light of native symbolic categories. Because of the prevailing state of controversy and confusion regarding the theoretical issues involved, an extended discussion of the position taken here has been necessary, and this is to be found in the Introduction and the concluding chapter. The study is based on field work done in the Mount Karimui area, Territory of Papua–New Guinea, from November, 1963, to February, 1965.

The ideas presented have emerged gradually during the course of the field work and subsequent analysis of the data. The specific form that they assume here was conceived in October, 1965, and during an attack of malaria in December, 1965, and was subsequently revised during the spring and summer of 1966.

My field work was carried out on a grant from the New Guinea Native Religious Project of the University of Washington, under the direction of Drs. James B. Watson and Kenneth E. Read. The funds for the Project were provided by the Bollingen Foundation and the University of Washington. The writing of the doctoral dissertation (at the University of Chicago) from which this book was adapted was facilitated by a NIGMS Training Fellowship granted by the University of Chicago.

I am indebted to Drs. Watson and Read for their happy choice of the Daribi, a people who represent the relatively little studied range of societies existing between the Highlands and the coast of New Guinea, as research subjects. Dr. Read showed sympathy and understanding in the problems involved in my embarkation for New Guinea, and Dr. Watson offered advice and encouragement during the course of the field work itself.

The Administration of the Territory, represented by the Department of Native Affairs, has been most cooperative. Dr. Charles Julius, the late Government Anthropologist, graciously extended to me every form of assistance during my passages through Port Moresby. Local officials in Goroka and elsewhere were likewise most hospitable. Patrol Officers Ernest Mitchell, Anthony Wright, and especially Michael Bell have done their utmost to accommodate my work. I am grateful also to Mr. Ivan Champion for the interview he graciously granted me at Konedobu.

I would like to thank very heartily those private persons who helped to make my stay in New Guinea a pleasant one, including especially Mr. David Cole and his wife Rosemary (formerly) of Bena Bena; Ken and Roselyn Mesplay; as well as Christie, Lisa, and Kent Philip, of Karepa Mission Station, Karimui, and Val Tolley and Angela, and Jack and Monica Frame of Goroka. The Trefrys of Walio and the Mac Donalds of Noruai proved themselves good friends and good neighbors.

The people of Kurube' and Hagani Clans, and indeed all the Daribi people with whom I came in contact, responded to me with unexpected warmth and sympathy and with that comfortable courtesy which their culture stresses. I should mention especially my informants as contributors to this study: Tąre, Hanari, Yapenugiai, Sąri, Kiru, Ogwane, Waro, and Pini. Kagoiano (frontispiece) of Kurube' has helped as informant, analyst, companion, and confidant to an extent for which any acknowledgment would be insufficient. My cook, Yul, of Kilau Clan, Gumine, has rendered service for which a warm friendship could only have been the basis. I should not neglect to mention the children who contributed elementally to lighten the difficulties of field work: Kiape, Kiba', Sobe, and Masizi of Kurube'; Sidawi of Peria; and Domuai of Hagani.

Dr. David M. Schneider is in a sense the *pagebidi* of this work. The theoretical position taken here could scarcely have been formulated without the insights communicated in his paper *"Some Muddles in the Models."* He very kindly undertook to receive and examine my field notes as they were produced, and, within the limits of the situation, to educate me in the field. His criticism and advice during the formulation and writing of the present work have been greatly appreciated. For all of this, and for his assistance generally, I should like to express my deepest gratitude.

Drs. Fred Eggan and Lloyd A. Fallers have also read the drafts and commented extensively when the main thesis was proposed. Each has offered, in addition, helpful suggestions and much appreciated encouragement, for which I offer my thanks. Dr. Milton Singer has likewise offered valuable criticism in the initial stages of the formulation.

I am deeply indebted to the Anthropology Department of the University of Chicago for its generously offered assistance and encouragement in the publication of this work, and wish to express my sincerest gratitude to all concerned. Special thanks are due to Dr. Fallers for his assistance in preparing and presenting the manuscript.

I would like to thank Professor Daniel R. Irwin, Mr. Tso-Hwa Lee, and Mr. John McHale of the Southern Illinois University Cartographic Service for their preparation of the contour map of Karimui. A final word of thanks is due to the geographer Kerry J. Pataki, of the University of Washington, for his help and advice in preparing the maps.

Contents

Illustrations

Figures

Plates

Maps

Tables

Introduction

In his history *New Guinea: The Last Unknown*, Gavin Souter speaks of a certain Captain J. A. Lawson, who in 1875 published a book in London announcing his discovery in the interior of New Guinea of a mountain higher than Everest, a waterfall more impressive than Niagara, and

daisies the size of sunflowers, spiders as big as dinnerplates, scorpions ten inches long, an "extraordinary fern bearing black fronds," deer with long manes of silky hair, a giant crimson lily whose perfume clung to Lawson's hands for several hours after he had touched it, an ox resembling the American bison, huge apes "repulsive in feature yet human-like to an extraordinary degree," a tree measuring eighty-four feet around the bole and a striped feline larger and more handsomely striped (black and chestnut on white) than the Indian tiger.[1]

Perhaps because it is "the last unknown," New Guinea has served as a promising *tabula rasa* for the projective imagination; negritoes, "Semitic tribes," and African lineage systems have been discovered there, and the average American maintains a colorful image of a landmass rife with harems, headhunters, and cannibalistic orgies.

Projection in itself, though possibly objectionable, is scarcely to be avoided; it is the means by which men, as participants in the various cultures, extend the realm of the "known" by applying

[1] Gavin Souter, *New Guinea: The Last Unknown* (New York: Taplinger Publishing Company, 1966), p. 3.

the range of their symbolization to the data and impressions of the "unknown." It comprises the mythic component of science, the scientist's intuition and hypothesizing, Tennyson's "fairy tales of science," and Goethe's *exakte sinnliche Fantasie,* as well as the imagistic fantasy of the poet. Science, however, in contrast to poetry, which judges the value of its creations in terms of their innate, imaginative appeal, must apply a critique based on fidelity to the data themselves. Thus, while the creations of the scientist are projections, they must be carefully controlled ones, formulated in the light of his investigations of the data and subject to criticism on that basis.

Even so, the practice of extending the realm of the "known" by applying one's symbolizations to the "unknown" can easily become a means of finding what one wants to find, especially if one's criteria of comparison are loosely conceived. If skin color and stature alone are considered, then New Guinea has "negritoes"; if a certain type of nose is of primary importance, it has "Semitic tribes"; and if some features of social structure are emphasized while others are ignored, there are African-type lineages in the Highlands. The criteria used for comparison, therefore, serve as a control on the scientist's efforts to consolidate his grasp of the "known" world by extending his symbolizations into new areas, just as the data themselves provide an ultimate critique of the content of his theories. The criteria are a function of his own outlook, his standards for what is meaningful in the data available; they provide, in short, an accurate and precisely defined framework within which the variation in observed data can be meaningfully dealt with.

In approaching an "unknown" such as New Guinea, it is important therefore to examine first one's own standards of comparison. To what kinds of data do they apply, and how great a range of variation do they admit? Are our standards sufficiently abstract to admit whatever we may observe which contrasts with known phenomena into an understandable pattern of variation, or will they force us to obscure the contrasts and differences by stressing instead those features which accord with an external, introduced type specimen? Within a loosely construed framework of evaluation, the application of "models" referring to actual, historical phenomena elsewhere and resulting in a kind of analogy has been the basis of much of the objectionable "projecting" mentioned above. Captain Lawson's mountain "higher than Everest" is simply a bigger and better Mt. Everest; and negritoes, Semitic tribes, and African lineages likewise furnish stereotypes which some have found useful in accounting for the diverse and "new" phenomena encountered in New Guinea. If we are to make sense out of New Guinea, we must find criteria within which its mountains, physical anthropology, tribal history, and social structure can be meaningfully compared to and contrasted with like phenomena elsewhere in the world, rather than explained away as merely additional "examples" of the latter. We are concerned here with social structure; let us therefore examine the problem of finding adequate criteria for comparison in this area.

In his article "African Models in the New Guinea Highlands," J. A. Barnes has characterized the ways in which New Guinea Highland societies as a type fail to conform to the features of the traditional models that have been proposed for a number of African societies. He is aware of "the mistake of comparing the *de facto* situation in a Highland community, as shown by an ethnographical census, with a nonexistent and idealized set of conditions among the Nuer, wrongly inferred from Evans-Pritchard's discussion of Nuer social structure" [2] and remarks that "this procedure gives an exaggerated picture of the differences between the Highlands and Africa." [3] Such a procedure would indeed compound the dissimilarities involved by adding the discrepancies which can be expected to exist between a model and a group "on the ground" to whatever differences may exist in the ethnographies of the two areas.

Barnes has instead chosen to generalize the "major differences in social structure" between Africa and Highland New Guinea in terms of the ethnographies available to him. Whereas the African societies seem to incorporate descent as a means of recruitment and stress a "lineage principle," he points out that

[2] J. A. Barnes, "African Models in the New Guinea Highlands," *Man* 62 (1962), p. 5.
[3] *Ibid.*

in most, though not in all, Highland societies the dogma of descent is absent or is held only weakly; the principle of recruitment to a man's father's group operates, but only concurrently with other principles, and is sanctioned not by appeal to the notion of descent as such but by reference to the obligations of kinsfolk, differentiated according to relationship and encompassed within a span of only two or three generations. In each generation a substantial majority of men affiliate themselves with their father's group and in this way it acquires some agnatic continuity over the generations. It may be similar in demographic appearance and *de facto* kinship ties to a patrilineal group in which accessory segments are continually being assimilated to the authentic core, but its structure and ideology are quite different.[4]

He goes on to contrast the general, large-scale characteristics of social structure in the two areas, particularly as regards the role of descent and group affiliation, and concludes that "in general this contrast might be phrased as between bounded affiliation in Africa and unbounded affiliation in the Highlands; or between African group solidarity and New Guinea network cohesion." [5]

Although it is sometimes difficult to distinguish between model and data in his article (as for instance in the matter of solidarity, which has been a central theoretical concern for many of the African ethnographers), Barnes has presented a convincing and detailed account of the divergent trends in social structure characteristic of Africa and Highland New Guinea respectively. The essence of his discussion is that the models developed for the description of African societies will, in the light of these differences, prove inadequate for the analysis of Highland New Guinea societies. This brings us once again to the matter of analogy and criterion, for the African models, if Barnes's observations are correct, bear the imprint of a regional ethnographic tendency and are hence too particularistic for our purposes. Are there other models which would be more appropriate to New Guinea? What standards have we, apart from the data themselves, to evaluate models, and what is the common ground on which all models of social structure may be compared?

[4] *Ibid.,* p. 6.
[5] *Ibid.,* p. 8.

The distribution of societies based on large, multifunctional segments over widespread but disjoined areas of the world has provided not only one of the surest and strictest tests of the theories of social anthropology but also an unfailing source of theoretical controversy in this area. To a large extent this controversy has been the result of the necessity for developing models to explain the social structure of particular peoples and of applying these models to other societies. Given the interests and commitments of anthropologists and theoreticians in our contemporary academic environment, such a procedure is to a large degree unavoidable; one studies the general as it is manifested in the particular, because generalizations about a social system should proceed from an intimate knowledge of that system. The difficulties and controversies arise from the application of models and generalizations derived for one particular society to others, although in fact societies of this type tend to base their social systems on principles derived from a limited range of basic concepts.

The nature of human critical thinking, which proceeds by the discovery of differences and similarities, coupled with this basic similarity of human societies, made it inevitable that the first attempts to compare and contrast social systems would be in terms of analogy. Our terms "marriage" and "descent" are in fact derived from elements which function in our own social system and are applied to functions which we take to be analogous within other systems. For a long time before and after the establishment of anthropology as a science, comparisons of societies were made in terms of such analogous functions or institutions; marriage among the Yakut or the Inca was contrasted with marriage in England, and the analogous institution (which had to be—broadly—defined) was "marriage." Customs differed, but the institution remained the same, for it was analogous. The relationship of marriage to the other elements of the social system was assumed—it was given by the place of marriage on the list of institutions. Malinowski, in his development of Functionalism, sought to relate the existence of such institutions to a paradigm of basic human "needs," substituting this as a framework of criteria over which the individual societies vary.

Since Malinowski, or more accurately since the work of Radcliffe-Brown, we have learned that beneath the superficial resemblances among certain institutions in the various human societies there lies a real diversity in social organization and that such a thing as marriage can play widely differing roles in different societies. It has become apparent that in societies characterized by large, multifunctional segments, institutions such as marriage and descent play vital roles in the political and social organization and that analogies drawn with institutions in our own society can scarcely furnish an adequate explanation of their interrelationship.

With the increasing sophistication of our views of social structure brought about by such realizations, specific models have been constructed for the description of societies characterized by segments, and these models have obviated the possibility and the necessity of drawing analogies between our own institutions and those of such societies. Yet the notions of marriage and descent, among others, remain the "common denominators" of these models; it is these "institutions" that we proceed to discover in all societies and use as points of comparison for the models developed to describe them. They are *de facto* criteria for the comparison of societal models. It is true that these notions are no longer based on analogies with usages within our own society. A great and still continuing effort has been made to define them abstractly enough to serve as broad categories within which differing conceptions may be compared; hence has arisen the proliferation of "types" of descent (unilineal, bilateral, double unilineal), of marriage (including "prescriptive" and "preferential" as well as positive and negative marriage rules), and of such things as postmarital residence.

Given such criteria, and their preordained subtypes, it is possible to label or classify each society encountered as having one kind of descent, a marriage rule, a rule of postmarital residence, and so on. Where a "new" kind of descent is encountered, the opportunity arises of adding a term to the list, redefining and broadening the category of "descent." Thus the problem of ordering and sharpening our criteria becomes a process of working out a satisfactory definition of descent or marriage, of dividing and articulating its subtypes in a satisfactory manner. It is also possible to describe a given social structure in a synthetic way by referring to such subtypes; one can speak of a system characterized by a certain kind of descent, a certain kind of marriage rule, a kind of postmarital residence, and proceed to show how the kinship system and its underlying symbolizations interrelate these usages into a logical whole.

Given this procedure, a picture emerges of a range of societies, each made up of bits labeled "patriliny," "prescriptive marriage," or "virilocality" in diverse but often recurring patterns. The variation among societies is manifested in the variety of combinations. With such a picture we can show how societies vary in a number of particulars, such as marriage type, but it becomes difficult when we wish to determine how they vary with regard to a number of interlinked usages, or as whole systems. Statistical correlations can be drawn up, showing perhaps that "unilineal descent and virilocality show a 12.8 per cent correlation," but these simply measure a frequency. We have no criteria for the variation among societies seen as whole systems, for the principles by which in each instance a "kind" of descent emerges in interaction with a "kind" of marriage rule, and so forth.

Yet, are these principles not the very essence of the kind of variation we are trying to measure? Is it not the total social system itself and the conceptions around which it is organized that determine the existence of something which we label "bilateral descent" and that combine it with other usages which we classify as a "negative marriage rule" in a viable organic unity? To borrow a phrase from mathematics, such principles of organization constitute the "second derivative" of the variation which we otherwise apprehend in the form of differing combinations of descent and marriage types.

The more complex models that have been proposed, those of alliance and descent theory, address themselves to the total social system, the matrix from which the various types of descent and marriage emerge in each particular case. These models show the elements of descent, marriage, and so forth as component, interlinked facets of a single system. In their comprehensive explanation of total social systems, these models are superior to the "classificatory" approach described above, but in their adherence to one "kind" of interrelationship of elements in each case, they sacrifice any flexibility in dealing with variation. They are models, not criteria, for social systems; either they fit a given instance, or they do not fit.

Schneider has effectively criticized the widespread, indiscriminate application of a "total system model"; he argues that "too much time, effort, and energy are spent in mending the model, in protecting it from new data, in insuring its survival against attacks." [6] Such models are particularistic, not primarily because of their ethnographic regionality, as are Barnes's "African models," but because each implies one and only one kind of interrelationship among the elements. What we miss is a set of criteria governing a range over which societies vary with respect to the ordering of such elements as descent and marriage into social systems.

As we have remarked above, it is these elements which provide points of comparison between models of social structure. But we have also seen that "elements" of this sort can be viewed as arbitrarily isolated portions of a total system, generated, as it were, by the principles which govern it. We can choose between a view of social systems as varying constellations of these elements or one which stresses the principles by which they are ordered and generated.

If we choose the latter, what criteria are we to use? They must be specific enough to denote the relevant functions toward which the ordered elements are oriented and yet sufficiently general to preclude the kind of theoretical particularism that we have seen in the application of "total system models." Societies of the type we have been discussing are characterized by large, multifunctional segments, which have been subjected to a varying treatment by theoreticians, ranging from the ideal categories of Lévi-Strauss to the venerable, quite English, corporate institutions of Fortes. Schneider has used the definition and interrelationship of these segments as ad hoc criteria in his comparison of the descent and alliance theory models. In speaking of alliance

---

[6] David M. Schneider, "Some Muddles in the Models: or, How the System Really Works," in *The Relevance of Models for Social Anthropolgy,* A.S.A. Monograph No. 1 (London: Tavistock Publications; New York: Frederick A. Praeger, 1965), p. 78.

theory, in which marriage interrelates the segments, he treats these as "issues":

> there are, then, two closely connected issues which create more unnecessary confusion than there need be. One is the issue of how the segments are conceptually defined, and of their "formal" relationship to each other. The conceptual definition has a "function," but it is not the function of a "degree of corporateness" as a concrete state of affairs. Its function consists of its logical implications at a conceptual level. The second issue is the issue of how marriage interrelates two segments.[7]

Unit definition and interrelationship, in this sense, are the functions toward whose fulfillment the entire complex of interrelated elements—descent, marriage, relationship, and so on—is oriented. They order or organize the relationships of these elements to one another, or, more accurately, they subsume a complex of relationships and rules which we variously identify as "descent" or "marriage." The composite picture of a society made up of units, conceptually defined and interrelated in certain ways, is, as it were, the result of the working out of such rules. We can, if we choose, describe such a society in terms of its rules of recruitment, marriage, or relationship, or we can approach the functions of unit definition and interrelationship directly, in an effort to find principles which order these details.

I propose to take the latter approach in the pages which follow and use unit definition and alliance, or interrelationship, as criteria for the comparison of whole social systems. As in alliance theory, the units are conceptual entities, but they may, in addition, correspond to groups "on the ground." I will treat the Daribi system of symbolic categories, as these have emerged during the course of interviewing and analysis, as the means by which the natives themselves conceptualize and deal with their social system; and these, together with specific examples from my field notes and experience, constitute the data to be evaluated in terms of the criteria. As the native symbolizations furnish the ultimate points of reference by which the details, or rules of the system, are determined, so we may apply these symbolizations to the functions of unit

[7] *Ibid.,* p. 56.

definition and alliance, in terms of which the whole complex of rules is oriented, and derive general principles for the system as a whole.

It would be unwise, however, to disregard the details of recruitment or marriage, for instance, and imagine that the system could be adequately described simply with reference to unit definition and alliance. Such an approach would lack analytic precision, for it would render impossible any kind of "breakdown" and detailed explication of the ways in which the principles themselves operate. We should rather recognize that the details of recruitment, marriage, and relationship are the specific ways in which the principles act and interact to fulfill the functions of unit definition and alliance.

Among the categories themselves which anthropologists have used to study such details there is a great diversity. "Descent," in the strictest sense of the term, is a "loaded" word, implying a fusion of the function of recruitment with one of the ways in which recruitment may be effected—that of connection through substance. In its less strict connotation, "descent" refers generally to connection through substance, which is a kind of native symbolization, a concept which can be more accurately rendered by the term "consanguinity." The term "recruitment," taken by itself, refers directly to an aspect of unit definition, and it is this which I shall use. I shall apply the term "consanguinity" to the native symbolization of connection through substance. "Filiation" and "complementary filiation" are parts of a model and derive from theoretical axioms which are at a variance with the approach taken here. "Marriage" and "affinity" are conceptions which can be universally applied, though they play varying roles, and will form part of our theoretical framework. I shall use the term "exchange" with reference to a kind of native symbolization as this enters into the conceptualization of social structure. Although there are no specific referents for such functions, the ways in which people may be related to each other, and the ways in which they may be related to units, might equally well be seen as details of the social structure, and these will also be taken into consideration.

What follows is an attempt to show how such details, ordered in terms of the generalized functions of unit definition and alliance, can be used to derive a set of ideal principles, based on native symbolizations, which govern the fulfillment of these functions.

It would require an extraordinarily talented and articulate person, and one with a great deal of experience, to express adequately the "soul" of Karimui, the emotional impact on a westerner of the landscape, overcast, with an often piercing melancholy, choked with life yet somehow immensely desolate, or of its people, with their dour, almost boastful pride in a culture which is a curse, whose demons are named for diseases, whose powers are the ill-wills of the wronged, whose triumph is the negation of a negation. There is no science for such an understanding, for there are no criteria by which to judge it, yet it is another, perhaps more satisfying, approach to the native culture. I have chosen an easier task.

I

On the Edge of
the Highlands

The Daribi and Their Environment

The Migaru Page Daribi, or "Daribi at the base of Mount Karimui," inhabit the Karimui Plateau to the west of Karimui Patrol Post and the adjacent limestone ridge-country lying farther to the west, at the intersection of the Eastern Highlands, Southern Highlands, and Gulf Districts in the Territory of Papua–New Guinea. Although the area under the jurisdiction of Karimui Patrol Post straddles the Papua–New Guinea frontier, it is administered for the sake of convenience from Goroka, capital of the Eastern Highlands District. The Karimui area comprises the Karimui, Bomai, Daribi, Pio, and Tura census divisions, with a total population which fluctuates in the neighborhood of 5,000, the bulk of which is concentrated in the Karimui and Daribi Divisions. The Patrol Post and its airstrip were built in 1960, after contact had been established with the people by a series of yearly census-patrols beginning in 1953. The first patrol officer at Karimui was R. B. Aitken, who, together with his successor, Patrol Officer Dwyer, managed to get in touch with all the native groups in the area. Some early patrols seem to have reached Karimui from Kikori, the administrative center for the Gulf District to the south, and one of these is said to have been mistakenly attacked by men of Masi Clan.

Much earlier, in 1936, the area was visited by Ivan Champion,[1] whose memory is preserved today in the given name Semene, a

[1] Ivan Champion, "The Bamu-Purari Patrol," *Geographical Journal* 96 (1940), No. 4.

Daribi version of "Champion." The name "Karimui" was first applied to the mountain by Champion, who adapted it from a language spoken by his carriers, from the Southern Highlands.[2] "Kari" is the term for "mountain" in that language; "-mui" refers to the mountain itself, and is perhaps a form of the Pawaia name for it, Mio. Somewhat before Champion's visit, Leahy and Dwyer passed through the area in the final leg of their epic 1930 journey through the Highlands. Like Champion, they found the natives remarkably friendly, though their account complains of the mud, the incessant overcast, and the sickly condition of the people.[3] These complaints are echoed in some of the early patrol reports. Daribi remember Leahy and Dwyer as "the two men who came with the big dog," and they also recall Champion's visit, but otherwise reports of contacts with Europeans passing through the region in this early period are difficult to identify. There seems to have been a "twilight period" of vague, general awareness of strange, light-skinned people living in peripheral areas during the thirties and forties; it was probably then that "a man named Korigiai, from the Pio, whose brother's name was Oro, told everyone that if they did a certain type of 'singsing,' the Europeans would come." The singsing involved men sitting cross-legged on the floor, with the women sitting on their laps, and also promiscuous intercourse. "Some men did this, others just watched." Daribi claim that they first heard of Europeans from the Tųdawe (Pawaia).

Karimui Patrol Post is staffed by a patrol officer, a small contingent of native policemen and translators, and a native clerk. A European Lutheran missionary and his family live nearby at the Karepa Mission Station, and the Seventh Day Adventists maintain a medical aid post on the station as well as out-stations at Iuro and Iogoramaru villages. Both missions maintain schools at the station for native children. Native "evangelists" of the two missions live in many of the major villages. A government medical aid post was established at the station in 1964, and the Lutheran

[2] Ivan Champion, personal communication (1963).
[3] Michael Leahy and M. Crain, *The Land That Time Forgot: Adventures and Discoveries in New Guinea* (New York: Funk and Wagnalls Company, 1937).

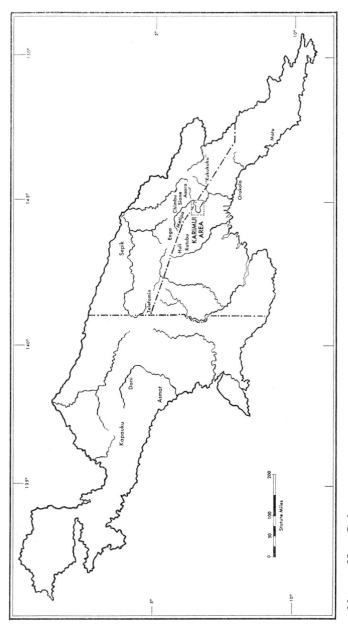

MAP 1.—*New Guinea.*

Mission plans to build a hospital at Karepa. Mr. David Trefry of the Summer Institute of Linguistics had been working with the Pawaia language at Walio, where he has lived with his family intermittently since the opening of the station. Mr. George Mac Donald of the same organization has since begun work on the Daribi (Mikaru) language at Noruai (Weriai), where he has been living with his family. Dr. Robert Glasse spent a period of about a month at Bosiamaru in September, 1962, studying social structure and its relationship to leprosy.

The people living to the west of the Patrol Post, by far the largest group in the Karimui area, call themselves Daribi. This name probably results from a combination of the word *dari*, translatable as "together with," and the particle -*bi*, which seems to function as a plural-marker for kinship terms, and may be derived from *bidi*, "man/men" or "person/people." An approximate gloss for Daribi would then be "those who are together," or "the together-people." The name Mikaru, used by the early patrol officers in reference to these people, has been retained by the Summer Institute of Linguistics and by other linguists, including S. A. Wurm,[4] especially with regard to the language. This term is derived from *Migaru*, the Daribi name for Mount Karimui, and its use probably originated with the word *Mengaru*, the name used by Chimbu-speakers to the north for the Daribi. The Daribi people at Karimui distinguish themselves by the term Migaru Page Daribi ("Daribi at the base of Mount Karimui") from the other groups of Daribi-speakers. These, insofar as they are known, include the Daribi who live on the volcanic Plateau of Mount Suąru in the Bomai Census Division to the northwest, and who have recently undergone severe depopulation, coupled with culture change as a result of the immigration of Highlanders from the Marigl area to the north; the Urubidi, a group probably of phratry size living to the southwest of Mount Karimui along the Bore River, a tributary of the Tua, who are presently in the initial stages of contact; and the Daribi-speakers

---

[4] S. A. Wurm, "Australian New Guinea Highlands Languages and the Distribution of Their Typological Features," *American Anthropologist* 66 (1964), No. 4, Part 2 (special publication; *New Guinea, The Central Highlands*, ed. J. B. Watson).

said to live at Lake Tebera, to the south. The southern and south-western limits of the language and its dialects are not at present known.

In addition to the Daribi, a pocket of perhaps 1,000 Tῃdawe-(Pawaia-) speakers live at Mount Karimui, in the valley of the Sena River to the east of the Patrol Post. It is perhaps significant that, although a very high percentage of these are bilingual, speaking Daribi as well as their own language, comparatively few Daribi speak Tῃdawe. The two languages do not seem to be related to any significant degree. Intermarriage between the two linguistic groups is so common that they may be said to con-stitute a single society. Although the main stock of Pawaia-speakers begins at the Pio River, to the south of Mount Karimui, evidence suggests that the Sena River group has been in associa-tion with the Daribi for a long time and that, as the Daribi claim, they reached their present location by moving eastward ahead of the Daribi along the northern side of the mountain, rather than spreading directly north from the Pio. Two versions of the origin myth which I collected state that the ancestors of the Daribi and the Tῃdawe lived together at Bῃmaru on the Tua River; and Obe, a very old Tῃdawe man of Iuro, claims that in the time of his father his people lived at Bosiamaru, and the Daribi lived at Boromaru, on the western side of Mount Karimui.

There is also evidence to suggest that the "center of gravity" of the Daribi population was at some time in the past located in the valley of the Tua, to the west of Mount Karimui. Daribi themselves maintain that the valley was once filled with clans and can name some of those which used to live there. In a myth of the origin of pitpit arrows which I collected, the hero, who lived on the Bore River, proceeds down the Bore to the Tua and then up the valley, giving pitpit shafts to each of the clans he comes to. The natural features of the Tua Valley are widely celebrated in Daribi legend. Souw, the Daribi creator and cul-ture-hero, is said to have lived originally on the Bore, and Sugage, the founder of Noru Phratry, lived at Bῃmaru, an unusual grass plain on the Tua. The Daribi who lived in the Tua Valley must have been predominantly a river people, relying on canoes for transport, as the Urubidi do today. Unlike the Highlanders, who also live inland, far from navigable water, Daribi still retain their knowledge of canoe-making. A move inland would have been facilitated by the introduction of the sweet potato; and the present distribution of the various Daribi-speaking groups, separated by the river valley, was probably clinched by the introduction of malaria into the low-lying lands along the river. A single settlement, Gɛnabi, composed of the remnants of Gɛnabi and Mabere clans, totaling twenty-eight souls, is situated in the valley today and maintains a precarious existence there, on the margins of two societies.

It remains difficult to estimate just how long the Daribi have lived in their present inland situation; a test-pit excavated by Mr. David Cole in a rock-shelter near Dobu Clan, in the southwest of the Karimui area, yielded evidence of human habitation down to a depth of only three feet. The Daribi population of Karimui appears to have spread outward by segmentation from a small core area in the southwest, above the Saza and Ababu Rivers, and six of the eight phratries can be definitely traced to this region.

The tribal environment of the people seems also to have changed in the past few centuries; legends of the time when they lived at Bᶙmaru in the Tua Valley tell of continual warfare with the Bᶏria (i.e., "Pangia," the Wiru people of Pangia Patrol Post), and trade seems to have been carried on with the Kewa' people to the south. More recently, emphasis has shifted to the Highland peoples of Mengino and Gumine to the North. Guri, a government interpreter from the Bomai, claims that the first polished stone axes were introduced there from the Highlands before his father was married. Guri is about thirty years old, and was born when his father "was an old man, with white hair," so we might estimate that the Highland peoples were first encountered sometime around 1900. Informants claim that before this *yazare huq*, ground river-stone axes, were used. Trade with the Highlands made available the high-grade salt produced in the Gumine area and opened up markets for the bird-of-paradise plumes, previously discarded, which are so abundant at Karimui. Contact with the Highlanders also prepared the way for other types of cultural interaction; the "singsings" and dance costumes now in use at Karimui originate in the Gumine area, and a series of cult-like practices, emanating from Mengino and Gumine, have swept through Karimui. The present Daribi initiation rite, with its flutes, a former ceremony called the *waianu*, and its successor, the present *gerua* dance, are examples of these.

Physically, the Daribi tend to be more wiry and more slightly built than Highlanders, and lack the deep, broad chests and bulging muscles of the latter. The general impression is one of tribal ectomorphism; I have seen only three Daribi in the course of my field work who could be called stout in any sense. There is a wide range of variation in stature, though the Daribi may well average slightly above the norm for New Guineans. There is likewise considerable variation in skin color; the skin of most Daribi is a dusky brown, but the very light skin and blond hair frequently observed in children does not always darken with age, so that remarkably light-skinned adults are often seen. I suspect that this is part of the normal range of genetic variation in the population. Daribi tend to have long, narrow heads and fine features and often have beautifully straight noses, of which they are justly proud. The distended spleen characteristic of malaria victims is very common, and other disorders are caused by protein deficiency. The rate of leprosy infection formerly reached as high as 15 per cent in some villages. Karimui has recently become the scene of an experiment aimed at the control of leprosy (Hansen's disease) through the use of BCG tuberculosis serum, and it is visited several times a year by a team of doctors from the Public Health Department. Large, untreated tropical ulcers contributed to the general impression of native debility received by early patrols into the area, but these have been largely eradicated.

The area inhabited by the Migaru Page Daribi lies between 144° 30′ and 144° 50′ East longitude, and 6° 30′ and 6° 40′ South latitude. The amount of land actually utilized by them totals about 160 square miles, and if we estimate their population to be about 3,000, this yields a density of 18.7 persons per square mile. The Karimui area is effectively circumscribed to the north, west, and south by the Tua River, which drains much of the territory in the Australian Highlands districts, and swings far to the west around Karimui to gather the waters of the Kaugel and Erave Rivers before turning east and south again to become the Purari. The land within this great loop of the river is dominated by Mount Karimui, which rises to a height of 8,700 feet, and its girdling plateau. Like its neighbor to the northwest,

FIGURE 1.—*Daribi everyday costume in Kiru's youth.*

Mount Suaru, Karimui exemplifies a group of dormant volcanoes which rise above the lower-lying ridge country on the southern approaches to the Highlands. Bosavi, Mount Murray, Duau, and Favenc are other members of this group, and these "pleistocene volcanoes such as . . . Mount Karimui . . . take the form of dome-like stumps of mountain clusters and are usually surrounded by a plain of volcanic detritus." [5] In their splendid isolation, they gather about them clouds formed from the warm air masses moving up from the Papuan Gulf and make their own brooding climates below. This very precipitation in an earlier time filled the intermittently active craters with sediment, so that the ensuing volcanic activity caused terrific explosions which blew out the sides of the mountains. Thereafter, the continuing rainfall smoothed down the contours of the rock and carved the deep radial pattern of drainage in the surrounding plateaus, forming the endless series of gorges, some as deep as 1,000 feet, which never fail to catch the attention of those on "patrol."

Mount Karimui itself has been superimposed on a much older series of low-lying limestone ridges, running northwest to southeast, and these form the predominant landscape in the area to the west of the mountain. On a clear day the continuations of this ridge country to the west and southwest can be seen from the western slopes of Mount Karimui, flat ridgetop after ridgetop, stretching endlessly to the horizon. This region, much of it unexplored, with its karst phenomena, caves, white outcrop, and underground rivers, makes up the backdrop for much of the folklore of the Daribi, and very likely was the home of their ancestors. Many of the clans at Karimui are situated in limestone country, and seven of them live within the hollow, fishhook-shaped ridge called Hoyabi, the western end of which, serrated in a peculiar sawtooth pattern, forms the MacGregor Peaks. Daribi maintain that their ancestors lived in the caves which honeycomb many of these formations, and several caves in the area of Dobu Clan are presently inhabited.

Except for areas under cultivation, or stands of second-growth covering former gardens, the whole of Karimui is overgrown with tropical rain forest. The plains of *kunai* (*Imperata cylindrica*) grass, found widely in the Highlands, are conspicuously absent. The size and composition of the forest-cover varies greatly with altitude and the nature of the soil. The upper reaches of Mount Karimui support a lush "moss-forest," grow-

[5] Great Britain, Naval Intelligence Division, Geographical Handbook Series (1945), p. 17.

ing over the hulks of ancient, rotten trees and a floor of debris; below, the zones of vegetation grade down through groves of pandanus until the level of the plateau is reached. This is covered with huge, massive hardwoods: oak, beech, and a New Guinean cedar, with trunks up to six feet in diameter, heavily buttressed. The upper limbs of these trees are interlaced with vines and epiphytes, "where marsupials like to sit." The forest covering the limestone country is less impressive; the trees are smaller, and more low, bushy plants of the pandanus variety are found. The limestone itself is often moist and crumbly, and minute, moss-like plants grow out of it. In the deep river gorges and the valley of the Tua the character of the vegetation changes again, and quite exotic varieties can be found.

The fauna likewise shows considerable variation with relation to altitude. Lowland and coastal species of birds, including the crowned pigeon, inhabit the Tua Valley; large flocks of hornbills nest in the cliffs here also, and in the dry season mass migrations of giant bats move up the river. Forest wallabies are found along the banks, and occasionally huge pythons drape themselves in the lower branches, awaiting the random incautious boar. Eels are the dominant life form in the river itself, and these are so numerous that Daribi class fish as a subspecies of them. Catfish are also found here. Farther up, the bird life changes, and Karimui has in fact an extremely high bird population density, including sixteen of the eighteen known varieties of bird-of-paradise.[6] These, as well as the black and red parrot, which is not found in the Highlands, and the cockatoo, very common at Karimui, furnish plumes for trade with the Highlands. Birds of prey are especially plentiful, and there are countless varieties of pigeons and parrots. Eggs of the bush-fowl, or megapode, found in the heaps of decomposing brush where they have been left to incubate, constitute an important source of protein. The marsupials living on the plateau and in the limestone country are mainly arboreal, and include varieties of cuscus (*Phalanger*) and tree kangaroo (*Dendrolagus*). These are hunted, as well as the larger game, wild pig and cassowary, the latter being very numerous.

[6] Rev. Kenneth Mesplay, personal communication (1965), quoting Jared Diamond, an ornithologist.

Karimui is also ideal reptile country; Daribi legends dwell fondly on the many varieties of snakes, and when a hunter can over-come the exaggerated local fear of them, they may be killed and eaten. The insect world has favored Karimui with a generous elaboration of phasmid and katydid-like forms. The upper reaches of Mt. Karimui support exotic fauna of their own, including still more varieties of birds and the spiny, egg-laying anteater *zaglossus*, a monotreme.

Many of the peculiarities of Karimui are explicable in terms of its situation on the edge of the Highlands; it is a region of overlapping influences from the Highlands and the low country to the south. In the bottoms of the deeper gorges, and the valley of the Tua River, still partially navigable by canoe, it is possible to grow sago, while sweet potatoes are grown throughout the area, and its higher ground approximates the Highland environ-ment; malaria is the nemesis of the limestone country and the lower plateau. Gẹnabi, on the Tua, the lowest Karimui settle-ment in altitude, is at 1,300 feet; Noru is probably below 2,000 feet, and over half of the forty-five or so Daribi clans are below 3,000 feet; Nekapo, the highest, may be above 5,000 feet. The climate is decidedly warmer than that of the Highlands, though the nights can be surprisingly cool during the dry "winter" season, from late May to the end of July. This is the *siburu si*, a lean period when the cyanide-bearing *siburu* nuts ripen. This is followed by a spell of unsettled weather in August, and then by a dry period in late September and October, when the breadfruit nuts ripen, at a time when this supplement to the food supply is much appreciated. Daribi tend to be more quarrelsome than usual during such hungry periods. Late October is a time of beautiful sunsets, the sidelit evening clouds anticipating the rainy season, the *waia si*, "pandanus season," which, beginning in No-vember, continues through April, interrupted only by a short December dry spell. This is a time of all-day rains, of long, gray days haunted by swooping showers, and of torrential noc-turnal downpours, but here, as always, there are unpredictable dry spells. During the waia si the various species of red or yel-low pandanus fruit (*waia*), so beloved by the Daribi, ripen, and also, later, pitpit, sugar cane, and bananas. Infrequent high winds (*mazhuku*) which "come down from the mountain" are greatly feared, for there are usually many dead, dry trees standing about, and at such times the emotional climate reaches a state of near panic. At all times, however, Karimui maintains an indefinable atmosphere of leaf-choked forsakenness, whether in the gray-blue overcast afternoons, with bleached, dead tree trunks reaching up into the dull sky, or during the pellucid late afternoon hours on clear days, when a brisk wind saws through the relaxed foliage.

Subsistence and Settlement Pattern

> How still it is; our horses
> Have moved into the shade, our mothers
> Have followed their migrating gardens.
> — W. H. AUDEN

One of the most persistent themes in Daribi culture is that of food, and the giving and sharing of food, particularly meat, is an important symbolic idiom. The people themselves give the impression of being always hungry; meat is especially welcome, and use is made of all manner of resources in the satisfaction of this hunger. Rats and small birds are shot by men during lax hours and small edibles are continually being picked up from the bush by Daribi of both sexes, although they do not go to the extreme of eating nondescript insects as the Kapauku of West Irian apparently do.[7] Even today, after the arrival of steel axes and the better grade of sweet potato introduced by the government, the food supply is erratic, and must be supplemented from many sources. Earlier, during the time of the polished stone ax, the work of cutting trees was harder; a *zibi*, or group of brothers, formed an ax crew, and often mass tree-cutting bees, *me bidigo gi ni gerigibizhu*, were made up of the men of allied or neighboring clans. Even at this time, however, and perhaps exclusively before this, when ground river-stone axes alone were used, men did not cut the trees at all, but searched for places in the forest where trees had fallen and made their gardens there. The size of

---

[7] Leopold Pospisil, *The Kapauku Papuans of West New Guinea,* in the series *Case Studies in General Anthropology,* ed. George and Louise Spindler (New York: Holt, Rinehart and Winston, 1963), p. 14.

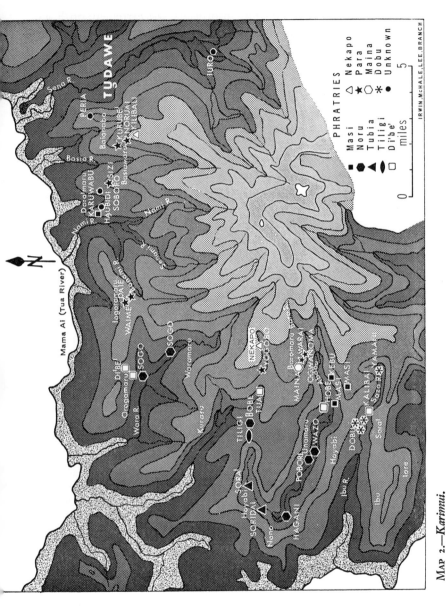

Map 2.—*Karimui.*

these gardens, as indicated by informants, was extremely small, and they were probably only provisional, sago very likely serving as the staple food. Several present-day settlements are said to have originated in such wind-cleared areas. Today it is possible for a man to clear his own garden land, and the staple food is the sweet potato.

Gathering of wild bush products is done matter-of-factly by everyone, and a Daribi going on any kind of errand in the bush will return loaded down as if coming from a supermarket. Pandanus fruit, fiber for the weaving of string bags, bamboo for cooking or water containers, mushrooms, butterfly larvae, and white wood-grubs are collected in this way. The grubs are kept alive in a packet of dried ferns until cooked and eaten.

Fishing is done in several ways. Eels are caught with a forked fishing spear ("comb-spear"). In small streams, fish are caught by using fish-poison or by damming the stream and picking up the fish in the area below the dam. In large streams such as the Tua a type of fishnet, woven like a string bag, with a frame, is used. Fish are collected from lakes and from ponds made by constructing earthen dams in small streams, through the use of *hogobi'a,* bamboo tubes with both ends open. These are scattered on the bottom beforehand, and the fish take up residence inside; later they are picked up with a hand over one end and emptied.

Hunting trips are made in family groups and last about three or four days. A small house of pandanus leaves is made as a shelter. The man goes out, with dogs if possible, and hangs the marsupials on trees as he kills them. The wife remains behind, gathers firewood, and cooks or smokes the game. Dogs are used to locate the hole or tree of a marsupial, and the animal is either smoked out or dug out. Treed marsupials are shot with arrows from nearby branches. Large quantities of marsupials and other game are killed and smoked over the fire in a small hunting lodge occupied by a group of men preparing for the *habu* ceremony; after a month or so, when the ceremony is to be held, an impressive quantity of meat has been accumulated. Small ground marsupials and rats are killed by falling-log traps (*kę*), and cassowaries are taken with noose snares or hunted with arrows. Birds are shot from blinds in trees or from an ingenious if ludicrous contraption (*węge*, "water-egg" or "puddle") consisting of a blind from which a bamboo shooting tube extends, pointing at a likely spot on a perch tied between two trees above a puddle, to which the birds flutter after bathing. Wild pigs are sometimes hunted.

Daribi claim that before contact with the people of Gumine they had no domesticated pigs, and indeed the word *kibu*, "pig," resembles *gibu*, the Daribi term for "bush." Before domesticated pigs reached Karimui, wild pigs provided the only available pork. The natives would make a path leading to a lair of wild pigs; at night they would kill the adults and catch the small pigs. When they grew up, a pig-feast was held. Daribi still have comparatively few pigs, though a moderately wealthy man may have a herd of six or seven. These are well cared for when small, but later are allowed to roam the bush surrounding the village, and are fed at intervals to keep them from going wild. When a sufficient number have matured they are killed, and a gerua dance and initiation are held. Dogs are much prized and are kept for use in hunting, but they are fed very scantily and usually wander about with their mouths tied to keep them from killing chickens. The latter have been introduced since contact, and are highly valued possessions.

Sago is cultivated wherever possible, in the low country and in the bottoms of gorges. Large stands of it occur in the lime-stone areas west of Hagani, and in some cases, as at Tiligi', artificial swamps are created for the planting of sago by damming streams. Where the land is too high to grow it successfully, clans maintain sago swamps some distance away in lower country. It is very likely that this crop was much more important in the past. Groups of men, often zibi, plant their sago in plots, which are subdivided for individual men. Nearby trees are ring-barked to clear a place. Holes one foot deep are dug with a stick, about ten feet apart, and a piece of rotten wood is put into each, after which a sago shoot is inserted. If it thrives, the ground is cleared around it and the rotting vegetable matter heaped around the young plant. When the tree is mature and ready for cutting, a party of clanmates and relatives of the owner arrives to begin work and takes up residence in small houses or shelters erected near the swamp. The tree is cut by the men and apportioned by the owner, much in the way a pig is sectioned, and the wives of the recipients set about chopping out the pith. The sago thus distributed is treated in the same way as pork is in regard to reciprocity. When the pith has been chopped out, the starch is leached from it by means of an elaborate funnel-and-strainer device erected on the site, and the kneading and straining is carried out by women. When the sago starch settles at the bottom of the basin into which the fluid drains, it is taken up and dried in a large net bag.

Other tree crops are planted, especially fruit-bearing pandanus (Pidgin *marita*), a valuable and much enjoyed source of fat in the native diet. This makes up a considerable fraction of the daily diet when it is in season, as do breadfruit nuts in the preceding season. Siburu nuts, which come into season in June–July are also important in this respect, but unless they are thoroughly leached in water, serious poisoning can result from eating them. Trees are planted, cared for, and cut by men, with the exception of *ugwa* trees, whose bark is used in making cloaks, which are owned and tended by women. Women plant and tend ground crops.

A garden is made on a flat piece of ground if possible, near water. When a man finds a suitable place for a garden, he breaks a stick to mark the spot. Then the women come to clear the brush away; the man tells them where he wants to make the fence, and they clear the ground up to his mark. Then the men cut the trees; first the small ones are cut, then some of the larger ones (often these are cut from a platform built high enough to avoid having to cut through the root-buttresses), and others are ring-barked and left. The women make a pile of all the brush and debris at the bases of the trees left standing and set fire to it. The bark of the standing trees is consumed in the fire, but the dried wood remains, to be used later for firewood. The large tree trunks and limbs which have been felled are merely left to rot. While the women are engaged in burning off the garden, the men build a fence around it, after which their work is finished.

The sweet potatoes are then planted; a small hole is dug by forcing the digging stick into the ground and pulling it sideways. Three or four sweet potato stems with leaves attached are put into this, and their bases are covered with earth. The next planting is made three or four feet away, so that the crop is planted indiscriminately, not in rows or mounds, but simply on the cleared ground. The women must also weed the garden, but the earth is soon covered with sweet potato vines and the women's duties are finished. The tubers are suitable for eating about six months after planting, but they may be left in the ground and harvested occasionally for a year or more afterward. Some gardens are planted a second time, in which case the sweet potatoes will "still be all right"; if a garden is replanted a third time, however, the crop will "come up rotten." Yams are planted like sweet potatoes, but the vines are allowed to twine around poles. Other garden crops include taro and the various edible leaf plants, planted by putting stems into the ground; sugarcane and pitpit, which are planted by putting lengths of cane into the ground; bananas, planted from shoots; and maize and beans, which are planted from seed. Manioc is also planted in the gardens.

Unlike the Highlanders, who shift their gardens periodically in a sort of fallowing system, the Daribi are true swidden agriculturists. Land is plentiful at Karimui, and the complex techniques of hilling, draining, and extensively fertilizing crops that have been developed in some parts of the Highlands are unknown here. A Daribi clan, consisting of about sixty to eighty persons, shifts its gardens about within an area of about two or three square miles as the soil becomes exhausted. The bush which is cleared away in making the new gardens may be either virgin forest or second growth which has arisen since some previous use of the land. Sweet potatoes may be left in the ground for a considerable period after they ripen, and it is usually possible to build another garden nearby when a previous one is exhausted, so the actual period of time spent by a clan at some particular spot depends on other factors, and may vary considerably. When moving to a new location within their territory, or when emigrating to a new territory, members of a clan build their new house first, generally on a high, easily defended point, while they are still living at their old gardens. At Soridai Clan, which was at this transitional stage in 1965, the men had moved into the new house in the center of their recently planted gardens, while the women were still living in the women's quarters of the old house.

The house erected in a new area is usually a *sigibe'* ("arrow-house"), a two-story longhouse elevated from the ground and originally built with a bark floor and walls supported by a wooden framework and roofed with sago leaves. Like a block-house, a sigibe' is built for defensive advantage; women live on the first floor (*aribe'*), while the second floor serves as the men's quarters (*bidigibe'*) and as an effective shooting platform in the local type of warfare, which consists in surrounding the house of the enemy. After the house is finished, land is cleared for the gardens. Traditionally "men's gardens surround the house"; in stories a person first "arrives at the garden," then "arrives at the house." The gardens form a ring around the house, often falling away down the slopes of the rise on which it is situated, and, as anyone who has had to cross one of them realizes, they

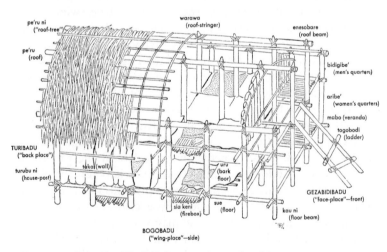

FIGURE 2.—*The Daribi sigibe', a two-story longhouse.*

constitute in themselves a most formidable defense system. The huge tree trunks and limb systems felled in the preparation of the garden are never cleared away, and the sweet potato vines grow indiscriminately over these, so that any path through the garden is a veritable obstacle course. The garden surrounding a house is usually divided into pie-shaped segments, each belonging to an adult male resident and extending outward from the house to the periphery. Around a large house, such as a sigibe', there may be many such segments; around a small house, holding a zibi or other small group of men, there may be only two or three. Alternatively, the whole garden is held and worked in common by all those in the house.

When the gardens surrounding the original house have been exhausted, the land is planted with pitpit, and also becomes covered with *kunai* grass, and the house population splits into smaller groups, which build *kerobe'* (a single-story version of the sigibe', with the men's quarters in front and the women's in back) and gardens in peripheral areas surrounding the original house and garden site. These houses may belong to individual men, to zibi, or to informal groups of men. Smaller sigibe' might be built here if there were danger of attack, or a new large one might be built to which inhabitants of the smaller houses could repair in times of danger. When these smaller gardens have been exhausted, the clan may decide to begin a new cycle and build a sigibe' at a wholly new location, or simply rebuild their smaller houses and continue the peripheral gardening pattern. This simple scheme, in which the clan radiates outward from its original location at the longhouse, is subject to a great deal of variation, depending upon the warfare situation, social pressures, and personal preference. Daribi prefer to live in the small, individual houses, where there is more privacy, for "the children fight and go crying around" in a sigibe', but they feel more secure in the latter type of dwelling. At a new location, therefore, when there is little cleared land and the people may not know the area well, or at any time when attack is possible or imminent, a sigibe' will be built.

At Hagani, in the MacGregor Peaks, the site of the former sigibe' is overgrown with kunai grass, and some of the people

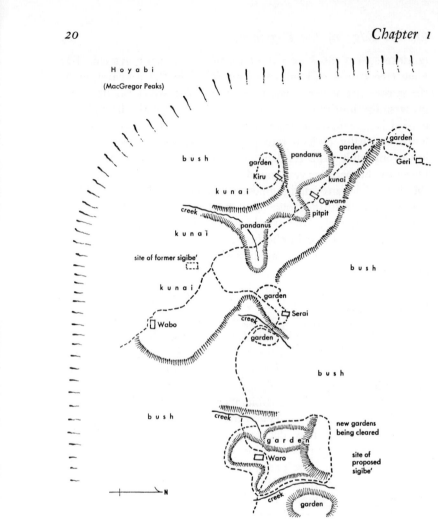

FIGURE 3.—*Hagani: house and garden distribution.*

live at Waro's large house, which is surrounded by garden segments. These, however, are becoming exhausted, and new gardens
are being cut above the present ones, in an area where Hagani
plans to build a new sigibe'. Other Hagani people now live in
smaller houses built in areas surrounding the old sigibe'-garden
region. These houses belong to individual men and are inhabited

by them and their families, and often by informal groups of other clan members and their families as well. Wabo's house, one of these, was originally located in the middle of a garden. By now the garden has been exhausted, but Wabo's son died in the house, and he does not want to build a new one because his "liver hurts" on account of his son. His garden is now built on the side of the MacGregor Peaks. Iogwa and Haru lived in this house from the time it was built, but made their gardens elsewhere. They are members of a different zibi than that of Wabo and his brother Dewi, another resident who is presently

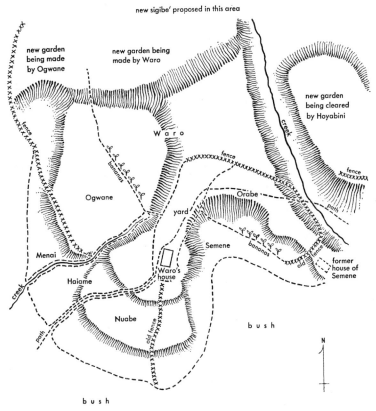

FIGURE 4. —*Waro's house and surrounding gardens, Hagani.*

away at the coast, on contract with Native Labour. The people
of Hagani have lived in the present situation for about four
years, and the major events in the present cycle seem to have
been as follows:

1960–61: Still in sigibe' with surrounding garden segments.
1962:   Individual houses made in peripheral areas with new gardens.
1964:   Ogwane's house torn down, new one (kerobe') made on site.
1965:   New sigibe' at gardens above Waro's house proposed.

This pattern of settlement, involving as it does continual shifting, regrouping, and dispersal, affords many opportunities for
segmentation and the formation of new groups. When the clan
assembles to form a new sigibe' group, certain members and
their families may not rejoin it, and in fact the clan itself may
be settled in two or more locations. At present, Sogo Clan is
divided in this way, some of its members living at Orogamaru,
near their affinal-maternal relatives at Di'be', while the rest live
at Waramaru, on land they formerly shared with their allies,
Kurube' and Noruai. The latter clans had also been subdivided
before their move to Baianabo, where they now live. Perhaps
because of warfare with the Iogoramaru clans, a part of each
clan moved to Baianabo, above their affines at Peria and Meyo,
on the Daribi-Tᵾdawe frontier. In the case of Kurube' this
included two sigibe', those of the Buruhuₐzibi and the Sonozibi,
whereas the Bapozibi and the Ozobidizibi had sigibe' at Waramaru. Later the Bapozibi withdrew to Suguai, on the Bonami
River, where it was joined by part of the Sonozibi, and each
group made a sigibe'. They were "coming slowly" to Baianabo
to reunite with the zibi there, but at this point contact was
made by the administration, and, following the suggestion of
the patrol officer, all of Kurube' moved to Baianabo, where they
occupied a single sigibe'.

The rapid shifting of houses and regrouping of occupants
reflect another feature of Daribi society: its accommodation of
high and capricious death rates. Ideally the grandsons of one
man could constitute in themselves an entire clan, subdivided
into zibi corresponding to their respective fathers. In fact, however, a given group of children will be cut down by more than

half through disease, accidents, and other causes as they grow up. Even after maturity is reached, the high death rate continues, so that those men who manage to survive to late middle age assume a truly patriarchal position, surrounded by the wives and wholly or partially orphaned children they have inherited from their less fortunate brothers. Which zibi will dominate a clan depends very much on the vicissitudes of chance. As an example of this, the five adult men of the Bapozibi, together with three sons of Bapo's full brothers, were the major force in Kurube' Clan when it lived at Waramaru and Suguai; today, perhaps ten years later, all eight of them are dead, and the power has shifted to the Sonozibi and the Ozobidizibi, the grandsons of Bapo's half-brother Haie. The continually shifting residence situation provided by the Daribi settlement pattern yields a setting in which the growth and disappearance of families and the continually changing friendships and alliances can manifest themselves in terms of residence groups. The flexibility of the pattern also renders possible the practice by which individual families, zibi, or sections of clans take up residence with other groups, affines, matrilateral or patrilateral relatives, and perhaps amalgamate with them, or by which whole clans occupy the same area to form the ephemeral *communities*. Essentially, this is a system predicated upon minimal ties with the land; there is ample land available to all, and therefore its control and distribution pose no major concern for the society. Daribi society is eminently flexible and portable, and the major considerations in establishing residence seem to be those of kinship, alliance, and intergroup relations. The shallow genealogical depth of Daribi social units, and the relatively low stress placed on patriliny fit very well with Meggitt's conclusion that "the degree to which social groups are structured in terms of agnatic descent and patrilocality varies with the pressure on available land resources." [8]

Clans which have adopted the pattern of single-family "line-houses" suggested by the first patrol officers (and thought at first by the Daribi to be compulsory because of an error in translation) are obliged to remain in one spot, and thus must

[8] Mervyn J. Meggitt, *The Lineage System of the Mae Enga of New Guinea* (Edinburgh: Oliver and Boyd, 1965), p. 279.

spread their gardens in an ever widening periphery around the village. In these cases additional small houses are built in the gardens. About half of the Daribi clans had moved into line-houses, but recently there has been a large-scale trend back to the original house types, the kerobe' and the sigibe', which are more comfortable and more economical to build than the line-house with its walls of hand-hewn planks.

Land and Property

Karimui is surrounded by large tracts of uninhabited bush which are seldom used except occasionally for hunting, and even in the settled areas there is enough garden land for all. There is, there-fore, no "struggle for land" at Karimui; the societal complex involving disputes over land tenure and inheritance, intergroup rivalry, and warfare over land described by Brookfield and Brown (1963) for the Chimbu and by Meggitt (1965) for the Mae Enga, and typical of many Highland areas, does not occur here. A territory of land, generally about two square miles or more, is held by each Daribi clan as a whole. Land use seems to be the basis of clan ownership; a certain area, bounded gen-erally by natural features, such as river gorges, mountains, or ridges, usually named, which has been utilized by a clan, and within which their various house and garden sites are serially located, is considered the property of that clan, and is associ-ated with it. This land is used for gardening, hunting, and other exploitation of natural resources; its disposal is entirely the privi-lege of the owning clan. Where several clans live together as a community, the territory, originally perhaps belonging to one of them, is subdivided among them. The territory originally belonging to Kurube' Clan is at Waramaru, in an area that was subdivided among the three clans of the community, Kurube', Noruai, and Kilibali. In former times, Kurube' moved about within their section, building houses and gardens in the tradi-tional pattern. When part of the clan moved to live near their affines at Baianabo, others lived between the two areas at Suguai, on the Bonami River. Now that the clan has moved to Baianabo, the land at Suguai is no longer considered their property; "Bosiamaru has taken our pandanus, bamboo there, now it belongs to all." On the other hand, they would like to move back to Waramaru someday; "Waramaru truly belongs to us, our ancestors were there a long time, we just settled at Suguai for a short time." Baianabo was given to Kurube', Noruai, and Kilibali in return for the marriage of its women to Peria and Meyo Clans, its former owners. Ţąre, an older man of Kurube', claims that Peria and Meyo are still owners of Baianabo; Kagoiano, another member of the clan, maintains that "now it belongs to us."

If a man wants to make a garden in his clan territory, he will generally inform other clan members, although he does not have to. He may make use of any unused land within the territory (though burial sites and old house sites are generally tabu). If a man wishes to make his garden on the site of an old, abandoned garden previously owned by another clan member, he should first ask the permission of this man, who may want to use it again "after the bush comes up." If denied this permission, he may go ahead and make his garden on the old land anyway. Use of land establishes a claim to it, but an ambiguity arises in the case of abandoned gardens; some feel that later users are obliged to ask permission, as the land is not in actual use; however, this claim is not enforceable. (In former times when cleared land was at a premium because of the use of stone axes, or before this because of the scarcity of good stone axes, this "residual right" may have been more frequently respected or even enforced.) If a member of another clan wishes to make a garden on clan ground, he must ask permission of the owners, who are apt to answer ironically in the hortative idiom "all right, go ahead, but we will make a garden on your clan grounds too." When Mara of Kurube'-Noruai tried to build a garden on Meyo's land, the Meyo men came and tore out his fences.

Land is always treated as the property of the clan as a whole, and any decisions or transactions which may be made regarding it must be made by the clan as a body. Otherwise, it may not be subdivided or sold, and there is no individual landownership, nor do the component zibi of a clan have any separate rights. The maker of a garden is recognized as its owner as long as he has a claim on crops growing within it; if he should die, the garden reverts to his wife. If she in turn remarries, she will make a new garden with her new husband. A person is felt to be the owner of anything he has planted, and has rights in it regardless of the land on which it happens to be growing, even if this should be included in a garden belonging to someone else. Sago, breadfruit, *haga*, siburu, and *dora'* (Pidgin *tulip*) trees belong to individuals (generally men) who have planted or claimed them, and are inherited patrilineally; the owner may designate before his death who among his brothers or children will inherit them. According to Kagoiano, "If I should die now, my two (full) brothers would get my sago, but if I married my children would get it." Women may own or inherit trees too, but give them up when they marry and move away. Ugwa trees, whose bark is used in making bark cloaks, part of the category of "female goods" used in marriage exchanges, may belong only to women. These, as well as bamboo groves, fruit-bearing pandanus, sugar cane, and pitpit, belong to the person who has planted them when they are "young," or the first time they bear. Later, when they are "old," they become the common property of all clan members (members of other clans may not use them; those of other clans in the community may, although they usually go to old gardens belonging to their own clans for such products). This "reversion" depends, however, on the planter himself; he may want to claim the "old" crops, and in this case they will not revert to the clan as a whole.

Pigs are generally killed upon an adult man's death, releasing their souls so that his ghost will not arrive empty-handed at *Yazumaru*, the abode of the dead. The pork is used in making death payments; any pigs remaining will be used to meet outstanding debts or to make a final payment to his mother's brother. If any remain after this, they will be divided among his brothers or children. Dogs likewise go to a man's brothers or children; often they are given to someone who had asked beforehand to receive them at the owner's death. Generally if a man admires some possession of another man, he will ask to inherit it in this way, and permission will be granted. Miscellaneous items of festive decoration will usually go to age-mates, and very personal items, such as a bamboo pipe, string bag, or

bow, are hung from the *tangets* planted at the site of the exposure-coffin, placed with the bones in a burial cave, or interred
with the body. A house is inherited by a brother, abandoned, or
is generally available to anyone who may need a house.

The wealth exchanged in betrothal and marriage payments,
payments given to the mother's brother, and in making restitution is called *sizibage* ("soot-things," referring to the white shell
ornaments worn to contrast with the soot which is rubbed over
the skin in the traditional Daribi festive costume). This category includes crescent shell neck-pieces (*ge*), shell headdresses
(*wiare*), other varieties of shell ornament, stone and steel axes,
bushknives, trade beads, and, lately, Australian currency. Pigs
and pork may also be exchanged for sizibage, as may smoked
marsupials and, since contact, chickens and tinned meat. The
"female goods" used by wife-givers in making counter-presta-
tions, bark cloaks (ugwa) and string bags (*wa*), are also valid
exchange items in this category, as are lengths of trade cloth.
Ordinary foods and tobacco (*sogo*) are classed as *tubu nai* ("edible things"), and these, together with fruit-bearing trees and
gardens, cannot be given in exchange for sizibage or any of
the other trade items in that category. People give food to others
when they have none, but the recipients are expected to reciprocate when their gardens, in turn, begin to bear. *Ba' nizi* ("bird
feathers") constitute a third category; these are valuable as a
medium of exchange in trading with the Highland peoples to
the north, and include various types of bird-of-paradise plume
and also feathers of the black and red parrot (*kaware*). Although
they may be used to obtain sizibage items such as axes or pigs
from the Highlanders, they are seldom exchanged for these at
Karimui or included in bride prices or other payments. They
may, however, be used to purchase baby pigs. Marsupial skins
(*haza ware*) may perhaps be assigned to this category, although
they are more often seen in bride prices. The exclusion of these
items from the sizibage category can be explained by the fact
that their potential as trade objects is realized only when they
have been transported to Highland areas where such bush products are scarce, and that the trip, always arduous, was particularly dangerous before contact. The assignment of subsistence

and exchange goods to separate categories accords with Salisbury's conclusion that

> . . . the presence in nonmonetary societies of discrete scales of value, each depending on a different standard of evaluation, is not an unfortunate accident. It is a simple mechanism ensuring that subsistence goods are used to maintain a basic standard of life; that free-floating power is allocated peacefully, with a minimum of exploitation (or disturbance of the individual's right to subsistence) and in accordance with accepted standards; that the means of ensuring flexibility in the society do not disrupt the formal allocation of statuses in the society or the means of gaining power.[9]

In addition to considerations of prestige and power, which are important at Karimui but less conspicuous here than in the Highlands, the system of exchange or prestation thus "sealed off" is involved in a very basic way with the social structure; it provides an effective criterion by which units are defined in contrast to one another. The circulation of the "pay" (sizibage) at the disposal of clan members corresponds fairly closely to the series of exchanges through which recruitment and marriage are effected, and these resources are therefore vital to the clan's future membership and its position in the society. Thus there exists in this type of society a large pool of circulating collateral which is used in expressing intergroup distinctions, quite without analog in our own society, and it is this which is distinguished from subsistence goods. Early theorists apprehended such exchange systems solely in economic terms; even Mauss, the first to realize their profound social implications, emphasized chiefly their role in maintaining prestige and in potlatching.

Anthropology first became aware of their involvement with the social structure as a whole in the investigations of bride price in African societies by Gluckman, Kuper, Evans-Pritchard, and others. In the writings of Lévi-Strauss, Leach, and Needham, the role of exchange in social structure comes into its own theoretically, but their understanding of it applies to "a certain type of society," Schneider's *segmental* (1965), where it symbolically

---

[9] R. F. Salisbury, *From Stone to Steel* (Melbourne: Cambridge University Press, 1962), p. 212.

expresses the relationship of units in a "continuing connubium." Among the Daribi the definition and interrelationship of units operates quite differently, but the role of exchange in this respect is no less important.

Law and Political Organization

A man starts a fight, and no matter how much one despises him, one has to go and help because he is one's relative and one feels sorry for him.[10]

We may view ethics, what one "ought" to do, as a set of sanctions or constraints setting the boundary conditions for motivation, what one "wants" to do, just as law, what one "must" do, sets the boundary conditions for ethics. Actually, however, this paradigm of social constraint is based on conceptions of our own which can be formalized in terms of the modals "want," "ought," and "must," and whose imposition upon a native New Guinean culture is at best rather arbitrary. Daribi expresses volition by the infix *-ainu-*, as, for instance, in the phrase *ena tuainubo*, "I would like to eat," or *ena tuainu-iai*, "I wanted to eat". Otherwise, modality is expressed by a range of inflected hortatives: *nage pau*, "you go!"; *aga nai tumainau*, "let him eat!"; *nage sę igio*, "don't you work!"; *nage bidaganio*, "you shall (in future) stay!"; *aga eragasogobeo*, "let him not come and kill!"; etc. Although used with a great deal of flexibility, as, for instance, in the sense of a dare, "go ahead, hit me! (I have friends)," these hortatives are essentially orders issued on personal authority; there is no implication in them (as there is in "should" or "must") of an external standard or compulsion. They are seldom obeyed as "orders," however; the total significance of their use involves the position of the speaker as well as that of the person spoken to, as the "orders" of a man are only one factor in a total situation. The effect of this usage is to relate such constraint to the immediate personal or social situation, reflecting Daribi law in general, based as it is ultimately on relative, political intergroup situations.

Daribi seem to be without the polar conceptions of "good"

[10] Pospisil, p. 57.

and "evil"; the absolutes "good" (*duagi*) and "bad" (*duare*) are used to express the relative fitness or excellence of a house, a piece of work, a bow, and so on. Duare connotes "bad" rather than "evil," *schlecht* rather than *böse* in Nietzsche's sense, in the way that a dull knife blade is bad. The term *ware*, similarly, means "fine," a word of praise, and *duai* means "of no account," or "useless." Lapses in moral conduct are spoken of as *pobaze* ("left," with the connotation of "crooked"), and those responsible are condemned as "bad" men. Models of correct, courteous action are given by a pair of stock characters in Daribi legends, generally portrayed as two cross-cousins (*aga hai 'nami si*), the *bidi mu*, or "true man," and the *peraberabidi*, or "man who breaks things."

The circumstances, motives, and means of interaction in Daribi law are all given by the social structure itself, and except in cases where an outraged group of bystanders interferes in an affair, there is no arbitration by any sort of external authority, and litigation merges with political interaction. The disagreements and squabbles which individuals for one reason or another bring into the open from time to time are referred to larger political units, but far from constituting some sort of court of arbitration, these units become the major litigants. At this point, other issues, relevant only in a political context, are brought in, and the incident marks a further step in the ongoing relationship of the two groups.

At Kurube' one evening, Nu, a young man, was playfully (and falsely) accused of stealing tobacco from my cook. Sezema, another young man, then insulted Nu, and the two fell to fighting, slapping at each other. Hanari, Sezema's father, then intervened, attacked Nu, and shouted accusations at him and those of his and Kaite's zibi. Kaite, sitting nearby, parried the accusations, and Enebe, of the Ozobidizibi, could be heard shouting that ghosts (*izibidi*) of Kaite's zibi were making his wife sick, and he began beating Kaite's sister. Thus, before this minor incident was closed, all four of the major zibi had been implicated, and the latest grievances aired. The charges and countercharges exchanged in such disputes are rationalizations, presenting "cases" in the light of a body of generally held values. The charges are often wild and are answered by irrelevant and equally invalid counter-charges, so that their number often carries more weight than their content. They may even be self-contradictory; after presenting a case demanding compensation payment for a Dobu man who had lived at Kurube' for a while before going to the Bomai, where he died, a party of men from Dobu Clan remarked, "Later we will ask the patrol officer whether he has really died or not."

Evidence is also presented to substantiate charges; grievances may be recorded by successive knots on a cord (*bonosezemo*), or by tying a rib-bone of a *pini* snake across the head of a man-arrow for each incident (*ozu ni*), and the resulting tally is exhibited to the opposition at the next flare-up. The men of Hobe Clan showed me the evidence that their councillor had been killed by the *kebidibidi* ("cassowary man," a kind of *sangguma* sorcery); it was a stick which the councillor had broken when the kebidibidi finally came to dispatch him. Divination was later to establish which was the guilty clan. The aim of this rationalization and presentation of evidence is the convincing of neutral parties and those of one's own group, so that they may rally to the cause, and the reinforcement of one's own convictions. Proof is in any case merely a sanctioned form of conviction, and in a society without formal institutionalized legal procedures, conviction will have to do.

Occasionally, as in the case of incest or some other outrage committed within the clan, the violation of the society's values will be so flagrant as to provoke an attack on the offender, or other important men will intervene. When Enebe committed adultery with Usuanu, the wife of Kebui, for instance, Enebe's elder brother Ţare joined the others in attacking him. Normally, however, fighting between brothers is considered an outrage. Eleven days after the dispute at Kurube' described above, Paro's dog was seen eating a chicken being kept by Sezema, the son of Paro's elder brother Hanari. Sezema threatened to kill the dog, whereupon Paro killed the dog himself. Then Paro's wife "spoke ill" of Sezema, who retorted angrily. Hanari tried to intervene on Paro's behalf, pointing out he had killed his dog, but this was too much for Paro, who began to rake up an old quarrel with Hanari. The two men then confronted each other; Paro picked up a length of cane, but did not strike Hanari, who charged at him repeatedly, slapping and grabbing. At this point a group of men arrived from Noruai and Kilibali, other clans of the community; Dono, an important man of Noruai, attacked Hanari, striking with his hands, and Sąri, the *Tultul* of Kilibali, shouted to Hanari, "He is your brother, you shall not fight him!" Such interference between clans of a community is the furthest extent of communal enforcement; when Dono of Noruai raped his mother-in-law he was condemned as a "bad man" by his clanmates, but when the men of his mother-in-law's clan, Meyo, slashed him with axes in retribution, the incident set off warfare between the community of Kurube'-Noruai-Kilibali and that of Peria-Meyo.

Ultimately, then, a zibi or clan has the obligation of rallying to the assistance of any of its members, opposing his assailant's group on a corresponding level, or settling the matter internally where the litigants are members of the same group. Thus a dispute among constituent zibi of a clan is settled externally for the zibi, internally for the clan. If a man should kill his full brother, the obligation to reciprocate rests with one of the remaining full brothers; "I would not like to live with a man who had killed my brother; it is better to 'back' the death [Hanari]." If Paro were to kill his parallel first cousin Kiape, a clanmate, the zibi of Kiape would come and kill Paro; if they did not do this the zibi of Paro would be obliged always to give payment to that of Kiape. Even if this should happen, the zibi of Paro would live in constant fear of being ambushed by those of Kiape's zibi, and might put Paro to death themselves to avert this. Just as the members of a man's zibi or clan are obliged to support him against outside groups, so they are likely to be killed in retribution for his acts. At Sizi Clan, Pubai fought with his parallel first cousin Huzukai and slashed him in the kidney. Huzukai feigned death, and Nabi, Pubai's elder full brother, fearing retribution, killed Pubai. When Huzukai got up again, his zibi was forced to give payment, pigs and a woman, to that of Nabi. If a man were to kill someone of another clan, his own clanmates would not kill him under any circumstances, but would give payment to the other clan. Daribi society places the greatest emphasis on the bond between siblings; if a child kills his father, the brothers of the man will reciprocate, and likewise if a man kills his wife, her brothers are the most directly concerned. If a man should kill his own child, he faces the hostility of his wife's clan, and she herself will leave him unless her clan is compensated. If a man who has no brothers is the victim of theft or other violation, and retribution is not made, he will say to the offender, "I can't fight you, you must reciprocate." If this is not done, he can do nothing further.

The eldest of a zibi, or group of brothers, is the *gominaibidi* (from *gomo*, the source or "head" of a stream), who is also called the *toburubidi* (literally "head-man"). He has the responsibility of protecting, providing for, and establishing his younger brothers as they grow up, especially if their father is dead. As the eldest, he is the first to marry and set up a household, and he should feed and shelter his younger brothers and see to it that they marry as they come of age. If he should die, his own wives will pass to them under the junior levirate. The younger brothers in turn should respect and obey him and offer him their services. If the gominaibidi dies, the next eldest brother will succeed to his position. The gominaibidi of its constituent zibi are the real leaders of a clan. Traditionally, the one of these who is closest to the gominaibidi of the previous generation, the eldest son of an eldest son, is the gominaibidi of the entire clan, and, although there are some complicating factors, this practice seems to be generally followed. Hanari, the gominaibidi (and also *Tultul*, or government-appointed village chief) of Kurube', is the eldest surviving son of the eldest son of a youngest son, and Waro, the most influential man (if not the village councillor, or Papuan "Tultul") of Hagani, is the eldest surviving son of the eldest son of a second son in the main Hagani line. The gominaibidi "talks to" the clan (often first thing in the morning), giving its members the orders of the day (*gominaibidigo po bogaza orau*, "you listen well to the talk of the gominaibidi!"). If a man should kill a member of his own clan, the gominaibidi would come and talk to him, but he will do nothing else in the way of punishment. This is up to the zibi of the victim. The gominaibidi leads his men in warfare and in other large projects, such as mass garden-clearing bees.

A "big man" in terms of wealth is a *genuaibidi*. A genuaibidi is not necessarily a gominaibidi, but there is considerable overlapping between these categories, as an elder brother has a good chance of achieving status and wealth. A genuaibidi will readily give wealth to those who need it (to be reciprocated later), and arranges marriages for the benefit of young men ("he would ask you if you were married; if not, he would help you"). There seems to be no requirement for prowess in warfare; during periods of fighting, Awi, an extremely wealthy man of Meyo "would take his (eight) wives and run away in the bush." There is considerable variation in the amount of wealth possessed by genuaibidi; Hanari, who has only three wives, was identified in this way, whereas Awi, with eight, commanding much more wealth and influence, is also placed in this category.

A Daribi clan is definable as a unit in terms of common participation in exchange activities; members share an obligation to contribute to bride prices and other payments raised for the benefit of clanmates and have a right to share in similar payments made to the clan. Although an ideology of patrilineal descent is used in connection with the clan and in relating the clans of a phratry, this merely refers to the normative means of recruitment, to be discussed in later chapters. Members who have been added to the clan through matrilateral ties are not discriminated against, and there is no attempt to conceal the basis of their relationship through genealogical fictions. Nor is residence a definitive factor; members of a clan usually live within one territory, but many clans retain their unity although split among several locations. A *community* is formed by two or more allied clans living in proximity and sometimes, in former days, sharing the same garden. Although patrilateral ties between clans on the phratry level are recognized, phratries are in no way functional units and are by no means exogamous. The processes of clan formation and alliance will be discussed in a later chapter.

Internally, a clan is composed of a number of zibi, usually four or more. A zibi can be defined as a group of siblings sharing the same mother and father, although all the offspring of one father are classed as a zibi named for him, as it is he who is responsible for their recruitment. Given the norm of virilocal postmarital residence, a zibi becomes ultimately a group of brothers. The component zibi of a clan are related to each other by close patri- or matrilateral ties, and since they themselves comprise members all of the same generation, the minimal genealogical depth re- quired for the full articulation of a clan is only three generations. Actually, however, the process of clan formation does not always proceed along schematic genealogical lines, and because of this and of irregularities in the birth rate, clans are articulated over a depth of four to seven generations. In addition to the major zibi, the membership of a clan always includes a number of orphans, adopted sister's sons, zibi who are growing up, and only sons. As a result of the differential ages of brothers in the preceding gen- eration, the zibi of their sons will mature serially, and the whole range of offspring of a long-lived man with many wives spans as much as twenty years, so that the internal structure of a clan is always something which is in the process of becoming, and seldom shows anything like the regularity of a kinship diagram. Addi- tional irregularities are introduced by high and capricious rates of birth and death and by the vagaries of residence and adoption. Even the odd and orphaned male children included in this way, however, are potential clan members and fathers of zibi, although, to be sure, they will not receive the same support and assistance as a man with many brothers.

As an illustration of Daribi clan composition, let us examine the structure of the two clans among which most of my field- work was done: Kurube', where my house and base of operations was located, and Hagani, over twenty miles away, at the other end of the society. Kurube', not too far from the Patrol Post, had at the suggestion of the government adopted the pattern of indi- vidual family "line-houses" shortly after the establishment of the post, and has had some contact with evangelists, while Hagani, one of the last clans to be encountered, still retains the original house and gardening pattern.

Kurube' is a member clan of the large Para Phratry, which has spread along the Karimui Plateau to the north of the moun- tain. It is presently in the final stages of separation from Noruai, another clan of the community, with which it shares a common great-grandfather. The third member of the community is Kilibali, allied to the others and derived patrilaterally from Nekapo Clan. Kurube' traces its interrelationship through the offspring of Kuru by his first two wives; his sons by a third wife became the ancestors of Noruai, and their sister was the mother of the founders of Kilibali. A certain distinction is drawn between the sons of Kuru by his first wife (Sawa) and their lines and the line of Haie, the son of Hwari, his second wife. Kagoiano speaks of Suabe, Kebui, Haria, and others as his "brothers" in contradistinction to the lines of Sono and Ozobidi, and actually since Suabe and Kebui were only two, and Haria an only son, they probably allied with their full parallel cousins, the sons of Bapo, to form a solidary group. Kagoiano's distinction is also generational, since he is a classificatory father to the sons of Sono and Ozobidi. Today all the men of the former group are dead, and Bapo's last three sons, Kagoiano, Nu, and Pobaze, are at the point of maturity. Two other zibi, the sons of Gaga (Węsinugiai) and those of Buruhuą, lend their support to the Bapozibi in intraclan affairs. The sons of Gaga were born at Dobu, where their father was living with his matrilateral kinsmen; when men of Kurube' went to Dobu to take part in the massacre staged there (*ca.* 1960), they traced the Gagazibi to their hiding places in the bush and brought them to Kurube' to live. Of this line, only Suabe has married thus far, one of the others, Webai, being merely betrothed. The Buruhuązibi, on the other hand, have all married, and Ma, the gominaibidi, is one of the most influential men in the clan. Their patriline is at Hagani, Buruhuą and his brothers having been brought to Kurube' by Gogo, their mother, after the death of their father. Of the sons of Haie, half brother of Bapo, Sono and Ozobidi became the founders of the two most influential zibi in Kurube' at present, and Hanari, eldest of the Sonozibi, is gominaibidi of the clan. The other sons have died without issue, except for Anuabo's son Yawane, who died, and Karoba's surviving son Huzukai, who is unmarried. Although they do not constitute a separate group, the Sonozibi and Ozobidizibi support each other in intraclan affairs. This is the wealthiest, most influential, and most numerous faction in Kurube' today. Sono's sons by his second wife Sumaia (Mebidiai, Kanama, and Yowinugiai, the half brothers of Hanari) have gone to Iuro to live. Thus the major factional split at Kurube' is that between the line of Kuru by his first wife (Gagazibi, Bapozibi, Buruhuązibi) and the line by his second wife (Sonozibi, Ozobidizibi). Although the alignment here is along kinship lines, it may not have always been so; the Bapozibi lived together with the Ozobidizibi at Waramaru, while the Sonozibi and the Buruhuązibi lived together at Baianabo.

Hagani is a member of Noru Phratry and represents the latest in a series of settlements which have moved westward within the hollow limestone ridge Hoyabi and budded off as separate clans. The Noru line at Hagani seems to have been derived from the line of Garo, founder of Noru Phratry; others of the Hagani group live at Noru Rest House and scattered through the bush between Noru and Hagani and consider themselves either Noru or Hagani in terms of clan affiliation. The other major components of the clan are related through women: the line of ("Moni") Gąwia, related patrilaterally to Denege Clan, and the Dobu line, whose fathers were childern of Wiribe, who was brought to Hagani as a child by his mother Sį at the death of Weare, his father. Although these two lines contribute the bulk of Hagani's manpower, the gominaibidi of the clan is Waro, of the Noru line; and Wabo of that line, the village councillor, also has a powerful voice in local affairs. Nuabe is the most influential of the Denege line, which lives at Waro's house together with Waro and other "odd" members of the main Noru line. The Yogwazibi of this line shares its house with Haru and Yogwa of the Dobu line, and these make up another faction. The main Noru line at Hagani contributes only four adult men to the total manpower of the clan, although it still has a strong potential, with many members presently in their teens. The seven adult men of the Dobu line make up the largest group of adult males; Kiru and Geri, the eldest of them, are well past their prime, and all of the next generation but Ogwane, Kiru's son, are quite young. Thus, because of this staggering, the next decade should see an increase in prominence of the Noru line as the adolescent members of this group mature, followed by another eclipse as the children of the Dobu line come of age.

2

The Curse of Souw

> With all its eyes the creature-world sees
> openness. Our eyes are however
> as if reversed, and are set around it
> like traps ringing its free escape.
> What *is* out there we know only
> from the animal's face, for at an early age
> we turn a child around and make it see,
> backwards, patterning; not the openness which
> is so deep in the animal's face, free of death.
> We alone see death; the free animal
> has its demise always behind it
> and before it God, and when it moves, it goes
> into eternity, as springs run.
> —Rainer Maria Rilke, *Eighth Duino
> Elegy* (trans. R. Wagner)

A World of Souls

In the beginning, according to the Daribi, man was immortal; he
lived an idyllic existence untroubled by death and the grief and
worry associated with death, and he was without the means and
practices of killing and the offenses, such as adultery and theft,
which give rise to the motives for murder. This ideal state was
terminated by a curse laid upon mankind by the culture-hero
Souw.

At a large river to the south of Mount Karimui called the Bore there
lived a widow and two young girls, Yaro, who had light skin, and

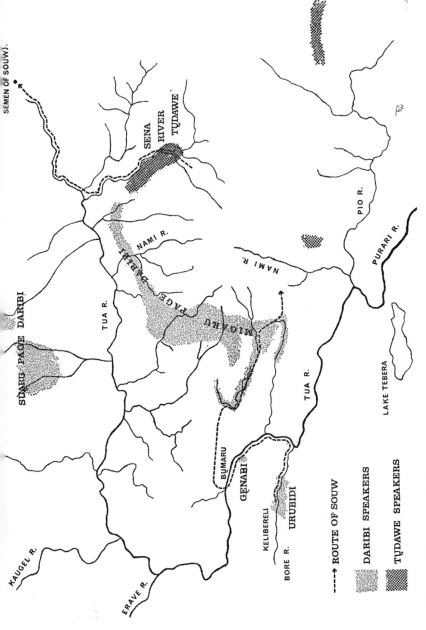

MAP 3.—*The route of Souw.*

Karoba, who had dark skin. A bird called the *kauwari* would often be heard calling; when people hear this bird, they know it has sighted a snake, and they go to the bush to find it. As long as the widow went into the bush when the kauwari called everything was all right; people did not steal, or die, or work sorcery. One day, however, the young girls went instead. When they arrived at the place where the bird was calling, they saw a large snakelike object approaching them. It was the penis of Souw, a giant light-skinned man who was the father of Yaro. The girls did not know what it was and were afraid. It began to copulate with Karoba, and she called out *yubidi, yubidi*, and Souw was ashamed and withdrew his penis. Before, when the widow had gone, she had known what the penis was, and had not cried out. Now, however, Souw was angry because the girl had cried out, and he got into his canoe and started off down the Bore. Yaro was working sago by the river and saw her father leaving, and she begged him not to leave her, but he told her to remain and that he would later come and visit her. He told her he had been working *animani* (sorcery) and had left the materials behind, and Yaro went back and brought them to him. He left then, taking his possessions with him, and as he left he cursed the people who remained: "Later you will have trouble, you will die, you will kill other men, you will work sorcery"; and he "threw down" the practices of stealing, adultery, fighting, sorcery, the kebidibidi, death in general, and the mourning customs (*yei*) of putting soot and clay on the face, among the people, who had formerly not known them. (In another version it is said that he also "threw down" his own skin, which would have conferred immortality upon men if they had taken it, but instead the snakes came together and took it, so that now they are immortal and do not die, but simply shed their skins and become young again, whereas men die.) Yaro followed her father, but Karoba remained behind on the Bore. After a while Souw came to the end of the Bore and followed a road, and as he went along this road he stopped again and again and made ridges to block it. As Yaro came along behind her father, she turned loose marsupials, fish, birds, snakes, pigs, and *pa* grubs in the bush. She took a knife (said in another version to have been left at the Bore by her father) and when she came to Hoyabi (the MacGregor Peaks) she cut it again and again, giving it the present saw-tooth appearance. When they came to the Peai or Saza River near Masi, she cut another mountain. As Souw walked about the ridges between Noru and Masi he scattered sago and dora' trees about. When he came to the site of the small lake near Noru, he dug his foot into the ground and hollowed out the lake bed. He also hollowed out the bed of the Ababu River in this way, and he planted pandanus and vines there. Then he went around Mount Karimui and cut the Nami gorge as a boundary between the Daribi and Tudawe (Pawaia) peoples. Yaro was the ancestress of all light-skinned peoples, and Karoba of all dark-skinned peoples.

Tales of "paradise lost" and "Pandora's box" are anything but rare in world folklore, but there is an appropriateness here which renders quite incidental any discussion of diffusion. The shaming of Souw is in its way a kind of original sin, and the resulting curse marks the point of origin for the interminable sequence of vengeance and countervengeance, of sorcery and the whole range of intrigues, of petty differences and disputes, and of chains of mutual recrimination which form the backdrop of traditional Daribi life. The story of Souw's curse is in fact an origin myth of the system of projective causality which characterizes the Daribi world view; in a culture which sees the world in terms of universal interaction, it provides the "cause of causes," the necessary beginning of the sequence which is operating today.

Many cultures approach the issue of man's relationship with the surrounding world in terms of individual constraint; what is feared is personal contamination, loss of *mana,* or indwelling force, the failure in personal effectiveness brought about by some slip in behavior, or "punishment" and reprisals by some outward force resulting from such a slip. This fear is overcome by keeping a close check on individual actions, disciplining oneself, praying, performing the ritual without mistake. For such cultures the chief source of anxiety and danger in the world is the individual himself; in his analysis of religious belief among the Gururumba, an Eastern Highlands people of New Guinea, Newman concludes that

. . . the Gururumba act on the world to a greater extent than it acts on them and they consider that the capacity to act derives primarily from forces present in their own bodies. Supernatural entities have their closest analogy with these inner forces, while ritual acts are most often manipulations of the human body or its symbolic exten-sions. . . . Ritual acts and symbols refer as much to the control, stim-

ulation and display of individual nurtural strength as they do to the
main divisions of the social order.[1]

For the member of such a culture, all the world is looking in at
him and watching his every move, and he himself is largely the
cause of what befalls him; the Daribi, on the other hand, peers
out into the world to find a cause for his misfortune at which he
may vent his spleen. For the Daribi, the individual is acted upon
by the world more than he acts upon it; sickness, weakness, and
madness result from the possession or "holding" of his soul by
outside forces. The world outside the individual is the major
source of anxiety here; the causes of his maladies are projected
onto real and imaginary beings surrounding him. Far from exer-
cising restraint, the Daribi reacts hysterically, relying on anger
to maximize the force of his interaction with the world; his tendency is to bring matters to a head, to push things to the breaking
point and let them break, to advance the causal process of the
world and "get it over with."

The ultimate spiritual reality recognized by Daribi can be abstracted to a field of *numina* (Daribi *noma'*), or souls, animate,
spontaneous, and sentient spirit-beings which move about inde-
pendently, interacting with one another in the manner of Leib-
nitz' *monads,* and thus precipitating the action in the world.
Souls are essentially spontaneous; they perceive, think, feel, and
act of themselves, and comprise each a complete personality and
will. The "causality" perceived by the Daribi is a recognition of
the fact that everything that happens to a person originates with
one of these souls. There are many kinds of such spirit-beings in
the world: those which animate human beings, the souls of pigs
and other animals; spirit-people, such as the *izara-we,* who live
underground; izibidi, or ghosts; noma' which have been liberated
upon death; and so on. They are normally invisible, and seeing
them is dangerous, usually causing sickness in the beholder.
Trees, plants, rocks, and such, are not believed to have souls.

Daribi do not believe in reincarnation; "a newly born child

[1] Philip L. Newman, "Religious Belief and Ritual in a New Guinea Society," *American Anthropologist* 66 (1964), No. 4, Part 2 (special publication; *New Guinea, The Central Highlands,* ed. J. B. Watson), p. 270.

doesn't have a noma' "; it develops within him when his skull hardens on top and his teeth appear. It is located in the heart (*hoburudu*) and is closely associated with the liver (*homu*) and lungs (*dinihomu*), although the latter are viewed as extensions, "the same as leaves." When a man dies and his noma' goes away, the empty space it leaves in his heart fills up with blood. The noma' is responsible for the operation of the *mobo,* or breath, centered in the heart, causing breathing and speech, and is also responsible for understanding (*korizaga*), or thought processes, linked with the liver. The Daribi expression for "I think" or "in my opinion" is *eno humugo,* "my liver says." As one informant put it, "If a man thinks 'I want to build a house' or 'I want to work in the garden,' it is not he himself that is thinking this, but his heart. If you didn't have a heart, you couldn't do anything, you would sit in the house just like a crazy man."

The most significant property of the noma' is its detachable nature; it may leave the body of its own accord, for instance when frightened, or be "held" or possessed by some other spirit-being. The word noma' means also "shadow," and it is used loosely to connote also "name" (*nogi*) or "picture," although there is no true identification of the personal name with the soul, and these expressions are metaphorical, working on an analogy of the soul with some separable part of a person's identity. If grown men go about shouting when a child has just received its noma', the child will become frightened and the noma' will leave, making the child ill. When a man is sleeping, his noma' leaves his body and performs the actions experienced in dreams. If a sleeping man is awakened, he is awkward for a while and does not have thoughts until his noma' returns. Once at Hagani, when my host Ogwane was dozing, I shouted to frighten his hunting dogs from beneath my cot; Ogwane woke up with a start, saying, "Do you want to frighten my noma'?" Temporary absence or possession of his noma', as when a man is waking from sleep, or when it has been "taken" in sorcery or possessed by a ghost, causes a person to be sick, awkward, and "without thoughts." Permanent removal of the noma', when it has been taken and not released by "bad" izara-we, when a man has been victimized by kebidibidi or other types of sorcery, or when it has been possessed in a child by a ghost, results in death. A noma' thus detached becomes an izibidi, or ghost (*izi-*, "die"; *bidi*, "man"), which lingers at the place of death if unavenged or unmourned, or goes to Yazumaru, abode of the dead, whence it may return at sunset (the "very witching hour" at Karimui) eastward along the river gorges to plague the living, or "talk to" them in whistle speech.

The susceptibility of the soul to external influence, its "detachability," is the definitive expression on the individual level of the Daribi world view, with its location of the spiritual "center of gravity" outside of the individual. The very component of a person's makeup which animates him and expresses his will and identity, the noma', is the part which is separable and affected by other entities; without it the body becomes merely a former residence, a relic to be mourned by his clanmates. The possession or "holding" of a soul by an external influence, or its temporary absence, entails sickness and abnormal behavior and is always a matter of grave concern, for prolonged absence can lead to death. As the external influence gains greater and greater purchase over a man's soul, it gradually loses its attachment to his body. Daribi dramatize this by saying that the soul of a dying man follows the Tua River until it comes to the abode of the dead; when a man is sick, but not yet dead, his soul is still "on the road," and has not yet arrived; when it reaches the abode of the dead, the man dies. If the soul should turn back, the man would not die. Possession of a soul does not always lead to death, however; the influence may be countered, or may only be imposed temporarily. A person whose soul is being "held" in this way falls into a socially recognized "state," sickness (*gazi*), insanity (*wabu habo*), epilepsy (*izara pabo*), or simply obeys the will of a ghost. The external, projective orientation of Daribi religion coincides with and reinforces a tendency toward hysterical reaction patterns among the people, and, as in Siberia, we find trance states and states of hallucination frequently occurring here in a religious context. Likewise, in the social sphere, behavior associated with outbursts of anger is rigidly stereotyped, almost to the point of ritualized drama.

Sickness is the state most commonly associated with possession of the soul, and it is always accounted for in this way. It can result from an encounter with a spirit-person, an izara-we or *uyabebidi*, a *gura'*, or spirit-snake, from sorcery (animani), from an attack of the kebidibidi, or sangguma, or from the attack of a ghost. Spirit-people and snakes may take a person's soul when encountered in their own territories in the bush; the sorcerer uses a special technique to gain a hold gradually on the soul of his victim, and the men who practice kebidibidi techniques are believed to kill their victims, releasing their souls, after which they are resurrected and allowed to return home in a sickened, stupefied state, dying a few days later. Epilepsy, izara pabo, is believed by some to be caused by the taking of the victim's soul by the izara-we. Insanity is caused by a ghost which "goes inside a man's liver and turns about." Ghosts are invisible and know more than living persons, and they retain an interest in their surviving relatives and clanmates, visit them, communicate with them, assist them, and use their special powers to chastise them, killing their pigs and children if dissatisfied. Like the living Daribi, ghosts have many moods, but they are more stubborn and harsh in their punishments than the living and seem to be slightly jealous of them. Although ghosts may come to almost anyone, they usually restrict their visits to spirit media, who may also be *sogoyezibidi* ("tobacco-spirits"), or shamans, with whom they have special relationships. An ordinary medium can "sing out" for a spirit, but a sogoyezibidi, who makes use of the spirit-familiar's powers in curing, brings on a trance state by smoking and seems to have more control over the spirit. The consequences of this contact for the medium are severe; one is reminded of the Siberian shaman, who begins his career often as a person who is subject to fits of arctic hysteria (*ämüräk* or *menerik*) and, as he becomes more adept, finds that he is less subject to uncontrollable fits, but is now able to "turn them on and off" at will. Rapport with an izibidi entails its possession of the medium. "The so-goyezibidi is first a man; he must die before he can become a sogoyezibidi." The onset is marked by sickness and diarrhea; when the whistling of the ghost is heard, the initiate smokes a great deal, and the ghost "strikes" and "kills" him; later, when he recovers, he is a sogoyezibidi. When the ghost of Nabia began to visit the medium Aruame, she became very ill, and had to be tied down to keep the ghost from taking her away (she is not a sogoyezibidi). While at Hagani I visited her one night to interview Nabia's ghost. She remained behind the partition, in the women's quarters. After I had asked her to get in touch with the ghost, a long silence ensued, after which shouting and the sound of people running could be heard outside; the ghost had "struck" Aruame several times and seized her by the neck, and when she went out into the yard to vomit, it "pulled" her away into the moonlit MacGregor Peaks, where she wandered for a day or so before being tracked down. Such behavior in the presence of an outsider is probably to be expected of a medium, but what is significant here is the relationship between spirit and medium. In her position as a mediator between the spirit world and the world of the living, the medium is obliged to submit to an ongoing or permanent possession by the ghost. This relationship is virtually the same as that between an attacking ghost and its victim, or between a sorcerer and his, with the exception that here the identity of the influence, the "cause" of the sickness, is known.

The Varieties of Influence

Although our own concept of "causation" has undergone much elaboration, this has been in terms of the primacy, or the categorical order of causes, and we do not distinguish origin, cause as a single, completed action, from a continuously operative cause, or influence. In Daribi, likewise, the term for cause, *page* ("base," Pidgin *as bilongen*) covers both senses. This term refers to the base of a tree or mountain, to the lower, pelvic-posterior portion of the human anatomy, and to the cause or origin of something by analogy with the base of a plant or tree, both in the sense that this is the point of origin for the plant and in the sense that the base supports and sustains the foliage. Thus an origin myth is called *po page*, "talk-base," and the page of a sickness is some malicious influence, the "root" of the matter. It is in this latter sense, as a continually active control or possession, that we encounter the notion most often in Daribi religion, and I will refer to this as an *influence*. With reference to our generalized model of the Daribi world view, the field of souls, we can speak of influence as any relationship of dominance or control among souls. In Daribi religion, an influence is a hold taken on an individual through possession of his soul by a malicious being or person, gradually weaning it away from its original connection with his body, until the person dies. Daribi religion can be reduced to a series of practices designed to counter or remove this influence. How then do such influences operate, and how are they opposed?

The idea of concealment and of the certainty with which an action is apprehended is a major theme in Daribi culture. Where the causes of all misfortunes are projected on the surrounding world and the individual is seen to be threatened on all sides by potentially hostile influences, the problem arises of where to project, of which external threat to focus upon. As we have seen in the previous chapter, Daribi frequently present "evidence" to justify an accusation. Evidence performs essentially the same function as divination; it provides a culturally sanctioned criterion for reaching a decision, for deciding where to place the blame. The Daribi language distinguishes a series of modalities indicating the relationship of an action to the perception of others, somewhat like that first discovered by the linguist Murray Rule at *Kutubu*,[2] and we can look upon this as a series of "degrees of concealment." "To be hidden" is expressed by the infix -*buri*- (*aga sogo turuburiare*, "he was smoking hidden"), "perhaps" by -*badi*- (*aga bidibadibo*, "perhaps he is there"), "to discover" by -*iza wai* (*eno aga suiza wai*, "I didn't see him, now I do"), and "to be found" by -*iai iare* (*aga iziai iare*, "he died and later was seen"). In a world where the connection between an effect, a sickness for instance, and its suspected cause is far from obvious, it can be expected that man will come to believe that a tendency toward concealment is part of the nature of things.

Ghosts can be said to be separated from the living by a "screen" of invisibility; Daribi say they are invisible, transparent "like the smoke of a fire," and the ghosts themselves have been heard to say, "We are just like men; we can see you, but you cannot see us." They can travel much more quickly than the living and thus "see" many things which would be impossible for a mortal to witness, and they also have the power to transform themselves

[2] Murray Rule, personal communication (1965).

into birds, insects, snakes, and other animals. Although they can see one another and perform actions in the world, human beings cannot see them except at certain special times. Whereas they have an unquenchable thirst for water, and water has a certain power over them, and they sometimes even request that pork be given them, the more usual offering is smoke from the bones of a pig or marsupial, and they are not nourished by ordinary human food. They inhabit a more elemental world, whose realities are the *animae* of this one, the abstracted world of souls described above. It is from their invisibility that they derive their power, for they are not innately strong; a ghost can kill a child or pig, but only has strength enough to make an adult sick. It is because no one sees the ghost, because he is behind the screen, that he is feared and is able to work his will among the living.

The screen may be penetrated and the world of souls entered by living persons only when they are able to interact directly with this world through the agency of their own noma'. This can come about in two ways. First, when a person is asleep, the noma' leaves his body and wanders about and experiences or "sees" the action taking place in dreams (*na*), including allegorical premonitions of future happenings. The latter are interpreted in certain standardized ways, and these call to mind the metaphorical nature of Daribi magical spells. Skills such as playing the flutes (*ona'*) used in initiation are revealed in dreams, and if one does not want to learn to play the flute, or to weave an armband (*mo*), "he pays no attention to the man in the dream who is explaining it." Certain members of the clan are known for their ability as dreamers and are asked to carry the pole to which a jaw is tied in the kebidibidi divination; they are called *ni-tuabo-na-iai-bidi* ("pole-holding-dream-making-men"). According to informants, a man who sees in his dreams where a dog has hidden part of an animal it has killed fits into this category, "because he has followed the trail of the dog and can follow that of the kebidibidi."

It is through a dream, too, that the second means of penetrating the screen is opened up, that of rapport with a ghost by a medium or sogoyezibidi. A person will say to a close friend or relative, "If I die, my noma' will come to you, I will not forsake you." A person who speaks and thinks well is chosen. Later, when the person who promised this has died, he will appear to the chosen one in a dream and say, "Remember when I was alive I told you I would come and make you a sogoyezibidi," and he will hand him a bamboo tobacco pipe (*sogonage*), the symbol of his trade. It is after this that the izibidi strikes and "kills" him, and he suffers the onset of the sickness that is the consequence of possession by a ghost and becomes a true sogoyezibidi. Although both the sogoyezibidi and the ordinary spirit medium may experience such possession and the consequent rapport with a ghost, and may thus penetrate the screen and obtain information regarding the world of souls, only the sogoyezibidi makes a specialized use of this information, in curing. The izibidi instructs a new sogoyezibidi in the ways of divination and curing. Whenever the sogoyezibidi undertakes a treatment he smokes a great deal to bring on the izibidi. A sharp rap on the floor often signals its presence. "The ghost does not come up to a man's face, it comes to his back, and when the man feels a little heavy it is because the ghost is there." The ghost sits on the head of the sogoyezibidi, who covers his head with a bark cloth "so he may look at the spirit." Between puffs on his pipe, the sogoyezibidi opens his mouth wide and sings *a-aa-aaa;* then the ghost may be heard whistling in the form of speech, and the sogoyezibidi interprets this. As my informants put it, "Just as you can read a book and we can't, so the sogoyezibidi can understand what the spirit is saying and tell us." Some sogoyezibidi claim they can "see" the cause of an illness.

As we have seen, ghosts rely on their invisibility to exert an influence upon the living, and sogoyezibidi make use of their rapport with other ghosts to penetrate this screen of invisibility and discover the cause of a sickness. It is not surprising, therefore, that penetration of the screen is often sufficient in itself to effect a cure; if a ghost is responsible for the sickness, it will "let go" of the soul of its victim once the sogoyezibidi has announced its identity. Two ghosts were detected in this way during a treatment which I witnessed, and I was told that "now that the sogoyezibidi has seen the cause of this sickness the sickness will go away, because the two ghosts wanted to cause it in secret. Now that they have been found out, they cannot do it anymore." A sogoyezibidi can also diagnose whether the patient is the victim of sorcery or the kebidibidi, but cannot determine the identity of the sorcerer himself.

Sorcery (animani) and the kebidibidi also derive their effectiveness from the secrecy with which they are practiced. These techniques are used to exact vengeance for an injury or wrong and rely on secrecy to conceal the identity of the sorcerer as well as to effect their ends. The sorcerer (*animani wawi bidi*) collects personal leavings of his victim secretly and dries them at his fire, gaining greater and greater purchase over the soul of his victim, who gradually sickens as a result. As a culmination, the sorcerer may kill his victim by throwing the material in a lake. The entire clan of a victim shares the obligation of finding out the identity of the sorcerer. When a clan member is sick, or has died, and sorcery is suspected, they will go around to close relatives, cross-cousins, affines, and others, and try to discover likely suspects by close questioning and sounding out rumors. Sorcery is private, only the sorcerer knows of it. A blood relative, affine, or close friend of the victim who is a clanmate of the sorcerer and who discovers the sorcery material in his house will wait until the sorcerer is away and then "throw it out." Then he will go to the victim and slowly, carefully tell him what he has done. The victim will ask him again to make sure, then collect some "pay" and give it to him. Often a friend or brother-in-law will visit a sick man and ask him why he is sick; if he doesn't know, the former will walk about and look for sorcery material. If he finds this, he will throw it out, and then return home. Later he will visit the victim and ask him if he has recovered; if the answer is "yes," he will ask, "At what time did you get well?" The erstwhile victim will tell him, and he will say, "Oh, that's just the time when I threw away the sorcery material."

If the victim or his clan is unable to discover the sorcerer by means of such contacts, an *animani po mibo* or "sorcery inquest" will be held by the clan. This is attended by the entire line; they question the victim closely as to whether he has had adulterous relations with women of another clan, or has stolen any pigs, trying to find possible motives. Brothers-in-law and other relatives who live elsewhere will come to "help in the talk." If a member of the victim's own clan is responsible, he will "throw away" the material at this time and ask the victim for a settlement in terms of "pay" later. If the sorcerer is not uncovered by the inquest, and the victim dies, the clan of the victim will go around to suspected clans and ask to eat with them. If, when the clan eats, the children of the victim's clan become ill, then the clan with which the food was eaten contains the culprit. Various other divination practices used by the Daribi work on the same principle, which is that the ghost of the victim, resentful of the fact that his brothers are eating with his murderers, whom they have not troubled to find out, attacks their children.

All blood relatives of a victim are susceptible to attack in this way; it is said that after eating with the unsuspected murderer's clan they will be subjected to epileptic attacks, after which they will contract leprosy. All those who are susceptible in this way can later demand payment from the sorcerer if they become ill, and a person who has epilepsy will search for someone who has worked animani against a close blood relative. If he does not find the guilty party, "his son will continue the search when he grows up." Such sickness can only be contracted if the eaters are ignorant of the sorcerer's identity. Relatives of a man killed by sorcery can also contract leprosy by walking near the lake where the sorcery material was thrown; the ghost of the victim will turn into a dragonfly with a red abdomen and bite them, causing the sickness. To cure this, a pig is killed and a small bamboo tube of water is broken over the head of the sufferer, while the name of the sorcerer who killed his relative is called out. The izibidi of a sorcery victim will also put his own hair and fingernails into the ears of those of his line who eat with his unsuspected murderers so that they will not hear the evil spoken of him. This is removed by the sogoyezibidi.

Whereas animani is private, and is the work of individuals, the kebidibidi takes the form of a small raiding party selected from the members of a clan or community. Although a clan is the minimal unit for recruiting a kebidibidi party, the raiding cannot take place within the community, and thus respects the limits of warfare. When selecting the men for the party, one man is taken from each of the constituent smaller groups participating, if possible one from each zibi; if a series of raids is undertaken by a community, the constituent zibi of each clan alternate in contributing men, so that involvement is spread as evenly as possible. This is done in the interests of secrecy, so that none of the groups will be in a position to inform on the others (through blood or

FIGURE 5.—*Kebidibidi.*

affinal ties, for instance). The allied clans of a community co-operate in making up kebidibidi parties for the purpose of eliminating their respective enemies, and thus besides secrecy there is also the motive of spreading the guilt as widely as possible. When, as occasionally happens, a clan "which has too many kebidibidi" is massacred by all the other clans in the society, each of these must send representatives.

Services can also be bought; if a clan is really outraged by adultery, it can take the payment given to it by the guilty clan and use this to bribe a clan which "has the kebidibidi" to kill someone of the offending group. The term kebidibidi derives from *kebi*, "cassowary," and *bidi*, "man," and alludes to the stealth necessary in this activity. A raiding party consists of four or five men, one of whom should have the knowledge of kebidibidi sorcery and possess a *kebidige* ("kebidi-egg"), which is used in the sorcery. The party ambushes a single, unarmed individual and "kills" him, releasing his soul, after which the victim is "resurrected" through the agency of the kebidige. This also eradicates the incident from the victim's memory, and he returns home, stupefied. Two or four days later he becomes ill, and the kebidibidi returns and dispatches him. The ostensible purpose of this procedure is secrecy, to make it look as if the victim died of sickness. Thus here, too, the action is "screened" from the victims by secrecy, and the major emphasis is on concealment on one hand and "discovering" on the other. Even where the kebidibidi is carried out as a simple raiding party with no sorcery involved, as I suspect happens in the majority of cases, this secrecy remains the key factor.

However much kebidibidi raiding does in fact take place, the number of deaths attributed to it is out of all proportion to the activity. Every sickness and death, no matter how "accidental," must have a cause for the Daribi, and every cause devolves upon the human soul and must have an agent. Most of the adult deaths which took place during the period of my field work were attributed to the kebidibidi. There are a number of omens which indicate whether a person has been victimized by the kebidibidi; when no arrowhead is found in the body of someone who has died in fighting, or when a sick person cannot eat pork, this is the case, and a sogoyezibidi can also diagnose this. After a body has been placed on the *ku*, "dripping pit," or exposure-coffin, no one talks in the sigibe'; at sunset, when izibidi are abroad, a close friend of the deceased will go to the door and shout *mena bidibauwe-e-e* ("where are you?"), and, if the deceased was a victim of the kebidibidi, a faint cry will be heard in the distance, *ena e bidibau* ("I am here"), the voice of his izibidi, which is at the place of killing. (Daribi otherwise recognize echoes, *i mugibu*, as the reflection of sound from cliffs.)

As with animani, the ghost demands revenge, and seeks to inform his clanmates: "If we sleep in the house of another line, and we awake all the time during the night to urinate, the line with which we are sleeping has killed one of our line, and the ghost of the dead man makes us get up all the time to try and tell us that this was the line that killed him." This guilt is usually determined by divination, however. When it has been established that the deceased is a kebidibidi victim, the mandible of a man known for his wisdom (*duagia-korizaga-iai-bidi*) when he was alive is tied to a pole from which the bark has been removed, together with some hair from the kebidibidi victim, with a piece of bark cloth, until it is completely covered. This is tucked under the arm of the body for the night. Early in the following morning a stick is put into the ground on each side of the ladder to the men's quarters, and the pole with the jaw is laid between them. A brother of the victim strikes the jaw with a leaf, calling out the names of the clans as he does so; when the jawbone stirs, the right clan has been found. A more usual procedure is that of using the

FIGURE 6.—*Sketches by Kagoiano of men performing the kebidibidi divination.*

pole to guide clanmates of the victim to the kebidibidi. In this case the men say as they are preparing the pole, "The kebidibidi killed you, now show us where he is," and the pole will become suddenly heavy, indicating that the izibidi is there. Two men hold the pole, which the izibidi "pulls" along the trail of the kebidibidi, stopping at places where he ate or defecated. A line of armed men follows. When they arrive at the house of the ke-bidibidi, the diviners shout, "You can't kill us anymore, now we have found you!" They may attack for revenge, or simply content themselves with a warning, but in any case the kebidibidi is a grave matter, more precarious than animani, as it always involves intercommunity relations. Yet here, too, as in the case of animani, the most effective information is provided by izibidi, although the sogoyezibidi may not be the mediator.

The influence operating on a victim of izibidi, animani, or the kebidibidi can be resolved into two components: the means or techniques by which a "hold" is gained on the soul, and the "screen" of invisibility or secrecy which conceals the action. The technique itself is relatively simple: "holding" the soul in the case of izibidi, gradually "stealing" it through personal leavings in animani, and removing it through sorcery done in personal contact in the case of the kebidibidi, and in each case would be obvious and easily countered were it not concealed by the screen. It is this second component, with its necessity for divination and penetration of the screen, most effectively by an izibidi, an in-habitant of the "world of souls," that gives free rein to projective tendencies and accommodates the system of social control. The primary problem here is knowledge, the identity of the perpe-trator, which must be discovered before action can be taken. Penetration of the screen resolves the anxiety as to the cause of an attack, and in many cases this in itself suffices as a cure or conviction. This type of influence provides the basic theme for a *genre* of Daribi legends, in which a man or spirit, by means of a concealed device or trick, kills one man after another as they are lured by the device, or go in search of their missing brothers, until finally someone learns of the device through a dream or spirit medium and, discovering the "cause," puts an end to him. The following story presents a typical example:

Once a man heard a kauwari bird calling, an indication that it had sighted some game, and went to where it was calling. There he saw a marsupial in a tree and shot it; he recovered it and began to gut it. Just as he did so he noticed that it was a man who had turned into a marsupial; the marsupial man got up quickly and killed him. Then he took the body back to his house and hung it in a casuarina tree. A second time the same thing happened; the third time a woman heard the kauwari calling, and her husband went and was killed. Soon the sigibe' of the clan was half empty. One of the remaining men had a dream in which he learned of the man who had turned himself into a marsupial in order to kill men; in the dream he was also told to go to a tree, where the marsupial would be next time he heard the bird calling, and paint the trunk with sap of the fruit called *hono.* Next time the bird was heard he found the tree and did this, and then climbed a nearby tree and watched. The marsupial-man wondered where he had gone, and turned back into a man and climbed down the tree to investigate; as he did so his two feet stuck to the sap, and he fell and hung head downward. The other man climbed down his tree and finished him off with a javelin and threw his body into a cave.

Another story shows a typical elaboration of this theme; here the hero removes his own vital organs (and soul) and places them in a waterfall for safekeeping, and operates by remote control, his own body rendered invincible by the absence of the soul. Daribi believe that water has the power to "hold" and also to sustain a soul which has been removed from the body; waterfalls (*ai sabo,* "stream-taking") are used in curing, to remove a possessing ghost, and the dead, who travel along watercourses, are believed to live in a lake.

Two men, who were cross-cousins, lived together. They went to a pig-feast, where one of them was given *husare* poison, after which they returned home, taking their pork with them. When they arrived they began to cook the pork, and the one who had been given poison died. Crying, the other made a dripping-pit and carried his cousin to it by himself. As he ate his pork he wailed for his cousin. Then he cut open his abdomen and took out his own vital organs, his liver, lungs, intestines, and kidneys, and put them into a black-palm sheath and placed them under a waterfall. Having done this, he filled his body cavity with stones. Then, wailing for his cousin, he took his bow and ax and went off to fight. He came to a house; the men there shot at him and missed, but when he shot he did not, and killed men, women, and children. Then he went home, and his enemies followed him. They shot and missed, but he killed them all. By himself he finished them off; he killed off Sizi Clan and wiped out the people at Iogoramaru. The men of Di'be' decided to ask a sogoyezibidi for help; the sogoyezibidi said, "Follow the stream; when you arrive at the garden, look at the waterfall; you will see there a man's vital organs. Kill these." When he had said this, they went and killed the vital organs. At this time the other man was smoking secretly, and he died. His enemies came to his house and saw that he had died. Thus was the cause of that fight.

Where the identity of an influence is known, or is not a matter of concern, the influence can be dealt with directly. Daribi religious ceremonial is based on the appeasement, frightening, or deception of ghosts; in the gerua dance performed at a pig-feast (*kibu da*), the *gerua* board, latest in a series of "cults" adopted from Highland peoples, is used to frighten ghosts and make them "let go" of the pigs. On the evening before the ceremony, a small gerua is hidden in the bush and "given" to the izibidi after having been paraded through the village. This is done to appease them, "so they will have a gerua of their own." In the habu ceremony, whose purpose is to "bring back to the house" the soul of a man who has died in the bush, and whose body has not been mourned over, a party of men spends a month or more in the bush hunting marsupials and preserving them by smoking. When the marsupials are shot, a pretense is made that they are held responsible for the sickness caused by the unmourned izibidi, and when a sufficient number have been accumulated, the habu men return to the house; the izibidi comes after, "following the smell of the meat," in the form of a rainstorm. The men approach the house as antagonists, *advocati diaboli* for the izibidi, and stage a mock combat with those who have remained behind; when they reach the house, the former spread the smoked game out before those who have been ill and say, "These black men have been making you sick." Ceremonies such as these deal directly with the ghost, frightening, appeasing, or exculpating him, and there are other, less impressive rites performed with the same end in mind.

Ghosts are inhabitants of another world, they are invisible, disembodied wills, and require special treatment even when dealt with directly. Otherwise, known influences are countered by means of reciprocity. A sorcerer works in secret, returning again and again to the house of his victim to collect personal leavings, which are mixed with husare poison and buried in the ashes of his firepit to dry. As this process continues and more and more material is added, the sorcerer gains a greater hold on the noma' of the victim, until finally, when he strikes the tube which holds it and throws it in a lake, calling out the name of the victim, the noma' goes with it and is "taken" by the "bad" izara-we resident in the lake. This is the mechanical process by which a sorcerer gains an influence over his victim, and, once he has been identified, it is this sorcery material which he is expected to throw out. Here, however, we encounter an influence which must be dealt with directly; the sorcerer undertakes his activity because of some grievance, and if he is to discard the material and remove the influence from his victim, he must be compensated. A problem is solved in the discovery of the sorcerer's identity, but the influence is finally countered by reciprocity; were he not compensated, the sorcerer might revert to the practice once more.

The influence of bush spirits is also countered by reciprocity. The izara-we ("epilepsy women") live everywhere beneath the ground, in ravines, and also in lakes; the smoke of their cooking fires rises from the ravines and forms the clouds on Mount Karimui. "Bad" izara-we live at "bad places" (*bege buru* or *amazi buru*), beneath sago swamps, in muddy places, and on the banks of the Tua River, and also in lakes, and are particularly prone to "take" human souls. Like izibidi, they have the power to transform themselves into insects, and thus they bite those who wander into "bad places," causing tropical ulcers. If a man eats, defecates, urinates, or has intercourse at a "bad place," or if his leg sinks deeply into the mud, the local izara-we will take his noma' (probably through the agency of personal leavings, as in animani). Then the victim marks the spot with a stick, and his brothers will lead a pig to the spot, play flutes, and call upon the izara-we to release the noma' of the victim, after which they kill the pig and let its blood flow into the ground. When ants appear, one of them will be caught and taken back with the men. A "road" is made of *sakegarebu* leaves by the men as they return, leading from the place of the izara-we to the victim's house, so that his noma' can find its way back. The ant which has been caught is put on the head of the victim overnight, and a string bag is put over it. If the ant is still alive next morning, the noma' of the victim has returned, and he will live; if not, the izara-we retain his noma', and he will die. If a child falls down in a garden or in the bush and cries, the izara-we have taken his noma', and his parents bring "pay," bark cloaks, net bags, pearl shells, etc., and place them on the spot. The izara-we are said to accept the payment, and give back the noma' of the child. Later in the day the parents return to the spot and obtain an ant with which to perform the divination described above, and they also apparently take back the pay.

The *gura'*, a type of two-tailed spirit snake, is said to live, like the izara-we, in "bad places," and also on the summit of Mount Karimui. Gura' will also take the noma' of those who trespass on their territories; when this is done, a pig is killed to placate the snake, and it may release the victim's noma'. The *uyabebidi*, or "leprosy men," live in various locations, on high ridges and in the tops of trees, like the harmless *sezemabidi*, but they also live along the Tua River. The places where they live are called *uyabeburu*, "leprosy places," which are infested with fireflies and mosquitoes. As Daribi learn in their dreams, the fireflies are really the torches of the uyabebidi, and if a person eats meat or has intercourse and then walks about in an uyabeburu, the uyabebidi will "burn him with their torches," and he will get leprosy. When this is felt to have been so, a pig will be killed and the uyabebidi called upon, and "the leprosy will go away."

Even where the influence, the cause of a sickness or death is known, an element of mystery remains, as in the uncertainty about the fate of a noma' taken by the izara-we, which is expressed in the ant-divination. This anxiety in the face of the external world can be understood in terms of the outward orientation of Daribi religion, of its view of the world as a highly dangerous place. That the source of a malady is somehow cloaked in mystery seems to be a key assumption of this religion, and it is only here, where the "root" of the matter has been diagnosed with some certainty that the influence can be dealt with in terms of reciprocity, as is done in the alliances and compensations of everyday life.

Influence and Reciprocity

What I have described here as "influence" is, of course, a construct of Daribi culture; it is a construed relationship between souls, between the noma' of the victim and an external noma' or spirit-being, both of which are also cultural constructs. We are dealing with a closed symbolic system, and if it appears to us as a curse, if we see a system in which only the sickness and death are "real," like Yeats's "imaginary gardens with real toads in them," then, like the curse of Souw, this is one which applies to all mankind, for all cultures project. Daribi religion amounts to a series of procedures for counteracting such influence, and I would like to explore further the nature of this "holding" or possession of the soul.

One of the major, if implicit and unarticulated, assumptions of the Daribi world view is the opposition of freedom and boundness, of that which is free to move and that which is rooted. I have characterized the Daribi soul as animate and spontaneous; it moves and acts of its own volition. All organisms capable of free and independent motion—animals and birds, fish, men, and insects—are thought to be animated by souls, noma', and are predicated by the state-of-being verb *bidibo* (from *bidi*, "man"), as in the sentence *kibu bidibo*, "a pig is there." Objects which are rooted in one spot, and have a place of their own, such as a tree, a leaf, a human hand or liver, a house, a road, or a mountain, do not have souls; with these the state-of-being verb *erarubo* (from *era*, "place") is used: *ni erarubo*, "a tree is there." With objects of the latter category which have been uprooted or disconnected from their proper places, as when a leaf is plucked from a tree, the verb *munarubo* (from *mubo*, "put") is used (this verb is also a positional, meaning "to lie on its largest surface"). A man's noma' is bound in intimate association with his body, and though it may leave through fright or during sleep, it usually returns because of this association. Through the mobility and spontaneity of his animating soul a man has these qualities and is able to talk, sleep, and nourish and protect himself. Should a man's noma' be weaned away from its association with him, through being "bound" or "held" by an external agent, the victim would gradually weaken, owing to the absence of his animating force, and would lose these qualities. Death is the result of the permanent breaking of the association and alienation of the noma'. Because the noma' is mobile and animate by nature, it cannot ever be "rooted" in a body, but only bound in association with it; likewise, even after death it never has a "true" place of its own. The izibidi may stay at the house of the sorcerer for a time, or linger in the bush near the place of death, and should eventually go to Yazumaru, the abode of the dead, but in fact it remains mobile, and may travel about at will.

Life, then, is for the Daribi a matter of retaining one's soul in its association with one's body, of keeping one's free will and mobility, and of holding at bay the world of influences and entities which would "bind" the soul and tear it free of its matrix. Where an influence is covert, it must be discovered and dealt with; where it is overt, it may be dealt with directly. As we have seen, many of the influences which threaten the individual are attributed to other human beings, who "cause" them for "legal" or "social control" reasons, so that it is not the supernatural alone which concerns us here, but rather something much wider in scope, a way of conceptualizing and dealing with the external world. To be sure, the "other world," the world of souls, is heavily involved, but this does not justify categorizing the whole system under the rubric of religion, for the influence to be countered may be of the natural or the spirit world, and the motives imputed for the influence may well derive from the world of everyday relationships of individuals or groups.

Payments made to a sorcerer or sogoyezibidi, or the pig killed to appease the izara-we, are drawn from the same "pool" of collateral that provides bride prices, betrothal payments, and payments made to the mother's brother. These payments are made to release the hold of some external entity upon one's person, just as divination is performed to discover who or what that entity is. Pigs and pearl shells are "counters" in a way for the vital substance of a clan; they can bring wives and therefore children, and they can "redeem" these children and make them members of the clan, and they may also be given to save a man's life and ward off the influences of sorcerers and izara-we. When a man's soul has been taken, he must draw on this reserve of "vital" wealth in order to redeem it, to substitute for his soul some satisfactory replacement. It is in the reciprocal sense of this type of exchange that the Daribi expression for betrothal, *noma' sabo* ("taking the soul"), is intended. One is reminded of Mauss' remark that "in this system of ideas one gives away what is in reality a part of one's nature and substance," [3] and "again, one gives because one is forced to do so, because the recipient has a sort of proprietary right over everything which belongs to the donor." [4] "Influence" is really a wide and diffuse category, including all the threatening forces in the world against which a man must defend and define himself to keep the freedom and mobility of his soul. Failure to do so would mean sickness or death, perhaps even loss of identity, as happens to certain heroes of Daribi legends who, shamed and unable to reciprocate, turn into some sort of bird or insect.

[3] Marcel Mauss, *The Gift*, trans. Ian Cunnison (Glencoe, Ill.: Free Press, 1954), p. 10.
[4] *Ibid.*, p. 11.

3

The Pagebidi

The Pagebidi's Curse

We have seen how Daribi conceptualize the danger in the world in terms of attack by external entities and how sickness, weakness, and death can only be the result of the direct or indirect influence of ghosts, spirit-beings, or human enemies. There is, however, another possible source for such malevolent influence: the *pagebidi* ("base-" or "cause-man"), a person's *awa*, or mother's brother. If a person falls behind in his obligations to his pagebidi, or does anything to displease him, the latter may curse him (*pagebidi i ora mabo*), either directly to his face, saying, "You didn't pay me, you will fall from a tree," or "You didn't pay me, you will get sick in your house," or, more likely, in his absence. As he pronounces the curse, the pagebidi plucks out some hair from his beard and throws it on the fire. Again, he may say, "May (Ego) be attacked by a pig," "May (Ego) be attacked by a cassowary," or "May (Ego) get leprosy." A man can also curse his sister's son with barrenness, or prevent his pigs from coming along well. Insofar as his pagebidi can curse a person in this way at any time, and does not require some special circumstance, we can assume that a man retains some sort of permanent influence over his sister's children. Moreover, it does not seem to matter whether the sister's child is aware of the curse or not, for the pagebidi may or may not speak directly to him, so this is not the sort of influence which depends upon secrecy for its effectiveness. What, then, is the means by which this influence is exerted? As in the case of animani, the agency through which a "hold" is gained on the victim here is that of personal substance; but, unlike sorcery, the influence is permanent and involves the concept of heredity.

Daribi recognize the role of sexual intercourse in conception, and seem to feel that more than one copulation is necessary for the creation of an embryo. According to their view, two substances are required for the creation of a child; the mother's blood (*page-kamine*, "base-blood"), and the father's semen (*kawa*). The mother's blood collects in the uterus (*wai' tabi*), where the semen joins it and flows around it, forming a container for it. The semen then forms the external parts of the body, the skin, muscle tissue, toenails, fingernails, teeth, eyes, and hair, while the mother's blood forms the blood and bones, and the liver, lungs, heart, stomach, intestines, and other internal organs. When a woman is in her period she says, "I am making a child, don't have intercourse with me." According to informants, "When a pregnant pig is cut open, the bones of the embryo are not strong, the joints have not formed yet; the blood of the mother is still making them." Accidental or unusual pregnancies occur frequently in Daribi legends; I have collected ten examples, which may be grouped into three categories:

1. (Four examples.) A woman becomes pregnant by drinking the sap of a banana tree, water collected in the leaves of a pandanus tree (a form assumed by her husband), or water from a bamboo tube in which a man transformed into an insect is floating. The banana is associated with growth and fertility, and the word for banana (*tq*) is the stem of the verb "to copulate" (*tqbo*). Its juice can be seen as the equivalent of semen, as can the pandanus water in another example. The insect-man simply transforms himself into an embryo.

2. (Two examples.) A woman injures her leg and binds it with a leaf, which fills with blood (in one case it is a banana leaf). She removes this and puts it aside and, returning later, finds that the blood has turned into a child. In this case the leaf performs the function of the semen in the uterus, forming a container for the blood.

3. (Four examples.) A woman has intercourse with an animal and (in all but one case, where she gives birth to various types of snake) bears human children. In another case not counted here a woman eats part of a giant monitor lizard and her belly swells up and bursts, disgorging all manner of hairless animals.

Except where the man transformed into an insect turns himself into an embryo, which is his own affair, each of these examples is consistent with the Daribi notion that both semen (or a functional substitute) and mother's blood are required for conception. Whereas banana sap, a leaf, or animal semen is substituted for human seminal fluid, nowhere is the mother's blood substituted for; this seems to be the essential element. Yet the mother's blood cannot form a child in and of itself; the other element must be present. In another legend, red yams grow at a spot on the ground where a woman's blood dripped in childbirth, suggesting that female blood has by itself a limited fertility. The noma' of a girl is said to come from her mother, that of a boy from his father.

Thus Daribi view a child as the result of a combination of maternal and paternal substances, and insofar as every different recombination of parents represents a unique genealogical constellation of such substances, each set of full siblings, those who share the same mother and father, are in this sense unique. In the same sense, of course, they are internally undifferentiated, for in each case they share the same combination of maternal and paternal substance (and this would also be true of all offspring of unidirectional marriages between the same sibling groups, though it would not be true of all the offspring resulting from a sister exchange, for although a brother and sister share the same substance, they pass on different portions of it). What we are dealing with here is essentially two distinct series of descending "blood" or substance lines, one of which is transmitted only by males and the other only by females; individuals, or sets of full siblings, occur at the intersections of these lines. Thus a man receives his "maternal substance" from his mother, through her blood, and shares this with his sister, and although he may not pass it on to his offspring, she will pass it to hers. For this reason

Daribi consider mother's brother to be "just the same as mother," for, as siblings, both "were made in the same bed" (the womb), and both were formed of the blood of one mother. A man shares this blood (page-kamine) with his mother and her brother, but not with his own father; it is said of mother's brother that "just as a plant comes up in one place and has fruits all over, so we came from this man (and are in another place)."

This sharing of blood, then, a bond of common maternal substance, is the basis of the pagebidi's influence and the agency through which his curse is realized: "When the pagebidi curses his *ogwa*, it is just as when you chop off the stem-base of a plant, and all the leaves and fruit die." The pagebidi can be seen quite literally as the "cause" of a person, both in the sense that he gave his sister in marriage, and in the more basic sense that he exerts a continual influence over his sister's children and, to put it negatively, is the "cause" of their not dying through his curse. Not only does the term pagebidi contain the Daribi word for "cause," page, but also the standard kinship term for "mother's brother," awa, may be used by itself to signify "cause" or "influence." Thus, in the Daribi version, the last sentence in the story quoted in the preceding chapter of the man who removes his vital organs to render himself invincible reads *te boi hweabo awa toru tama tiwai iare*, "that fight-striking mother's brother thing thus made," or "the cause (mother's brother) of that fight was thus." The relationship between Ego and mother's brother can be understood very clearly in terms of the notion of influence analyzed in the preceding chapter. The pagebidi is the page of his sister's son, and can very well also be the page of a malicious influence acting upon him; he is like a sorcerer living at some distant place who possesses a permanent and inexhaustible supply of sorcery material. This idea of an ongoing substantial relationship with the mother's line can be seen in the following story, where it is expressed in the necessity for mother's milk. As a substitute for his mother's milk, the child comes to depend on his father's semen, until finally, when he reaches the age of weaning, he prefers this to ordinary foods, and, driven by his need for maternal substance, he devours the vital organs of his pagebidi (Daribi are forbidden to eat the flesh of their pagebidi, although

Making a canoe paddle, Genabi

Waia, of Noru, with traditional decorative comb and shoulder strap

A man of Iamani Clan "eating smoke"; the fern headdress is popular in the Iamani area

Members of Tua Clan in their sigibe'

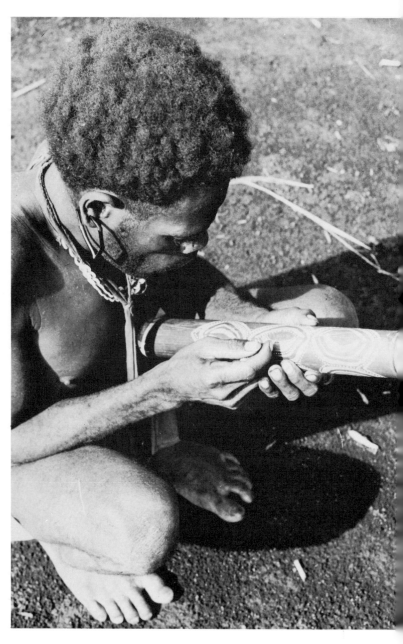

Enebe decorates a green bamboo pipe; Kurube'

Children, Kurube'

The village councillor of Tiligi' Clan rolls a smoke; the west face of Mount Karimui is in the background

A happy pagebidi: Habuare of Sogo and son with a death payment

Kụ, or dripping pit, burial; Tua Clan

Late afternoon at Dobu; a kerobe', or single-story longhouse

Steam-cooking pandanus at Kurube'; Mori and her daughter Masizi

they may eat that of their father's brothers), thereby becoming monstrous and inhuman, and he turns into a bat.

A man and his wife were living together, and they had a son. They took good care of him, but then one day the woman died. The child cried for its mother's milk, as it was still small. The father offered it sugar cane, sweet potatoes, and bananas, but the child did not touch them and continued crying. Then the father went to sleep, and the child came to him and began sucking on his penis. Later, when the man woke up, the child continued this habit, and the father would allow him to do it. Then one day, when the child was about four, the father prepared to go to a pig-feast at a nearby clan. He left all kinds of food, sugar cane, bananas, and so forth, in the house with the child and left. The child began to cry, and followed his father to the place where the pig-feast was being held. When he arrived, he began searching about for his father, and found him sleeping, wrapped in his bark cloak. He removed the bark cloak and began sucking his father's penis. The father woke up and thought, "This isn't my house," and was ashamed, so he covered the child with the bark cloak. The child's awa had died at this place and his body was lying on a dripping-pit nearby. The child went to the dripping-pit and ate the liver and vitals of his awa. Later he vomited blood together with the viscera. He then began to flit about in trees, and soon turned into a *pogebage*, a kind of flying fox. This flying fox is believed to cry when a person is dead or about to die. It lives in caves, and on the mountain *Dogu*.

Although the Mae Enga idea of conception is somewhat different from the Daribi notion, the theme of this story recalls Meggitt's observation that, among the former

semen and mother's milk are regarded as antithetical forms of a vital fluid that resides in people's skins. Coition during the suckling period automatically spoils the woman's milk, and the baby either dies or remains sickly or mentally deficient for the rest of its life.[1]

Among the Daribi, semen and mother's milk represent antithetical substances.

The word pagebidi also means "owner"; the owner of a pig or an ax is its pagebidi. By the same token, a man is the "owner" of

[1] Mervyn J. Meggitt, *The Lineage System of the Mae Enga of New Guinea* (Edinburgh: Oliver and Boyd, 1965), p. 164.

his sister's children; he calls them "his" children, and addresses them as "son" (*ogwa*) and "daughter" (*wegi*). These, of course, are the terms by which a father or mother refers to his or her off-spring, although the term of address used here is a reciprocal. A father and child call each other *aia*, which is also the term of reference for "father"; mother and child call each other *ida*, the corresponding term for "mother." A father and child are referred to by a third person as *aga aianami si*, "two persons who are each other's aia," and this form may be used for all reciprocals. (*Kili* and *kimi* are given as third-person referents for "father" and "mother," respectively.) By contrast, there is no reciprocal term of address between mother's brother and sister's child; a man may address his sister's child by name, or use the term "son" or "daughter," but the latter must always address him as awa, and is forbidden to call him by name (though it must be admitted that Daribi seldom address or refer to an older person by name, but rather use kinship terms or teknonyms). Joking is permitted be-tween a man and his awa, but Ego's relationship to his pagebidi is one of restraint and often anxiety; he must, at all costs, avoid displeasing or provoking this man.

Paying the Pagebidi

As with the other influences which Daribi see as threatening a person from the outside, that of the pagebidi must be countered if the person is to retain his freedom of action. Every member of a clan has, living at the clan of his mother, a pagebidi who is permanently bound to him by a tie of common maternal sub-stance and who in a sense "owns" him. As with other overt in-fluences, this one is countered by means of reciprocity; payments must be made to the pagebidi from a store of wealth representa-tive of the vital potential of the clan if he is to relax his claim. It is as a substitute for the possession of his sister's children, which a man could otherwise legitimately demand as their "owner," that this payment is tendered. The situation here is no different from that of the "possession" of a man's soul by a sorcerer or an izara-we, for all such instances involve some external "claim" on the individual which must be satisfied by this kind of substitution. Now it should be obvious why a person's awa may simply take any of his possessions without so much as asking (as he may, in fact, do), for he may demand whatever he wishes as a substitute for his sister's child; to quote once again a very significant passage of Mauss, ". . . one gives because one is forced to do so, because the recipient has a sort of proprietary right over everything which belongs to the donor." ² Such payments made to a pagebidi do not by any means wipe out the bond of common substance which unites him with his sister's children, but merely serve to keep him from making claims on them by virtue of this bond. His influence, however, does not extend to the sister's son of his sister's son, who also shares this substance; the maternal substance in this case now belongs to his sister's son's clan, for that is where the child's page is located.

A pagebidi always retains a certain claim to the possession of his sister's children. In the Daribi tale of the *dugumaru*, a kind of giant bat, a man gives his sister to this bat, who has special powers, in order to propitiate the bat and keep him from blowing the house down. In spite of the fact that the dugumaru is a formidable being and offers him magical pigs and pearl shells that will multiply of themselves, the man demands one of his sister's children in lieu of payment, and the dugumaru is forced to comply. When a man's sister has children, he comes to look at them, and if she should die, he could go to her husband and say, "I want to take my children." The husband, in turn, may reply, "No, I have given you payment." When a mother dies, her brother becomes the closest matrilateral relative of her children, and can press his claims. In this event the father of the children may offer payment to the pagebidi in return for waiver of his claim. This payment is made for custody of the children, and is distinguished from the payment which a man should make to his brother-in-law on the death of his wife. Otherwise, a compromise may be reached according to which the pagebidi adopts the children for a while, after which they are returned to their father: the latter may say to their awa, "You take care of the children; when they grow up, they will come to me and you will be paid," so that the pagebidi receives his payment upon delivery of the children.

² Marcel Mauss, *The Gift*, trans. Ian Cunnison (Glencoe, Ill.: Free Press, 1954), p. 11.

Failing this, the awa will take the children home with him and raise them as his own. Here there need no longer be any question of payments made to the awa, for, as he has been given "his children," there is no longer any need for substitution. If a man's wife dies, and the children have no awa, another wife of their father may take care of them, or perhaps a childless couple will, or, like Paro's children at Kurube', they will be entrusted to the care of an older, widowed woman living with the clan. Often when a man dies his children will be taken back together with their mother to live with their awa, for his claims now supersede those of anyone in their father's clan, whose other members will be concerned with making payments for their own children. Nevertheless, the children may be adopted by others of their father's clan, especially if their mother passes to another man under the levirate (who will then undertake to pay for them), or if they have no awa, or if for some reason their awa should not want them. The allocation of a child depends to some extent on its age, for a small child will not be separated from its mother, whereas a son who is almost grown will be able to raise his own payments to the pagebidi. Thus, allocation is the primary object of payments to the pagebidi when his sister's son is small; later, when he grows up, their object is to avert his curse.

Insofar as they determine whether a child is to be allocated to the clan of his father or to that of his mother's brother, the payments made to the pagebidi may be regarded as "recruitment payments." The membership of the clan is normatively recruited by a payment made for the custody of each child by one group of its consanguineals to the other; as this payment is made by the father's group to that of the mother's brother, we may speak of the system as "normatively patrilineal" ("normative" in this context denotes that which is culturally prescribed or expected, the "rules" of recruitment). By virtue of his consanguinity a father retains "first option" on his child, and if he pays consistently, the recruitment of the child to his clan is assured. It is only if the payment is not made that further claims to the child on the basis of consanguinity may be entertained. As Daribi clans are exogamous by definition, a man will always obtain a wife from outside his own clan; her brother, the pagebidi of their children, will almost invariably be a member of another clan, and the payments to the pagebidi will be transferred from one clan to another. Thus, if we can speak of a definition of the clan through exogamy, this "recruitment payment" is but a further instance of such definition; the one payment, the bride price, defines a unit in terms of who may contribute to it and who may receive it, and the recruitment payment frees the members of that unit of the consanguineal obligations incurred through previous marriages. If the pagebidi should receive the child, he need make no such payment to the father, however, for the latter has in this case already given up his option on the child.

A father is, therefore, primarily responsible for the payments made on behalf of his young children to their pagebidi, so that he must either provide the necessary collateral from his own resources or solicit contributions from other clan members. Insofar as he is obliged in any case to make continual payments to his brother-in-law, the awa of his children, there is a tendency to make payments specifically on behalf of children on occasions which focus on them particularly, such as the life crises of births, marriages, and deaths. In general the payments are given in one lump sum, consisting of wealth solicited among members of the father's clan, especially his brothers, and this is received by one of the child's mother's brothers and distributed to all those who stand in the relationship of pagebidi to the child. The payment given by the father must be sizibage, in the form of "male goods," pigs, axes, pearl shells, and shell ornaments and headdresses; this is reciprocated with "female goods," bark cloaks and net bags.

A total payment equaling about four pigs is said to be sufficient for each child during his lifetime, although this can vary greatly with individual circumstance. The first payment is large and is made either during pregnancy or shortly after birth. I have seen a huge pig given to cover such a payment. Another payment is given "when the child grows up a bit." If the child's mother should die, as mentioned above, a specific payment should be made by the father to retain the child; when Paro's wife Yabare died, he gave one fair-sized pig, one ax, and one *taraba* shell disk ornament to her brother Sege in order to retain her two small children. As Paro's other wife was nursing a small child at the time, he placed the two children in the care of Gereli, an old, widowed "sister" of Kurube'. When a boy is initiated, another payment is made to his awa, probably consisting of pork or wealth obtained in exchange for pork at the pig-feast which accompanies an initiation. Likewise, a portion of the "pay" given to her father when a girl is "marked," or betrothed, must be given to her pagebidi. When the pig given as a betrothal payment for Pagarabu's wife's daughter was killed, her mother's brother, Saza, and her mother's mother's brother's son, Ebinugiai, a classificatory awa, each received a strip of flesh, while the breast and forelimb were sent to Wabo of Hagani, the child's real father (*aia mu*). When the girl marries, a portion of the bride price must be turned over to the pagebidi; this amounts to about a tenth of the bride price or more. At Noruai, out of a bride price totaling fifty-two countable items (each roughly equivalent to a pearl shell), seven were turned over to the bride's pagebidi to be distributed; at Kilibali, of fifty items, five, including a steel ax, were sent to the pagebidi. After marriage, payments made to a woman's awa on her behalf will cease, for she is no longer a member of her father's clan. A man, however, must continue to pay his awa, though now this is sanctioned solely by the pagebidi's curse, rather than his claims for possession of his sister's son. The payments made now are small, consisting of a few items of wealth, and are made fairly regularly, as in the case of the payments a man must continually make to his wife's brother. At the death of a man, unmarried girl, or child, a death payment must be made to the pagebidi. For an adult man this may amount to a share of the pig killed at his death. When Maruwe died at Kurube', Peria clan demanded that her bride price be refunded, for she had left her husband there because of ill-treatment by an elder co-wife and returned to her father to live. At the same time, it was necessary to make a death payment to her pagebidi at Sogo, for she was not living with the clan of her husband. The payment given to Peria included twenty-five items, each roughly equivalent to a pearl shell; that given to Maruwe's pagebidi at Sogo totaled twenty. Contributions to both payments were solicited and received from men of all zibi at Kurube'. There was concern lest the Sogo men would consider their payment of less value than that given to Peria, so Ţare of Kurube' secretly slipped a jar of husare poison beneath some of the trade cloth included in the payment to Sogo.

Husare is a powdery poison, "white, like salt," which is usually kept tied up in leaves and is administered by secretly sprinkling it into bamboo water containers standing around in the house of the intended victim. A sorcerer will mix husare with the personal leavings of his victim which he has collected in order to perform animani. Husare is obtained from the Tudawe people who live on the Pio River. It is considered extremely dangerous, and always changes hands secretly. The giver will tell the recipient, when the latter is leaving after a visit, to allow his wife to go first, and to follow her at some distance. Then the giver will follow him, come up behind him, and put the husare quietly into his net bag without being seen. Then he will say, "All right, I will go back now. I was just following you to get something from the bush. I put some tobacco into your net bag. Don't keep this in a house where there are children." (Husare is so powerful it will cause sickness in any children who stay near it, and it also brings success in hunting; when Ţare's batch was brought from the Pio, two cuscus and a cassowary were sighted and killed.) Husare is classed as sizibage, "the same as pay"; it is rare and difficult to obtain, and makes a singularly appropriate item of "vital" wealth, for, in addition to its value in buying wives and children, it can also be used to avenge the deaths of clan members. Because the possession of such material by men of other clans could be dangerous, care is taken that it will not fall into the wrong hands (not immediately, at any rate). "Husare is only given to men who have given their sisters to you, other men might bring it back and give it to you (as poison)." As a man is indebted to his wife's brother and must constantly give him "pay," the latter would scarcely want to kill him, besides which wife's brother is the pagebidi of one's children and has virtual power of life and death over them anyway, which he could exercise regardless of the husare. Ţare's husare came from a man of Iuro, and "this man of Iuro has many children, and has given this husare to their pagebidi. Now a child of Kurube' has died, and it is given to her pagebidi at Sogo." Like all such "male" wealth, husare therefore circulates in the direction opposite to that of women, but the circumspect way in which it is handled, coupled with the fact that it may only be given in this direction, gives some measure of the importance of the pagebidi and of the significance attached to the sibling bond.

The Kin Category Pagebidi: Consanguineal Alliance

The nonreciprocal nature of Ego's relations with his mother's brother—the fact that the latter is felt to have a permanent, on-going influence on the former and therefore must be deferred to, the anxiety about being taken away or cursed on one hand, and the feeling of possession on the other—all these reflect the essential two-sidedness of the pagebidi relationship, for it is here that the two basic principles of Daribi kinship, substance and reciprocity, oppose each other. From the standpoint of the sister's son, the pagebidi maintains an influence which is to be countered (unless, of course, he becomes a member of the latter's clan); from the standpoint of the mother's brother, sister's child is "his" child, and he has legitimate rights in him by virtue of this. On his part, sister's son relies on the payment to discharge the claims, whereas mother's brother, on his part, depends on the con-sanguineal tie to press the claims. Thus, there are two major aspects of the pagebidi relationship; it involves, like marriage, an exchange of wealth between clans, wealth which is gathered and distributed like a bride price, and it also involves a bond of con-sanguinity, which relates Ego to the clan of his mother. Again, from the point of view of Ego's paternal clan, his pagebidi repre-sents another external influence or claim which must be settled if Ego is to retain his membership. It is a matter of recruitment; every member born into a clan has such a pagebidi who must be paid, and the clan itself may be seen as a body of men pooling its wealth in order to define its membership against such claims. From the point of view of Ego's maternal clan, he is a con-sanguineal of theirs who happens to have been born in another group, a kinsman, and they relate to him and conceive of him as such. Should they be able to press their claims to him success-fully, through default of payment for instance, he would be incorporated into their group; should they not be able to do so, they will receive as a substitute "vital" wealth which may be used to secure the membership of their own wives and children; in either case, a man relies on his sister's children for recruitment potential.

Recruitment, therefore, involves both Ego's father and his pagebidi, for it is the wealth given in recruitment by the former to the latter which allows him, in turn, to pay for his own children. Yet the pagebidi relationship is not solely a matter of recruitment, for, as we have seen, the payments given to a pagebidi do not by any means annul his consanguineal bond with sister's child, but only satisfy the claims he makes by virtue of that bond. The bond cannot be annulled, for it is one of common blood and substance and continues as long as those whom it unites are alive. A man retains his consanguineal bonds with both his father's and his mother's lines for the duration of his life, whatever may happen. It is this union of two hereditary substances, present also respectively in the father and mother's brother, in one person or set of full siblings, which forges the alliance bond in Daribi society. Thus it is not marriage which allies two units in this kind of system, although the units define themselves in terms of exogamy, but the conception of children, which necessitates the union of two substances; exogamy serves simply to determine which units may contribute substance to form such an alliance. Like the Word of God, then, the Daribi alliance is made incarnate; it begins with a living human being, whom both the paternal and the maternal lines call their "own" child. Recruitment merely serves to allocate this child to one clan or another; it cannot change or annul the consanguineal bonds.

Consanguinity relates two clans through the bond of common substance existing between mother's brother and sister's children, and this is effected through a complex of relationships which is generated as a consequence of this bond. The sum of these kin relationships, with their concomitant obligations and privileges, constitutes what I shall term alliance. The pagebidi relationship therefore embodies the primary link in this alliance relationship; in order to explore this aspect of it more fully, let us return to our model of descending "lines" of paternal and maternal sub-

stance. We have seen above how Daribi describe the two substances necessary for the conception of a child; the father's semen
and the mother's blood are present, respectively, in all their
children, but only the sons can pass on the paternal substance to
their own children, and the daughters alone can pass on the
maternal substance to theirs. We may represent this graphically
by a model of descending substance-lines, transmitted respectively
by males and females, and branching off but not continuing in the
case of a man's daughters or a woman's sons. Insofar as a child
is normatively recruited to the father's clan by purchase, the
transmission of paternal substance provides an idiom for clan (and
phratry) membership; as this is a norm, however, and not a rule
of recruitment, patriliny is only an idiom and we cannot speak
of descent here. A child or group of siblings is represented by the
crossing of such substance-lines, and in each case two paternal
lines are bridged by a connecting link of maternal substance.
Most of our discussion thus far has dwelt on the nature and importance of this direct linking of mother's brother and sister's son
through common substance; now we will consider the ways in
which such a bond relates members of the two lines other than
the awa and his ogwa, and the range of those whom Ego may
call pagebidi.

I have noted above that alliance for the Daribi is based on the
conception of children, the merging of two substances representa-
tive, respectively, of the father and mother's brother in the child
who is a "son" or "daughter" to both of them. These two men,
who call each other *baze*, are allied through their consanguineal
bonds with a third person. I propose to call this type of relationship a "cross-substance tie." The cross-substance tie between baze,
pivoting on Ego, is indicated by "1" in Figure 7. It is not a tie of
consanguinity in the usual sense, for it is drawn through a
descending rather than an ascending generation, and is therefore
not acquired by birth; it represents merely the clinching of a
contracted alliance. As in the case of husband and wife, baze remain affines of one another. Yet baze do make claims on one another relating to their cross-substance tie through a child, and
these constitute the first aspect of the pagebidi relationship discussed above, that of recruitment. In return for the payment he

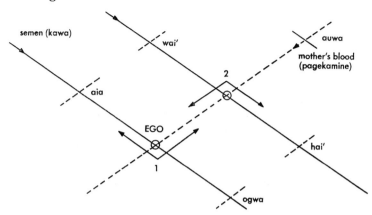

Figure 7.—*Cross-substance ties: same generation (here I have expressed the Daribi notion of mother's brother as the "source" or "cause" of a child by indicating a direct connection of maternal substance between him and the child).*

gives to his wife's brother, the child's father expects the latter to relax his claims to the child on the grounds of consanguinity; and the pagebidi, on his part, expects the payments as a substitute for "his" child. If this payment is not made, neither of these expectations is fulfilled, this particular cross-substance tie between baze breaks down, and the claims of the father's clan, which was to provide the payment, are nullified. (The actual consanguinity cannot, of course, be dissolved.) The inverse of the cross-substance tie between baze is that connecting cross-cousins, who call each other *hai'* (Fig. 7, "2"). Here we can speak of consanguinity; the relationship is one of "common sonship," it is acquired by birth. Daribi say that hai' are "the same as brothers," and the man who is aia to a child is at the same time awa to the hai' of that child and calls both "his" children; just as baze are linked because they share a child, so hai' are linked because they share a "father." The bond between hai' involves the second aspect of the pagebidi relationship, that of consanguinity; unlike the tie between baze, it cannot be broken through nonperformance of obligations. It exists by virtue of a man who was "responsible" for the births of those whom it unites through the bond of substance he shares

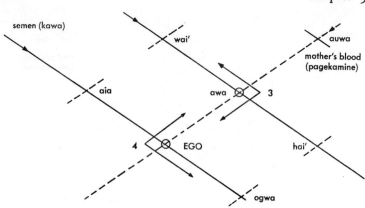

FIGURE 8.—*Cross-substance ties: different generations.*

with each. Both of these ties are comparatively important, for they relate members of the same generation and express alternative aspects of the pagebidi relationship. There are, however, two additional kinds of cross-substance ties, linking persons of different (alternating) generations (Fig. 8). Ego and his mother's father are each related to Ego's mother and mother's brother by a direct bond of substance, although in each case it is a different kind of substance, so that they are also related by a cross-substance tie (Fig. 8, "3"). Persons related in this way call each other *wai'*, the reciprocal used between grandfather and grandchild. A very similar kind of tie, inverted this time so that it pivots on Ego rather than his awa, unites his son with the latter (Fig. 8, "4"); as in "3", the reciprocal wai' is used here. In each of these instances, I will consider the tie to be one of consanguinity, since it involves a descending sequence of substances.

These four cross-substance ties share a number of features in common; each involves the use of reciprocal kin terms among those whom it relates, and each includes both Ego and his awa, pivoting on one and relating the other to some third party. Each one of necessity includes the bond between mother's brother and sister's child, for all of them serve to relate one of these two to someone in the allied clan not included in the direct link of substance between them. This consanguineal bond between Ego and his awa thus generates all the relationships involved in alliance, for it is, in fact, the only consanguineal link which can unite separate patrilines. The cross-substance ties are necessary if the alliance is to involve members of the two patrilines other than those united by the bond of common maternal substance, so that altogether the alliance relationships involve three categories of kin in each patriline: the sister's children, their father and children, and the mother's brother and his father and children. The two cross-substance ties relating mother's brother to the patriline of his sister's son pivot on Ego in our diagrams ("1" and "4") and are comparatively weak. Relationship "1" exists between two affines, and is therefore contingent upon fulfillment of contractual obligations in the form of the recruitment exchange; "4" relates a man's child to his awa, and is of importance only if he and his child are incorporated into the awa's clan, or if Ego should inherit the wife (and children) of his hai', for it gives Ego's child a "grandfather" in Ego's mother's patriline, and by virtue of this the children of hai' share a common grandfather. The two ties which pivot on the awa, "2" and "3", are stronger; they relate Ego to men of his mother's brother's patriline through the latter, his pagebidi, and Ego also calls these men, the father and son, respectively, of his awa, pagebidi. They are Ego's only true male pagebidi beside his awa, and together with the latter they make up the range of close male consanguineals in his mother's patriline. Thus, in terms of the complex of alliance relationships generated by the bond of maternal substance, Ego's maternal kin, as a patriline, relate to him as pagebidi, whereas to his awa, he and his line are either affines, baze, or consanguineals, sons or grandsons. Ego's orientation toward his pagebidi emphasizes his obligation or the payments made to satisfy it; the orientation of his pagebidi toward him, on the other hand, emphasizes consanguinity.

According to informants, a man has four kinds of pagebidi: a "true" or awa (mother's brother) pagebidi, a hai' (cross-cousin) pagebidi, a wai (grandfather) pagebidi, and an *auwa* (grandmother) pagebidi (Fig. 9). Each of these four categories of pagebidi is empowered to curse Ego if neglected when payments are due. As we have seen above, the wai' and hai' pagebidi are related to Ego by cross-substance ties through his awa. His auwa

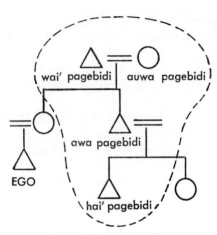

Figure 9.—*The range of pagebidi.*

pagebidi is, of course, related to him by a direct tie of maternal substance, likewise through his awa (and thus, of course, his mother). Ego's mother's brother's daughter is not one of his pagebidi, for she will marry out of her clan of birth and initiate a new pagebidi relationship with some other group, and it is in terms of this other relationship that her major role in alliance will be fulfilled. Continuing relations with her would in any case involve Ego's clan in a whole series of complications with the clan that has purchased her, a third party. By the same token, however, Ego's maternal grandmother, who is both related to him through common maternal substance and a member of his awa's clan, is one of his pagebidi, for it is through her that the substance was brought into that clan. Similarly, Ego's mother, a member of his own clan in this respect, is not his pagebidi, although she will be pagebidi of his sister's children.

As a girl reaches maturity, she outgrows whatever claims her pagebidi might make to custody of her as a child, and upon marriage she effectively passes out of the ken of the alliance relationship between her natal clan and her pagebidi, and a final payment is made to the latter to mark the event. A boy, too, outgrows his pagebidi's claims to custody of his person, but, unlike his sister, he remains a member of his natal clan for the rest of his life and retains his role in the alliance relationship between it and the clan of his pagebidi. He must, in other words, continue to pay his pagebidi, not, in this case, to effect recruitment by countering the latter's claims on his person, but to secure himself from the ongoing influence which his pagebidi maintains over him, and which may be activated in the form of the pagebidi's curse. I have described the nature and effect of this curse at the beginning of this chapter; it is lifted upon Ego's giving pay to his pagebidi, but there is no ritual involved.

All payments given to the pagebidi are given, in a lump sum, to the awa pagebidi, who then distributes them among the other pagebidi. When a child is born, the payment given is intended for all the child's awa pagebidi as a group, as well as for the other categories of pagebidi. As the child grows up, payments to his *awa soro* ("the group of his awa") will continue, although one particular brother of his mother, closest to her in lineal position or affection, may be favored. When a boy reaches maturity and becomes an adult member of the clan, when, in other words, he is permitted to marry, and hence is able to solicit pay on his own behalf, he may ask one of his awa for a contribution to his bride price. This may be done only once, and the contribution must, of course, be reciprocated later. The awa whom he approaches in this way will then become his "true awa" (*awa mu*), an exchange partner, and all of the payments he gives to his pagebidi will henceforth be made to (or through) this man, who thus fulfills all the functions of an awa as far as he is concerned. If Ego has no brothers and many awa, he will tend to choose as his "true" awa the one who was closest to his mother in affection or lineal position. If there are several sister's sons, and more than one awa, they will pair off, corresponding to respective lineal position: "Our gominaibidi has chosen the eldest awa, I will choose number two," and so on. If a group of brothers has only one mother's brother, he may visit each of them in turn on separate occasions and collect pay. Usually, however, in this case some classificatory awa will be chosen as awa mu, and represent the claims of the mother's clan. This is not to suggest that consanguinity is ignored here; choosing an awa mu is simply a matter of arranging exchange partners, of delegating a representative in the maternal clan to receive the payments on behalf of all the pagebidi. In this way the term pagebidi may be extended to classificatory mother's brothers (*me awa*, "other awa"), although this sort of extension does not apply to other kinds of pagebidi. Because Tąre, of Kurube', does not have any true mother's brothers, Boro and Egaiano, his mother's half-brothers, are his awa soro (they are sons of his mother's husband by her sister, Kari, and thus share Tąre's maternal substance). Egaiano is Tąre's awa mu; Boro is the awa mu of Enebe and Kų, Tąre's younger brothers (Fig. 10). "First Tąre began giving pay to Egaiano, then Boro said, 'You two are friends and exchange pay, I will try the other two now' and he became the awa mu of Enebe and Kų." A son of Ego's awa mu becomes his "true hai'" (*hai' mu*), also a pagebidi, and the two become exchange partners, too. The full implications of this relationship will be discussed in a later chapter. Habuare of Sogo Clan has selected his mother's eldest brother, Hobonugiai, as his awa mu, and his hai' mu is Bora, the second son of Hobonugiai (Fig. 11). Tabaia, the half-brother of Hobonugiai, is the awa mu of Piabo, Habuare's younger brother, but has no sons as yet. Bomai, who is younger than Tabaia, is the awa mu of Nogoba, the youngest brother of Habuare, and his son Dilibi is Nogoba's hai' mu.

Under normative conditions, when all exchange relationships

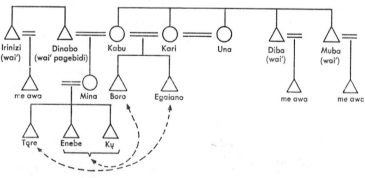

FIGURE 10.—*Selection of awa mu.*

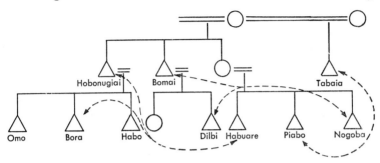

Figure 11.—*Selection of hai' mu.*

have been satisfied, every Daribi man and child will have a pagebidi in the clan of his mother, from whose consanguineal claims his clan membership or personal safety must be continually redeemed through exchanges of wealth. What of married women then? We have seen how a woman in marrying out of her natal clan effectively passes out of the relationship between it and the clan of her mother. Are married women, alone in this society, without pagebidi? As it turns out, there is yet a fifth category of pagebidi, for when a woman has married out this term refers to her brother, who, of course, remains with her natal clan. Just as in the case of a sister's child, a married woman is connected by a bond of common substance to her pagebidi, who lives elsewhere, and her membership in her husband's clan must be secured by payments to satisfy claims made by virtue of this bond, for "all women are like branches of a plant that come from the same base, and all (their husbands) must give pay here." Marriage, too, is thus conceived by Daribi in terms of the pagebidi relationship; a woman is taken away from her brothers in the same way that a child, who "belongs" to them, is "taken away" from its awa, but, like her child, a married woman is linked to her brothers as the branches and foliage of a plant are linked to the base of the plant. The bride price, for a woman, serves the same purpose as the recruitment payment for a child; it is a payment to counter the claims of the pagebidi, and this payment in both instances is made from a stock of wealth shared among clan members which, as the currency of such payments, may be said to represent the unity and potential of the clan.

As the Daribi individual maintains the freedom and mobility of his soul by countering external influences upon it, so the Daribi clan secures its membership by opposing the claims of respective external pagebidi to each of its members; this is not to say that Daribi religion "determines" the social structure or that the social structure is "expressed" or "dramatized" in the religion, but rather that these are two manifestations of a basic mode of symbolic orientation, of cultural symbolism. The kin category pagebidi emerges in the light of this symbolism as the group of those people whose claims on a clan member must be opposed, and the structural implications of this symbolic category concern our analysis of Daribi social structure.

Recruitment and Alliance

Insofar as marriage is also phrased in terms of the pagebidi relationship, we are entitled to ask whether this relationship itself is not essentially one of affinity, for the bride price and the recruitment payment are derived from the same stock of wealth, and, in the case of a mother and her children, are given, respectively, to the same pagebidi by the same man. We have seen, however, that the Daribi consider these as separate payments; they are not merged in one here as they are in the South Bantu *lobola*. Yet, is it not by virtue of these very payments that the clan membership, not only of the mother but also of her children, is determined? Are not a man's children, whom he buys, like his wife, from her natal clan, therefore primarily his affines? What we know of the Daribi theory of conception belies this suggestion, for the substances of the two parents each play a part in the formation of the child, which is henceforth related to its father and mother through common substance. The recruitment payment made on behalf of a child does not "relate" the child to its father, it merely serves to cancel the claims made on it by the mother's brother; the child is permanently related to each by consanguinity.

Reciprocity does not correspond to, or carry out, a preordained symbolic interrelationship here as it does in certain ("segmental") societies, it merely defines and delimits; as in Daribi religion, it is the aspect of reciprocity which satisfies obligations, rather than that which creates them, which is emphasized here. Wealth is given to an outside agent, a pagebidi or sorcerer as a sort of ransom, to "buy off" his influence upon oneself or one's children. Such reciprocity does not "relate" so much as it opposes relationships; rather than bridging a preordained gap between distinct descent lines, it imposes boundaries upon a network of consanguineal ties. Thus the pagebidi relationship cannot be subsumed under the category of affinity; rather, the opposite is true. Instead of deriving the pagebidi relationship from affinity, we may consider marriage itself and the whole issue of affinal kinship as well to be involved in the pagebidi relationship as a sort of prelude, the beginning of an alliance. Hence Schneider's question, and his answer: "What is marriage for a system without 'a prescriptive marriage rule?' This is the innovative, inaugurative relationship which 'creates'." [3]

How, then, is affinity involved in the pagebidi relationship? This is the relationship between the initiators of an alliance, between a man and his wife and her brother, her pagebidi, as well as that of her children. From the time a man begins to "take the soul" of his future bride in betrothal, he must give payments to her parents and brothers to oppose their consanguineal claims on her. These payments should continue as long as the marriage remains in force. As children are born to the couple, each of these will represent a cross-substance tie connecting the father with the mother and her brother. As it cannot by any means change the constitutions of the two parents, who have inherited their personal substances from birth, this cross-substance tie cannot be termed consanguineal in any conventional sense of the word; it nevertheless unites them through the fact that each is a consanguineal of the child. The relationship between the father of the child and its mother's brother expresses both consequences of this bond; because of their common "parenthood," they are

[3] David M. Schneider, "Some Muddles in the Models: or, How the System Really Works," in *The Relevance of Models for Social Anthropology,* A.S.A. Monograph No. 1 (London: Tavistock Publications; New York: Frederick A. Praeger, 1965), p. 58.

united in terms of the child, and insofar as they are not consanguineals of each other but affines, the relationship is carried out through the medium of exchange, in the form of recruitment payments for the child. As a man and his wife have more and more children, the recruitment payments tendered to the wife's brother by virtue of these children, the measure of the strength of the relationship, increase. Yet, although we may speak of this relationship before as well as after the birth of the children as "sustained" by the payments, it is only in a negative sense, by opposing consanguinity, that they do this. Affinity in each case is a matter of one generation only; the father is not really part of the pagebidi relationship, although he initiates it, and he has his own pagebidi elsewhere to pay. In the next generation, that of his children, the relationships pass over into those of consanguinity. Whether in the case of a woman and her brother or of a child and its awa, the pagebidi relationship always opposes reciprocity to consanguinity; the father is involved in it only insofar as he gives payments to effect recruitment on behalf of his wife and child. Thus, for the Daribi, "affinity" is a matter of demarcation, of separating a woman and her children from her parents and brothers, recruiting them to the clan of her husband. As such, "affinity" does not by any means constitute the bond of relationship conventionally denoted by the term, and I would prefer to use a more general one, exchange, for this principle. The exchange system, defined by the circulation of wealth, constitutes one of the major organizing principles of Daribi society, categorically separate from consanguinity but opposing it in operation.

A Daribi marriage is the creator of consanguineal ties, but only in the next generation; it is weak because affinity here is not primarily a means of relationship. Yet we should not imagine that because this relationship is structurally weak, because a father is only an affine of the pagebidi of his wife and children, the alliance bond is necessarily ineffectual. A child's consanguineal ties with both his father and his mother's brother, a wife's ties with her brother, remain in effect regardless of what transactions do or do not take place. The cross-substance tie between baze, plus the fact that they are not really consanguineals of each other, means simply that their relationship will be carried out all the more in terms of the interest of each in their common children. This interest, by contrast, is by no means structurally weak, and it may in fact be very intense. The possible conflicts arising from this shared interest are mediated by the payments given by the father to his baze, the mother's brother; he makes them by virtue of his own tie with his son, to "protect" the latter and secure his claims to him, while the mother's brother, on his part, demands the payments by virtue of his own tie with the same child. The relationship between these two baze is therefore a flexible and controllable one; it is weak in proportion to the claims to the child made by each party, and strong in proportion to the settlement of these claims, the exchanges made between them.

Daribi affines are always related through the opposition of consanguinity by reciprocity, even though the consanguinity that is opposed does not connect them directly. This is the meaning of the cross-substance tie between baze and of the "negative" sense in which reciprocity applies here. Only substance can "relate," only reciprocity can discharge. The father and mother's brother confront each other as representatives, respectively, of the two aspects of the pagebidi relationship mentioned above, exchange and consanguinity. They interrelate by the opposition of exchange to consanguinity, although they are not consanguines. The key to this whole complex of relationships, centered around the concept pagebidi, is the intersection here of these two basic principles. An alliance is made, mingling the substances of two separate lines to form one child (consanguinity); yet the child can only be recruited to one of these, and recruitment is determined by the fulfillment or nonfulfillment of the father's obligation to pay for his child's membership. If the father makes the recruitment payments, he retains both the child and the obligation to make further payments (which will be taken up by a son when he comes of age); if he does not, he loses the child and ceases to interact on its behalf with the pagebidi, although, of course, he will still be related to the child by consanguinity. Thus, the two major issues, recruitment and alliance, are summed up in the pagebidi relationship; it interrelates two lines and provides the claims and obligations through which recruitment is effected. Both are consequent upon the mingling of two substances in the conception of a child; though without reciprocity there would be no means of definition, no separate groups to ally, and no means of recruitment. Like Daribi kinship as a whole, the kinship of the pagebidi relationship is formed by an interlocking of the two principles, exchange and consanguinity.

The interrelationship of these two principles, the obligation of paying the pagebidi, constitutes the theme of a large class of Daribi stories, in which the failure or inability of a man to pay his wife's pagebidi for her, and later for her children, leads eventually to tragedy, usually involving the children born to them. Just as the alliance begun by a marriage is sealed in the blood bond created through the conception of children, so, in these stories, the consequences of a bad marriage are felt in this way. Ordinarily if a man does not pay his baze, the latter will come and take his sister back, or claim or curse her children; in these stories, however, the husband does not come by his wife in the usual way, but steals her away from an unwilling mother-in-law, who has no husband or sons. Thus, to begin with there is no pagebidi relationship. This is the case in the delightful story which follows.

Two brothers named Baurebe lived together in a sigibe'. They turned into beautiful butterflies and flew around over the water. A young girl and her mother went fishing at the stream. The girl saw one of the butterflies and admired it, and she called to it, "Oh, you come!" The butterfly flew up to her and fluttered around her, settling here and there and then getting up again and fluttering. Her mother had caught a whole net bag full of fish, and the girl stole four of them and put them on a rock for the butterfly. As they left the stream, she kept looking back at the butterfly. Later, at the house, when the girl's mother was cooking the fish, she said, "There are four fish missing from the net bag; where are they?" The girl said, "I don't know." Then her mother said, "I saw you looking at the butterfly. Did you give them to it?" Her daughter replied, "Yes, I liked the butterfly very much." Her mother said, "A butterfly is not a man; you shouldn't have given it fish." The girl just said, "I liked the butterfly, so I gave it the fish." Then she and her mother ate the rest of the fish she had caught. In the morning the girl went back to the stream where she had left the fish and saw that they were gone. "It was really a man," she thought, and she went back to her mother and scolded her: "See, the fish weren't there; the butterfly was really a man." Later the girl was sitting on the veranda of the house making a net bag, and the butterfly came to her, took all the white cord she was using, and flew away with it. Then it returned and perched on her leg. She admired it, then took some cord and put it down next to her, saying, "If you are really a man, take this cord." The butterfly flew away with it, and she was happy. Another time she went to the garden with her mother, and then slipped back to the house alone, and saw the butterfly perched on the veranda. She said to it, "My mother isn't here; if you are really a man, turn back into one." She went into the house and, when she turned around, saw a man standing in the doorway. She cooked him some food, but he refused it. Then he said, "I won't ask you to come with me, but if you want to come, you may," and he gave her directions for finding his house. He said, "I ate the fish you gave me, and I took your net bag cord and put it around a tree near my house so that the *nṵ* larvae would come and sleep there." Then he went away. The girl's mother came back and was angry with her for going back to the house alone, but the girl said, "Why are you angry? There are no men around here." At night, when her mother was asleep, the girl gathered all her possessions, decorated herself, and then left the house at the crack of dawn. She followed the road the man had described to her, and arrived first at his garden, then at his house. She saw the two men up in the house, and moved into the aribe'. The men didn't have any pigs or pay, and couldn't give them to the girl's mother in payment for her. When the girl went to the garden with her husband, he didn't try to have intercourse with her. She thought, "What is he trying to do? He isn't my brother." Once they went to the garden and she embraced him, saying, "You aren't my brother; I am another woman; copulate with me," and she hit him. He became sick and went home. Another time they went to the bush to cut some bamboo, and the girl took off her string skirt. Her husband saw her genitals, became aroused, and copulated with her. When they went back to the house, the man became very sick. The girl had taken his soul. She took some ginger and some salt, put them together in a little bamboo tube and shook them in the tube at the place where they had copulated, then gave them to the man to eat, and in the morning he was well again. Then the woman had a child, and it looked very much like its father. At the same time, one of the nṵ larvae in the cord "cocoon" the man had made for it turned into a butterfly. From then on, every time the woman had a child, another larva would hatch into a butterfly. This went on until the woman had ten children. Then the man and his wife went to a stream to fish, and the woman said to her husband, "Butterfly, you never did 'back' the four fish I gave you that time." The man said, "I didn't ask you for the fish," and the two were angry. They went home and ate the fish they had caught. They looked into the cord cocoon, and all the larvae were turning into butterflies. In the morning the woman said, "My mother brought me up, then I got mad at her and left her and came to you, but you didn't pay her for me." The man said, "It wasn't my idea; you gave me the fish, then you came to me of your own accord." Saying this, he heated a stone in the fire. Finally the stone burst with the heat, and the man, his wife, and all their children turned into butterflies. At the same time, the remaining larvae in the cocoon turned into butterflies. The man said to the other butterflies, "We will all flutter around over the water," and they went there.

Here the man's identity is somewhat ambiguous from the beginning, for he may turn into a butterfly at will. It is in this form that he meets his wife, and she makes the initial prestation, the fish, which begins their relationship. He takes the white cord she is using and forms a cocoon with it for butterfly larvae, thus enhancing symbolically the inversion of sexual roles, for the white cord is analogous to the semen, which in Daribi conception theory forms the container for the mother's blood. Finally, she takes the initiative in sexual relations. Each time a child is born to them, a butterfly counterpart hatches out of the cocoon of white cord. When the issue of the marriage payment comes up, the woman addresses her husband as "butterfly," for it was in this form that he began the relationship. The woman has no pagebidi in this story; she takes the man's role, while the man, unable to conform to the normal male role, forms a contrast to her assumption of this role by interacting with her in marriage and procreation as a passive, somewhat female, butterfly. When the woman begins to realize what the situation is, she quarrels with her husband, shaming him, and finally in the ensuing fight all turn into butterflies. Another version of this theme is presented in the following story, in which "bad blood tells."

An old, light-skinned woman called the *taumuzi* was living in a sigibe' with her daughter, named Soraborame. The old woman lived in the men's quarters and her daughter in the women's quarters. The taumuzi was a strange kind of woman, and did not wear a string skirt, but wore an old piece of bark cloth in front, and a tanget in back (like a man). She caught men, cassowaries, and pigs, and hung them up in a *yogo* tree, the kind that grows in lakes, until they were truly dead. One day she brought a young man home and her daughter said, "Don't kill him; I like him very much." The old woman hung him in the tree anyway. The elder brother of the young man then learned of his fate in a dream and came to the old woman's house looking for him. When he arrived at the house the daughter blocked up the holes in the ceiling of the women's quarters so that her mother would not see him, and told him, "My mother kills men, and has caught your brother and hung him up in a tree. You come back here at night." At night he came and had intercourse with the girl, then she told him to come back again the next night. The next night he came again and had intercourse with her, then he told her to go outside, and set fire to the house. The old woman said, "What are you trying to do?" But the fire burned her up. Then the girl pulled down the yogo and found that the young man was still alive, although the other people there were dead. The elder brother married the girl, and they waited before leaving until the illness of the younger brother was over. The elder brother and the woman had two good children first, then later they had another who was light-skinned, just like her grandmother. The father told his wife to throw the child away, but she did not. Later, when the child had grown a bit, the mother went to the garden to get some food, while the father stayed at the house, making a belt. The light-skinned child stayed close to her father, watching him. Her father said, "You look just like your grandmother," and beat her with his bamboo pipe until she began to bleed, and she cried. Her mother came and asked him what he was doing, and he said, "I was sitting here making a belt, and she was watching me, and she looked just like her grandmother, who killed men, so I struck her." The mother said, "True, she looks just like her." Then the whole family turned into yogo trees.

In this story the men are normal, but the woman is the daughter of the taumuzi, one of the varieties of ogre-like monsters which inhabit Daribi folklore. Here it is the taumuzi who plays an inverted role, for she lives in the men's quarters and dresses and hunts like a man. The elder brother and the girl cooperate to destroy this monstrous woman, and thus he claims the girl as his wife, without being able to pay for her. Their first two children are normal, but the third is the very image of her grandmother, the taumuzi. The woman's maternal line has not been paid, and the influence of the taumuzi, her blood, reasserts itself in the child of the couple. When they both realize what has happened, the whole family turn into yogo trees, symbols of the taumuzi's monstrous behavior. Failure to define oneself against an influence, to divert and buy off that influence through reciprocity, leads to the triumph of the influence, and finally to complete loss of identity.

Each person in Daribi society is ultimately a compact, a union of two groups, and serves to relate them in some sense. Even the dead express such alliances, like moldering and forgotten treaties, and, as a whole, the groups which seem as if they had been imposed on this great human gridwork are interknit again and again, for they are made up of nothing but unions. Yet to remain distinct, to define themselves, these groups are obliged perpetually to nullify the compacts, to tear up the treaties, and it is the tension between connection and definition, between freedom and boundness seen here, which informs the relationship between Ego and his pagebidi and is repeated again and again in the religious, domestic, and political aspects of Daribi life.

4

The Zibi

The Brother-Sister Bond

In the preceding chapter we have seen how the pagebidi relationship is at the focal point, so to speak, of both recruitment and alliance and embodies the fundamental opposition between consanguinity and exchange, the two basic principles of Daribi social structure. A person's pagebidi is simply a consanguineal relative living at another clan who must be paid if he is to retain his membership in his own clan, an external "influence" upon Ego who operates by virtue of ties of substance. The pagebidi may be either a mother's brother, together with his parents and sons, as in the case of a child or an adult man, or the brother of a married woman. A wife and her children share the same pagebidi, and it is part of a man's role as husband and father to give payments to this man in order to secure their membership in his clan. Insofar as these payments are made by the same man and to the same man in each case, we might, as suggested in the preceding chapter, consider both cases to be aspects of the same relationship. Correspondingly, both aspects of the pagebidi relationship, that of the wife and that of her children, may be traced to her initial separation from her brother, to the sibling tie which links her, and her children through her, by virtue of consanguinity, to the pagebidi. Thus, in every case the relationship between a person and his pagebidi is traced through a sibling tie, through a tie between brother and sister. In the case of a married woman and her brother, this is the tie itself; in the case of a child and its awa, the sibling tie between the child's mother and her brother forms the connection between the two clans. It is, therefore, primarily this sibling bond, concomitant with the symbolic notion of mother's blood, which is opposed by the bride price and recruitment payments and which nevertheless provides the ongoing "influence," the tie of substance which allies two clans. To put it differently, the pagebidi relationship itself can be viewed analytically as a function of the strength of the sibling bond, and this emphasis on the sibling bond is coincident with the conception of two lines of heredity. As the pagebidi relationship is of decisive importance in the delineation and interrelationship of clans, so, we might argue, the sibling bond, of which it is a function, is a fundamental tie of Daribi kinship.

In his Introduction to *Matrilineal Kinship*, Schneider implies that the strength of the tie between husband and wife is inversely related to that of the brother-sister bond. In patrilineal societies, the functions of recruitment and of jural authority are both exercised through men, and it is consequently in their fate that the interests of the patrilineage lie. In matrilineal societies, on the other hand, these two functions are separated; whereas authority is vested in males, children become members of their mother's unit by birth, and the unit therefore depends on its sisters and daughters for recruitment. Because of this separation of functions, a matrilineal group requires the services of its members of either sex; a man, who exercises jural authority by virtue of kinship, finds his closest lineal descendants in his sister's children, and the brother-sister link is thus vital to the interests of the group, so that "this dependence of a matrilineal descent group on both its male and female members might be phrased as an interdependence of brother and sister." [1] Thus a matrilineal society is limited to a certain rigidity in this respect, whereas

patrilineal units cannot afford to relinquish control over male members, who fill authoritative roles as in matrilineal descent groups, but they can afford to lose a considerable degree of control over their female members, provided that they gain proportionate control over

[1] David M. Schneider and Kathleen Gough, *Matrilineal Kinship* (Berkeley: University of California Press, 1962), p. 11.

the women marrying into their group. Thus the patrilineal descent group can lose complete control over its female members in exchange for complete control over its wives. This follows from the stated conclusions that female members of a patrilineal descent group cannot add members to their group.[2]

In the case of patriliny, there is a range of possibilities; the bonds between brother and sister may be completely loosened, as suggested above, to provide greater control over a woman by her husband. On the other hand, some degree of dependence between brother and sister may obtain, for

the real or symbolic interdependence of brother and sister is by no means distinctive to matrilineal descent groups but occurs among patrilineal descent groups as well. Where patrilineal descent groups practice marriage by sister exchange the interdependence of brother and sister is clearly evident. Among such people a woman's marriage may be directly dependent on her brother's marriage, and where one fails the other must necessarily fail too. Similarly, among those patrilineal people where bridewealth is a significant element of marriage, the marriage of a man may depend on the bridewealth which his sister brings in, so that in some groups brother and sister may be paired off and the brother cannot marry until his sister's marriage brings in the bridewealth necessary for his marriage. Also, the partial dependence of a woman on her brother's protection is quite clear in many patrilineal groups.[3]

Recruitment in Daribi society is not determined by descent, but rather in terms of an interaction of consanguinity and reciprocity; nevertheless, insofar as the recruitment payment is an option of the father's group, we may speak of "normative patriliny" and compare the Daribi situation with this second example. A Daribi child is linked by consanguinity to both his father and his mother's brother, hence each of them has a claim on him; as in patrilineal descent, the father traces his consanguinity directly to the child, and, as in matrilineal descent, the mother's brother traces consanguinity through his sister to the child. Both types of connection and both possibilities of recruitment are recognized

[2] *Ibid.*
[3] *Ibid.*, p. 12.

here: the normative, obligatory patriliny expressed in the bond of "paternal" substance and the maternal tie, representing the interdependence of siblings, symbolized by the notion of mother's blood. The payment which arbitrates between these claims effects recruitment by compensating claims of the mother's brother to his sister's children, just as the bride price compensates him for the loss of his sister; in other words, marriage and normative recruitment, as we have remarked above, are brought about through the husband's efforts to fulfill his wife's obligations to her brother. The wealth which he uses to make good these obligations is, in turn, derived from payments made to compensate him for his own sister and her children, and thus in Daribi society the claims of siblingship on one hand are balanced off against the demands of marriage and recruitment, of one's wife's siblingship, on the other. Daribi society incorporates the interdependence of brother and sister within its "normatively patrilineal" scheme; a man relies on his own sister and her children to provide him with the collateral to establish his own paternal succession, to "buy" someone else's sister and her children. If no "pay" is exchanged, the man reclaims his sister and her children; a limiting case of this, if, for instance, all wealth were to suddenly disappear from the society, would result in a *de facto* system which would be completely matrilineal, like that of the Nayar of India.

It would be a mistake to assume that any sort of patrilineal "descent" in the conventional sense is "purchased" with the exchange of recruitment payments, for, unlike certain African societies, the giving of a specified amount, either as bride price or as recruitment payment, does not automatically assure the allocation of a wife or child to one's group. As we have seen, such payments merely oppose specific claims of the pagebidi, whereas the relationship tie, the basis of these claims, cannot be broken or dissolved, for it is one of consanguinity. Though a son be recruited to his father's clan, the influence of the pagebidi always bears upon him, and the only way to ensure the child's safety and membership is to keep his pagebidi satisfied. Daribi consanguinity remains a permanent, lifelong tie, over and above all recruitment payments; it relates, but does not recruit. We have seen how the emphasis on the sibling tie yields a situation similar to that found in matrilineal societies. A man's sister and her children are lifelong assets and sources of support; he may make claims by virtue of them. His own children, by contrast, must be safeguarded and sustained against the demands of their own mother's brother; a man has rights in his sister's children, obligations to his own.

Kin Attitudes and the Family

The asymmetry implicit in this pattern of kin obligations can be seen clearly in the conventional attitudes toward the various categories of kinsmen. Perhaps the most succinct revelation of the basic orientation of these attitudes came in the form of an informant's response to a question of mine regarding attitudes toward the father's sister and the mother's brother; father's sister was said to be "closer to a person than his awa, because she is like a father." Mother's brother, on the other hand, is more distant, because he is "just the same as mother." This is not to suggest that Daribi go in fear of their mothers, or experience some aversion to them, a sort of polar opposite of American "momism," but rather that these are comparative valuations and express only a relative inclination toward the father's line. A child will be comparatively close to both parents and will respond to each with affection, and they, in turn, each show a great deal of concern for him, simply by virtue of being his parents. Both may chastise him for wrongdoing, but it is a significant observation of my informants that when one parent attempts to punish a child, the other will invariably become angry and confront his spouse.

There is, in other words, a certain tension or rivalry here, and the major concern is for the child. Authority over a child is for the most part exercised by the father, though the eldest brother, the gominaibidi, may come to take over this function as the child grows older, and jural responsibility and authority in the case of an adult man is always vested in his brothers. If a child eats the food of its parents, brings dirt into the house, insults or annoys another man, or fights with other children, its father will punish it by hitting it with his open hand on the side of the face. Informants say that a child is "a little afraid" of its father because of such punishment, and also of father's brothers, but not of father's sister. This location of jural authority with the father is simply another result of the family situation; there is no part-time avunculate here, a child is either brought up in its father's family, the preferred alternative, or elsewhere, with its mother's brother. Control of the children by the father is unavoidable if they are to be "his" children. Thus, certain aspects of Daribi kinship attitudes, the affection toward both parents, the reaction to the father's authority, may be derived from the nuclear family situation. They do not reinforce the "asymmetrical" pattern of preference for the father's line mentioned above, but then neither do they give a complete picture of the relationships involved, for they are far too general and may be predicted for any situation where a child is raised largely by its father and mother.

What this view fails to take account of is the relationship between husband and wife, the third side of the triangle. We have seen above how this relationship involves a certain rivalry over the child, and we may recall in this regard the conflict of interests involved in the cross-substance bond between a man and his wife's brother. A man is, of course, linked to his wife by the same cross-substance bond, since brother and sister share the same blood, but here the relationship is different, since it remains "in the family" and does not cross interclan boundaries. Nevertheless, it is the same interest which a man must oppose in both cases, the result of the inability of marriage to sever the sibling tie, and this interest is phrased symbolically in terms of mother's blood, which unites the pagebidi to his sister's children through his sister. It is against this sibling tie, this bond of mother's blood, that a man's energies are directed by his insecurities regarding possession of his children. How these insecurities are resolved in the case of the wife's brother, the children's pagebidi, constitutes the substance of the preceding chapter; in the case of the wife, the resolution of such insecurities involves intrafamilial relationships. Let us, therefore, briefly examine the structure and relationships of the Daribi family.

An infant may not be separated from its mother for any length of time until it has teeth. She will carry it about with her everywhere, cushioned in her net bag. After a child gets all of its teeth and can walk and talk, it is told it cannot nurse and is given sugar cane to suck. After this the child is no longer carried around by its mother, and, if a boy, may move into the men's quarters. The mother, however, continues to work, either in the garden, or in the house when there is no garden work to be done. It is at this time that the father preempts the child, calling to him early in the morning if he happens to be sleeping in the women's quarters, and he quickly learns to respond to this interest. While I was sleeping at Ogwane's house at Hagani I grew accustomed to being awakened in the morning by his three-year-old daughter Domuai as she rushed in from the women's quarters past my cot to her father, with whom she would spend the day. One night I was awakened much earlier—by Ogwane himself, who was calling out his daughter's name over and over again in his sleep. This pattern was repeated in every Daribi household I visited; Kiru's small son Toge at Hagani would begin to whimper unless he was brought into physical contact with his father, and Tạre's four little daughters at Kurube' followed him about like a small satellite system. A father will talk to his children, try to amuse them, cut their hair, delouse them, give them food, take them on visits with him, and be very anxious about their whereabouts when they are away from him. In the words of Kagoiano:

I know how it is with grown men; when they are first married they are very close to their wives and spend all of their time with them. Later, when the woman has children, the man spends much of his time with them, and his wife becomes jealous of them. She will often be angry with them because of this. A man is closer to his children than his wife is, and he is closer to them than to his wife.

A family is most solidary when isolated as a residential unit, during a hunting trip in the bush or when living together in one of the smaller, peripheral houses built after the exhaustion of the sigibe' gardens. Such isolation does not last long, however; visits are made, others come to share the house, and the family members gradually lapse back into their more congenial relationships with same-sex age-mates. Women generally seem to rely upon co-wives and special friends among other village women for companionship. Unmarried men form the closest and most solidary group insofar as friendships are concerned, and the terms *age* ("branch") and *hainamu,* "age-mate," are heard most commonly among them. Married men rely the least upon one another for companionship and are the loneliest persons in the society. Though they, too, may have special friendships, their closest "friends" are usually their children and wives, in that order. As a Daribi man marries and grows older, conflicts of interest tend to separate him from his age-mates and brothers, and as the latter die out, the number of his wives and children increases, until he finally assumes the position of a patriarch, a sun surrounded by many planets. Thus, a father gradually falls more and more into the role of sustainer, father of a zibi, the protector of his children and wives. He must continually strive to bind them to him.

A man's daily activities are a great deal less monotonous and rigid in this society than those of his wife. His work includes the cutting of trees and the building of houses and fences, as well as hunting and, formerly, warfare, and, though he may occasionally help his wife with the garden work, he is by no means obliged to spend most of his time on the tedious labor of food preparation and close work with the soil as she is. A man thus has more free time than his wife, and he is at greater liberty to decide what he will do, and when it is to be done. He may also use his authority to tell his wife what to do, and beat her if she does not comply. A man uses this liberty and authority to his advantage in the rivalry with his wife over their children, though I doubt that this is done in a spirit of conscious competition. It is rather that his insecurities regarding the children come into play here, and his attentions to them resulting from these insecurities gradually develop a bond of affection which both father and son rely upon. Thus the very fact of his predominance in the household, the fact that he exercises jural authority within the domestic group, is used by the father to bind his children to him. Although he may chastise the child, he will use his power also in a positive way to win his affections.

A child thus cannot be viewed as an independent variable in the formation of his kinship attitudes; he does not simply move through the world cathecting to relatives on his own, but is manipulated here, as in other parts of the world. The father's insecurities derive from anxieties regarding the possession of his children, which must be constantly re-established, and thus are ultimately also a function of the sibling tie, the bond between his wife and her brother. If there is anything in the way of internalization of his attitudes on the part of the children, then surely this attitude toward the mother's line will be internalized. Such internalization on the child's part could only reinforce the awa's symbolic role as an external "influence" upon him, and the father's attitude itself, that which is adopted by the child, is, in fact, a reaction to this role. When a boy comes of age, he, of course, assumes the obligation of opposing the pagebidi's influence, which therefore has a bearing on him all his life.

The Zibi

All the relationships we have been discussing, those of the pagebidi as well as the attitudes within the family, are manifestations of the sibling bond which derive their importance from the strength of this bond in the face of the separation through marriage of those whom it unites. To be more specific, they are manifestations of the bond between brother and sister. What then of the siblings who are not separated by marriage? Is the tie between brother and sister simply enhanced because it functions in alliance and recruitment, or does it derive its importance from the fact that they are siblings? To answer this question we must examine the role played by the sibling bond in Daribi social structure as a whole. Bearing in mind our observation that Daribi conceive relationship in terms of the sharing of common substance, let us recall our discussion of the Daribi theory of conception in the preceding chapter. A child is the result of a combination of male and female substance, of semen and mother's blood. These two substances, in turn, relate him to a male and a female line, through his father and mother, respectively, and thus give him a set of consanguines and a place in the society. Because they share the same paternal and maternal substance, because they "were made in the same bed," a group of full siblings are as one person in terms of heredity; they share the same mother and father and hence the same set of consanguines and the same place in the society. Furthermore, siblings are the only members of Daribi society who share full heredity with one another; a parent by contrast has only one kind of substance in common with his children. Insofar as these substances symbolize definite kinds of relationship, that is, definite kinds of obligations and prerogatives, we can translate the consanguineal unity of siblings into a shared complex of rights and duties.

We have seen that ties of paternal substance relate a child to its father's line, those of maternal substance relate it to the mother's line, and the joining of these two substances in conception forms an alliance between the two lines; in terms of consanguinity, then, a sibling group shares the same relationship to its father's line and the same relationship to its mother's line, and therefore all its members together create the alliance relationship between the two lines. We have also seen that claims made by virtue of paternal substance should normatively be "redeemed" by recruitment payments, whereas those made by virtue of maternal substance should be satisfied or "opposed" by these payments; in terms of the exchange principle, a group of siblings share the same recruitment—the payments are made on their behalf by one man, their father, to one awa soro, their common pagebidi. If these payments are made, they are recruited to their father's group; if they are not made, they will be recruited to that of their mother's brothers. As the offspring of the same mother and father, a group of siblings "relate" as a unit and are recruited as a unit; they share the same pagebidi relationship, and, insofar as they are internally undifferentiated in these respects, may be considered the nuclear unit of Daribi kinship.

Such a sibling group is known to Daribi as a zibi. This term may be used in connection with the name of a man or woman to denote all of his or her offspring; thus the Sonozibi are the children of Sono. It has the connotations of "line" or "lineage," and, like all Daribi words of this sort, may be extended by analogy to cover broader categories, so that, for example, all womankind may be referred to as the *wezibi*, the "line" or "group" of women, and the class of all furred or feathered animals is the *nizizibi* (*nizi* means "hair," "fur," or "feathers"). It may also be extended in this way to cover broader groups of kinsmen, a set of parallel first cousins for instance, or a line of descendants within a clan, but in the strictest sense it refers only to a set of siblings. In this sense, however, it may denote all the offspring of one father, regardless of their mothers, all those, in other words, whose recruitment payments are made by the same man, or all the offspring of one mother, all those who are "sister's children" of the same pagebidi, though it is only where these two relationships overlap, in the case of full siblings, that the whole significance of the sibling bond obtains. It is from this type of "nuclear" kinship unit, to which all the senses of the term zibi apply most fully, a set of full siblings, that the term derives its symbolic meaning. I shall, therefore, use the term zibi in this symbolic sense, to denote a set of full siblings which, after the marriage of its female members, becomes a set of full brothers. Such zibi constitute the minimal consanguineal social groups in Daribi society. Where a man has children by several wives, the resultant zibi are distinguished from one another by referring to their mothers; thus, at Kurube' both Tạre and Ba' are sons of Ozobidi, and therefore of the Ozobidizibi, but Tạre and his brothers are also sons of Mina and constitute the Minazibi in contradistinction to Ba' and his brothers, who form the Hagizibi.

As a unit of kinship the zibi is thus defined both generationally and lineally; a man is not a member of his father's zibi, nor is he a member of his son's zibi, and his first cousins also belong to separate zibi. In all of its kinship denotations, as opposed to metaphorical extensions, the term refers to siblingship by virtue of a common parent or set of parents. As a social group, the boundaries of the zibi may be extended to include half-siblings, which is the limit of the range to which the terminological distinction may be applied, although even here the actual genealogical relationships will not be overlooked, and internal distinctions will be made. This kind of extension occurs especially in cases where a man's sons by one of his wives are not numerous enough to form an effective group, and they, therefore, add their strength to that of their half-siblings by another mother. Another instance of this extension is the choosing of mother's half-brothers as awa mu or exchange partners in the pagebidi relationship, described in the preceding chapter. As we observed there, this involves merely the selection of certain individuals to fill the symbolic role of pagebidi and not a deliberate ignoring or denial of consanguinity. Similarly, where the term zibi is extended to include half-brothers, it is done in this sense of fitting persons into a symbolic role, or if you prefer, of phrasing a social group in symbolic terms. Given the preferred form of polygyny, in which a man marries cumulatively two or three true sisters, a child's patrilateral half-siblings, the children of his mother's full sisters, would be the consanguineal equivalents of his full siblings, for their mothers transmit the same mother's blood as his own. Likewise, given the operation of the junior levirate, which is also "preferred" or normative in this sense, a child's matrilateral half-siblings, the children of his father's full brothers, would also be the consanguineal equivalents of his full siblings, for their fathers transmit the same paternal substance as his own. An explanation of the extension of the term zibi to cover half-siblings, that is, all the children of one man or of one woman, could be based on these "normative" usages.

Just as the symbolic significance of the pagebidi relationship derives from the bond of mother's blood, so that of the zibi is based on the intersection of both kinds of hereditary substance, the sharing of full consanguinity. Since Daribi conceive of relationship in terms of substance, full siblings, the members of a zibi, are the most closely related persons in the society, for their shared consanguinity is exactly twice that of any other consanguineal bond. Thus, such rights and obligations as are consequent upon consanguinity will apply most fully to one's siblings. Because two kinds of substance are recognized, however, it is rather in terms of the intersection of two substance lines that the unity of the zibi is expressed, for the consanguineal relationships of its members to other groups will be in terms of only one kind of substance tie in each case. It is, in other words, the interplay or balancing off of the two sets of obligations, those of patriliny and the maternal sibling tie, that zibi members share. We have seen above how this takes place with relation to groups in the ascending generation; members of a zibi share the same father and the same mother's brothers, the same pagebidi, and thus they relate as a unit and also are recruited as a unit. They relate in a similar way to groups in descending generations, for just as the substance lines converge in the former case to form the zibi, so they diverge here in the generation of its descendants. As they relate to both their father and their pagebidi as children, so do they relate to both their sisters' children and their own children as "parents." The situation in each case, in other words, is that expressed in our model of "cross-substance ties," shown in Figure 7 of the preceding chapter; Ego is a pivotal member in both the cross-substance tie between his aia and his awa ("1") and that between his own child and his sister's child ("2"). When we extend this to the zibi itself, however, we find that, while all members share their pagebidi and their sisters' children in common, each man is responsible for the recruitment of his own children. Yet, in terms of the substance tie, a child is just as closely related to the brothers of his father as he is to his mother's brothers. What then is the relationship of the zibi of a father to that of his children? Is this expressed solely in terms of the father himself, or is there some way in which the groups interrelate as such?

The pagebidi relationship, in contradistinction to that with a father, always relates a group of children to a group of mother's brothers, for there is only one father, whereas mother may have several brothers, all equally related to her, and the group of her children are likewise all equally related to her, and thus to her brothers. The bond of consanguineal alliance between clan and clan thus relates all the members of two zibi equally to one another. Relationship within a clan is thus traced through one of its members, that between clans is traced between zibi; if a woman should return to her natal clan with her children, she would once again be a member of the zibi of her brothers, and the connection of her children to her clan would be traced through her as such, rather than through her brothers. Thus, it is the sibling tie which relates all of a woman's children to all of their pagebidi equally, for they are equally her siblings; it is by virtue of a single substance tie, through one member of a group, however, that membership in a clan is expressed. Men share their sisters' children in common, yet relate their own children to their clan and redeem this relationship by means of recruitment payments.

We have seen in the first section of this chapter, however, that a man relies on the bride price and recruitment payments obtained through his sisters to provide collateral for his own marriage and recruitment payments and that he therefore depends on the sibling bond to sustain his own marriage and the recruitment of his own children. But we also know that all the brothers in a zibi are equally related to all their sisters and all their sisters' children. The men of a zibi are thus mutually dependent upon the same set of sisters and sisters' children for their marriage and recruitment payments, and thus all of their claims made upon them are the same claim. While the wealth they receive by virtue of these claims may be shared with other members of their clan, it is they, the zibi, who determine how it is to be shared or whether it is to be shared. Although Daribi do not practice polyandry or group marriage, the wives of its members are thus in a sense wives of the zibi, for their marriages have been made through its common consent, and their children are in the same sense children of the zibi, since the collateral which is given for their recruitment payments is wealth which belongs to the zibi as a whole. It is in this way, then, that a zibi relates to the children of its male members, and the groups are related as father to son. This is also the expression of the sibling tie among male members of a zibi; by virtue of their common interest in their sisters and their children, they have a common interest in each other's wives and children. The formal means through which this is expressed is the junior levirate; since the eldest brother of a zibi, the gominaibidi, is the *primus inter pares* and wields authority, he has the responsibility for seeing to it that each of his brothers is provided with a wife when he comes of age. Since the gominaibidi matures first, he will marry first, and often marry several wives, some of whom may be given to his brothers as they mature. If he should die, his brothers would have first claim on his wives, and the same is true of any of the other members of the zibi. Wives should normatively pass to a younger brother in each case, but often an elder brother will inherit them.

It is partially because of the sharing of claims made through their common sisters by members of a zibi that sister exchange is frowned upon by the Daribi, for if a man gave a common sister (*horobo ape*) to another man in return for a wife of his own, this might afford an excuse to cancel the payments due to each as a baze, and the man's brothers would not get a share. In a sister exchange, therefore, Daribi insist that the payments be given and also that the men who have actually exchanged sisters may not keep any of the wealth themselves and must give it all to their brothers. The payments exchanged by men who have exchanged sisters are thus made directly to each other's brothers, as compensation for their own shares in their respective sisters. Those who have exchanged sisters, together with their brothers, also become pagebidi of each other's children, and the two lines would thus be in a position to make demands upon one another, a situation which might end in a deadlock, the only things exchanged between the two lines being curses. Thus, according to Daribi, a zibi should not stand in the relationship of both wifegiver and wife-taker to another zibi, and it is the zibi, rather than the individual man, which is the minimal unit in the giving and taking of women.

Just as the members of a zibi are the "children" both of their fathers and their mother's brothers, so they are the "parents" of both their own children and their sisters' children. Just as they may be recruited to either their father's clan or that of their pagebidi and are the objects of the payments made by the former group to the latter for the purpose of recruitment, so they make claims on their sisters' children for the purpose of recruiting their own. Based as it is, also, on the sibling tie, the junior levirate is a sort of equivalent within the zibi of the pagebidi relationship between groups. The latter represents the claims of a zibi made by virtue of the sibling tie with its sisters; the former represents the claims made by zibi members upon one another by virtue of the common siblingship they share with each other and their sisters. One is made through a cross-sex relationship, the other between members of the same sex.

Zibi are the building blocks of Daribi society. They are the internally undifferentiated units of consanguinity, composed of members who share in common the same relationships with other zibi. They are "sons" to some, "grandsons" to others, "fathers," "brothers," "cross-cousins," or pagebidi to others. The term *soro* is used to designate a zibi related to one in a certain way; thus one's awa soro is the zibi of one's awa. Insofar as zibi are recruited as units, either to the clan of their fathers or to that of their mother's brothers, clans may be seen as aggregations of zibi, those of its "children" being added successively with the passage of time. Thus a clan may include zibi related to it through female as well as through male members; it may be seen as a large zibi itself, made up of individual units which are themselves zibi. Similarly, the network of consanguinity, of intersecting blood lines which is Daribi society, may be viewed equally as a network connecting individuals with one another or a system linking zibi in the same way, for members of a zibi share the same heredity.

Together with the pagebidi relationship, which may also be seen as a consequence of the sibling bond, the zibi constitutes one of the key symbolic notions of relationship in Daribi society. As the pagebidi relationship exists by virtue of the opposition of exchange and consanguinity, so the zibi exists through the congruence or working together of these principles. The former is traced through one kind of substance and opposes payments to claims made by virtue of consanguinity, of mother's blood; the latter is formed by the presence of both kinds of substance, and there is, therefore, no opposition of this sort among those whom it relates, who share instead their rights and obligations.

Organization of the Zibi

We have observed in an earlier chapter some of the jural sanctions which apply to zibi members; brothers are primarily responsible for the protection of each other and their sisters and share the obligation to defend them and exact vengeance for wrongs done to them. If one of a man's brothers should kill another, another full brother would be obliged to put the offender to death in retribution. The zibi will also unite in support of any of its members against an outsider, and, since zibi members are considered jurally equivalent to one another, any one of them may be killed in retribution for a wrong committed by any member of his zibi. Fighting among members of a zibi is considered an outrage by Daribi, and if such a fight should break out, others of the community would step in to stop it and punish the offenders. A zibi will also exact vengeance for wrongs committed against its sisters who have married into other clans; if a husband of one of them should kill his child and not give adequate compensation to her brothers, she would leave him. Even where two zibi are related as father and son, each is considered responsible for its own members in opposition to the other; if a man kills his father, it is the brothers of the latter who are obliged to kill him. If the father has no brothers, then this obligation falls to another son of the father.

The strength and political effectiveness of a zibi depend on the number of men it contains; its wealth and marriage and recruitment potential depend on the number of its sisters, daughters, and sisters' children. Both factors are dependent upon the birth rate to some extent; a zibi with few members may combine in political matters with some other closely related zibi, and one which has few or no sisters will rely on the contributions of others of its clan for its bride prices and recruitment payments, but in either case the position of the zibi is weaker than it would be if it had more male or female members, for other zibi have primary obligations to their own members and may not always be able to give it sufficient support. Daribi recognize three gradations of zibi according to size. A small zibi, of about three or four members, is called a *sera'digibidi* ("three men"); a larger zibi, of about six or so members, is a *geninama';* and a very large one, of perhaps ten or so members, is a *bidi hauwabage* ("a great many men"). Most clans contain a few sera'digibidi and one or perhaps two geninama'.

There will often be a great variation in the ages of the members of a zibi, especially if it is a large one. For this reason it will often take on the aspect of a lineage, with elder and younger members. The jural obligations within the zibi are therefore arranged in terms of seniority, in terms of the obligation of elder members to sustain and support their younger brothers. In the second section of this chapter we saw that the career of a Daribi man has several stages; as a child, he is the close associate of his father, who befriends him and makes recruitment payments to his mother's line on his behalf. A devoted father will often, in addition, "mark" or betroth a small girl as the future wife of his son. As the boy reaches maturity he will assume responsibility for both the payments made to the pagebidi on his behalf and those for the girl who is betrothed to him, whom he may then marry if she is of age. If he does not marry at this time, or has not been betrothed, he is classed as an *ogwabidi*, or "boy-man," and will associate largely with his age-mates until he does marry. When he marries, a man will begin to raise his own children, and his activities will be increasingly bound up with his family, until finally he assumes the position of a patriarch, the father of a zibi. It is largely in the intermediary stage, that is, at the prime of life, that the zibi assumes its major role as protector and organizer, for here the young men have taken over responsibility for their own affairs. If the father should die while a boy is still young, of course, his elder brothers would take over the father's responsibilities with regard to him. Because the father is responsible for a small child, Daribi often say that such a child is a member of his father's zibi until he grows up. It is in his capacity as an adult, married man that the eldest brother of a zibi is best able to help his younger brothers, and efforts are made accordingly to set him up in this way first, his younger brothers serving as his helpmates and supporters in this respect. He, in turn, manages the wealth which comes to them as a group by virtue of their sisters and sisters' children and uses it to buy wives or distributes it among them.

The firstborn of a group of full siblings is called the *gominaigwa* or gominaibidi if a boy (*gomo* means "head" or "source," a *wę gomo* is the source of a stream; -*gwa* is a combining form of *ogwa*, "boy," or "son"). The term *toburubidi* (from *toburu*, "head") may also be used; a gominaibidi is literally the "headman" of his zibi. If the firstborn is a girl, she will be called the *gominaiwegi* (*wegi* means "girl" or "daughter"), and the first son born after her will be the gominaibidi. Middle sons are called *tomubidi*, and middle daughters are called *tomuwegi* (from the word *tomu*, "inside"); the last child is called *sabigwa* or *sabibidi* if a boy (*sabi* means "namesake," which may or may not be relevant here) and *nozariwegi* (a "later girl") if a girl. If a man has several wives, each set of children will have its gominaibidi and so forth, and the gominaibidi of the first wife, the gominaiwe, will predominate jurally over the whole group if need be. Terms like gominaigwa and gominaiwegi refer to small children; a gominaibidi is a grown man, the "head" of his zibi, a gominaiwe is a grown, married woman, her husband's first wife. When a gominaibidi dies, his next eldest full brother, a tomubidi or perhaps a sabibidi, succeeds to his position and becomes gominaibidi of the zibi.

The gominaibidi has the responsibility of looking after his younger brothers and has authority over them. He leads them in work projects, such as the clearing of land and house-building, and takes them to live with him in his house in order to safeguard them. His wives cook food for them, which comes from his gardens. If a younger brother refuses to obey his gominaibidi, the latter will forego this protection and refuse to share his food and house with him. When the younger brothers grow up, marry, and have gardens of their own, they bring food for him to reciprocate the food he gave them when they were small. The gominaibidi has the responsibility of providing wives for his younger brothers; after his own marriage, he will "mark" women for them and help them accumulate their bride prices as they attain maturity. He may also (alternatively) give them wives of his own. Where a pairing-off of hai' mu occurs, the gominaibidi will take charge of arranging this. As "head" of the zibi, he thus exercises authority in the use and distribution of the wealth obtained through claims made on its common sisters.

Upon the death of a man, his wives should pass to his younger brothers. In practice this is subject to the situation at hand and the desires of all parties concerned, though a younger brother has the strongest claim. A wife may pass to an older brother, a cross-cousin of the deceased (this will be discussed in the following chapter), or another man of the clan (who should compensate a man with a stronger claim for this privilege). If no one has a strong claim, or if the widow refuses to remarry, she may return to her own clan. This is sometimes stipulated by the bride's father at marriage, for if a woman should stay at her husband's clan without being claimed, she might well become a "wanton," and sleep around freely. The inheritor of a widow also inherits the obligation to continue the payments made to her father and brothers.

When her husband dies, a woman is asked whether she wants

to marry the man with the strongest claim on her; if not, another man from the same zibi, or from another zibi of the same clan, is selected, and she is asked again. When Pagarabu died, the logical inheritor of his wife (since he had no brothers) was Kagoiano, since she was once married to an elder brother of the latter. Although Kagoiano was urged on by the older men, and she, in fact, attempted to seduce him, he refused to accept her, and she moved in with Enebe, a former adultery partner, who is somewhat less strong-willed than Kagoiano. Enebe finally accepted her, although he already had a wife. When presented with a similar choice, Tạre's (and Enebe's) mother Mina did not want to remarry, and she remained with her grown sons at Kurube', where she lives alternately with them.

When a woman passes to another man, he should not theoretically take her over directly; first she must return to her own clan. The man who wishes to claim her then comes to her with mourning clay smeared on his face; she thinks he is in mourning, but is asked if she would like to follow this man. If she answers "yes," then she is free to do so. The man must give a payment to her line at this time, but there is no ceremony (as there would be at a first marriage). Actually, in most cases this procedure is not followed, and the woman simply goes to her new husband. When Suabe, who had three wives, died, they should have gone to Kagoiano and his brothers, who were his closest surviving relatives. In fact, however, they were appropriated by older men; the first was married to Ma, the second to Hanari, and the third to Kaite. Nụ, Kagoiano's younger brother, stole back the wife taken by Ma, although she is an old woman. When Hanari married the second wife, he gave a large pig to Kagoiano by way of compensation and another to her brother at Sogo. Kaite, who did not compensate Kagoiano and his brothers, later gave the third wife, whom he had married, to Kiape, who compensated him.

The junior levirate also indicates channels along which wives may be passed on without being widowed. There do not seem to be any particular rules for this, but it usually involves an older brother giving his wife to a younger brother. A gominaibidi, if he has more than one wife, may give one to a younger brother, who will give him payment (i.e., whatever he has retained for his own bride price) in return. When Enebe was caught having adulterous relations with the wife of Kebui, he was severely punished, by his elder brother Tąre among others. Nevertheless, Tąre gave Enebe a wife of his, Samuai, to keep him out of further trouble, and Enebe paid him for her. Similarly, Paro had been an adulterer when young, and Hanari, his elder brother, gave him one of his wives, Dini, and Paro paid him for this. The gominaibidi in any case has the responsibility of providing wives for his younger brothers; if he does not, and they become adulterers as a result, the fault is partly his, and in any case he is liable to revenge as a member of the adulterer's zibi. Giving the latter one of his wives is a solution of this. The following story, which has come from the Tųdawe, makes a case for this kind of exchange:

Once among the Tųdawe there were two brothers; the elder was married to two women, but the younger did not have a wife, for he was too young to marry. One day he went marsupial-hunting in the bush; he came to a tree with a hole in it and began copulating with it. He did this for a time and then went on his way. He called the tree his wife. When his elder brother's wife cooked some sweet potato and gave it to him, he took it to the tree and put it into the hole. One time his brother followed him when he went into the bush and saw him address the tree as his wife and copulate with it. He said, "That isn't a woman, that's a tree; what are you trying to do by copulating with it?" He said this to himself, and put a sharp sliver inside the hole. His younger brother came back after a while and copulated again, and the sliver went up into his penis. He was in great pain and ran around the bush; at night he had to sleep doubled up, like a cassowary. When he woke up in the morning he found that his penis had swollen tremendously. For two days he hid from his brother; then, when his brother went down to the water to wash, he took his brother's two wives into the house and told them to take off their pubic aprons and spread their legs. When they did so, he had an erection and his penis burst. The elder brother came up and said, "I put the sliver in the hole, when I saw you copulating with the tree." His brother was furious with him, but then he gave him one of his wives and asked if this would straighten things out. The younger brother said it would.

The pattern of exchange in the junior levirate is indicated in the kinship terminology. Siblings of the same sex address and refer to each other as *ama'*; those of opposite sexes address and refer to each other as *ape*. A man and his elder brother's wife, whom he may inherit, refer to each other as *sare* and may not address each other by name. A man addresses his sare as *ama'go we* ("brother's wife"); a woman addresses her sare as *auwago ogwa* ("grandmother's son," for she calls his mother "grandmother"). A man may accept food from his sare, but may not joke with her. A man and his sare's father call each other *wąi* ("father-in-law" —"son-in-law") and may not joke or speak each other's names. A man and his sare's mother call each other *au* ("mother-in-law" —"son-in-law"), and practice complete avoidance, including a tabu on each other's names. These are the standard Daribi relationships with wife's parents, for a man's sare is his potential spouse, and the avoidances are strictly observed. A man and his sare's brothers call each other baze; he calls her sisters *baze-we*, and her brothers call his sisters the same. Again, these are the standard terms for a spouse's siblings. Baze should not joke or address each other by name; they call each other baze. A woman calls her sare's parents, who are the same as her husband's parents, wai' and auwa, "grandfather" and "grandmother," respectively, and they call her wai'; there are no avoidances observed between them. The term sare is also used between a man and the wife of any man in his clan outside his zibi, together with the accompanying terms for sare's parents and siblings, for he may also inherit these if their husbands' younger brothers waive their respective claims. The term sare may, therefore, be glossed as "potential spouse under the levirate," and the restrictions between sare seen as safeguards against adultery.

A man and his younger brother's wife call each other wai' ("grandfather"—"grandchild"), and, as noted above, there are no avoidances between wai'. A man may accept food from his younger brother's wife, but would not marry her "for shame." He calls her parents wąi and au ("father-in-law" and "mother-in-law"). He and her brothers call each other baze, and he calls her sisters baze-we, since the two zibi are in a wife-giver–wife-taker relationship. A woman calls her husband's brothers' wives *abere*, their siblings ama' and ape, and their parents aia and ida. Abere should not joke with one another, but otherwise there are no restrictions.

The use of grandparental terminology toward her husband's parents and elder brothers on the part of a woman has the effect of grouping them together and raising them in generation; her parents-in-law are raised one generation, her husband's elder brothers two. Calling a person wai' puts him in a category of somewhat distant relationships, with which there are no extreme restrictions, but which nevertheless precludes sexual contact. The term sare imposes restrictions, but at the same time implies the relationship of potential spouse, for sare relate to each other's parents and siblings in the same way as husband and wife. The restrictions may be seen as directed against the possibility of adultery, for sare are not yet married, whereas the terminology implies that they might be so.

Just as the organization of jural authority in terms of seniority within the zibi imposes order on the claims made upon one another by zibi members, which might otherwise lead to devisive competition, so that of the junior levirate channels the claims they may make on the succession of each other's wives, wives in whom they share a common interest insofar as the bride price through which they were obtained came from a "pool" of wealth claimed by virtue of their common siblingship with their sisters. As it governs the inheritance of wives, so the junior levirate also prearranges the adoption of children, for these, especially when small, accompany their mother. Thus, a man upon inheriting his brother's wife also inherits her children and the obligation of recruiting these children, which are, therefore, recruited to their father's group, and recruited to it by payments of wealth which came from the same source, the same father's sisters, as those made by his father.

The pagebidi relationship relates people by consanguinity across the lines delimited by exchange; the zibi unites people by consanguinity in opposition to its affines, or relatives by exchange. A group of brothers share pagebidi relationships through their sisters, and they are bound together with relation to their wives by virtue of common siblingship with their sisters, hence the junior levirate. The pagebidi relationship, the zibi, and the junior levirate are all functions of the sibling bond, and their existence correlates with the emphasis placed by Daribi society on this bond.

5
Consanguinity: The Principle of Relationship

Substance and Relationship

In the preceding two chapters we have seen that Daribi conceive of relationship in terms of ties of shared substance. Relationship, in turn, has two major aspects; it represents a degree of "relatedness" or connection through bodily substance between two people, and it also legitimizes claims made by virtue of such relatedness. There are, moreover, two distinct kinds of bodily substance recognized by Daribi to be present in all persons, one of which is transmitted by males, the other by females. It is in terms of this contrast of kinds of substance that the normative claims made on relatives are phrased; the tie of mother's blood is "opposed" by payments, that of paternal substance is "redeemed" or reinforced by payments. Thus, in the pagebidi relationship the claims on a child made by his mother's brother are satisfied by the substitution of wealth for the child himself, redeeming in this way the father's claims to his possession. Yet, in spite of the satisfaction of these claims, the mother's brother remains related to the child, for it is his claims alone that have been satisfied by the payments. Because of this continuing relationship with the child, the pagebidi can, in turn, make further claims to the child at a later time, so that the redemption of paternal ties becomes a lifelong proposition. If the payments are not made, the pagebidi retains the right to dispossess the father of the child or to curse the latter through his "influence" over him by virtue of the blood tie. What remains constant here is the fact of relationship, what is subject to variation is whether or not the "normative" claims are met; a man is always the "son" of his pagebidi and his father, regardless of which clan he belongs to. Consanguinity always relates those who share some kind of substance bond between them, whether or not the normative payments are made. The claims themselves are always based on relationship, so we can speak of our first aspect of relationship, which I will call consanguinity, as the broader and more general of the two, encompassing the other and existing on a higher level of abstraction. It is because the two "kinds" of substance relationship are of the same category, and can be equated in this way, that we can speak of cross-substance ties.

As a test of this proposition, that consanguinity is an essential category, and that ties of maternal and paternal substance may be considered as subcategories, or contrasts made within it, we might consider whether claims may be made in terms of consanguinity which is not either distinctly maternal or paternal, that is, in terms of cross-substance ties. We have seen that a child's father and mother's brother, both related to him as consanguineal "parents," relate to each other as affines, for they are not consanguineals by birth. What then of cross-cousins, our second cross-substance relationship? They are related as consanguineals through ties of substance to the same person, who is "father" to one and "mother's brother" to the other. Although they share no one substance in common, they share together the substance of the same man and are both his "sons." Daribi say that they are "the same as brothers." Can they claim the rights of brotherhood in one another? Let us examine the relationship between cross-cousins.

The Daribi Alliance Bond

We have seen in the preceding chapter that the obligations between brothers are expressed formally through the junior levirate, that is, through rights in the succession of each other's wives consequent upon their common claims on the wealth brought in through their sisters. If cross-cousins are "the same as brothers," then, we should expect that such rights would obtain between them also. Daribi men may not marry their cross-cousins; it would be incestuous, for they are "the same as sisters." Instead, a male hai' should give his sister "somewhere else" and give to Ego some of the "pay" he receives. The same rationale is used between brothers. Hai', in fact, should always treat one another as brothers. If their clans should happen to be at war with one another, a man should shout a warning to his hai' as he is approaching his house that he is coming and does not want to shoot him. In stories the two heroes may be either brothers or cross-cousins; the distinction is immaterial. The two culture-heroes, Iwai and Mawa, who shot the sun and moon into orbit, are cross-cousins. Hai' may joke with one another, as brothers may, and, as in the case of brothers, they may address each other by name, although most people prefer to use the kinship term (Daribi seldom use names in addressing each other in any case). Hai' are also obliged to exchange wealth (sizibage—"male goods") when they visit each other, and may ask each other for "pay" in the form of contributions to bride prices and recruitment payments as often as they like. Thus, in addition to his brothers, a man may go to his hai' whenever he wishes to marry and solicit contributions for his bride price. When a child is born, a man will go to his hai' and say, "I would like to pay this child's awa, give me pay," and his hai' will give him some (since the hai' relationship is reciprocal, Ego's hai' has, of course, the right to ask the same of him).

The wealth which hai' are obliged to exchange with one another has, moreover, a definite purpose; a man gives "pay" to his hai' to secure leviratic rights in the wife of the latter, to "buy" the right to inherit his hai' 's wife when he dies. If these payments are made, a man has leviratic priority over the elder brothers of his hai' and also over his classificatory, or "clan" brothers, although not over his younger brothers. When his hai' dies, therefore, a man can ask for the woman "for whom he has paid." If, in spite of his payments, the wife is inherited by a brother of the hai', Ego can go to this brother and say, "Give back all the pay I have given to your brother, you have taken his wife," and the brother will be obliged to do this. A man may also cancel his hai' 's right to inherit his wife after his death by giving him a pig; if, however, the giver has no brothers, his hai' has the right to refuse the pig and thus retain first priority in the inheritance of the wife. If a man sees that his hai' does not have any brothers, he gives him "pay" all the time, jokes with him a great deal, and gives him food, for he knows that if his hai' dies he will get his wife. If his hai' has brothers who might inherit his wife, the man will not give him pay "all the time," and will be less cordial.

Thus, hai' share all the rights and obligations of brothers, with the qualification that leviratic claims must be "redeemed" by payments. This qualification is a result of the fact that hai' will normatively be members of different clans and that clans define themselves by exchange; and the direct transfer of women from one clan to another would violate the limits set by this—it would transfer a woman paid for by the wealth of one clan, without remuneration to that clan, to another. The levirate between hai' is in the nature of an option, which must be fulfilled by payments, and this is necessitated by the facts of clan membership. Otherwise there are no qualifications to the "brotherhood" between hai'. Brothers, of course, share wealth and privileges as a result of their common siblingship with their sisters, and the same is true of hai', who are "brothers" to each other's sisters. This is, therefore, also the source of their leviratic claims on each other's wives. Brothers give "pay" to each other when they share their sisters' bride prices, and these are shared among hai', too. Hai', however, must exchange additional wealth to validate their leviratic claims. "Hai' live a long way off, ama' lives with one, therefore pay is always given to hai'." A man gives "pay" to his ama' when his child is married and gives him pork when he kills a pig; he buys baby pigs from his brothers. When a man receives payment from his baze, he divides this among his brothers. This is not reciprocated; his ama' says, "Wait until my little girl gets married, then I will pay you." A hai', then, is the same as a brother; when a man asks his hai' for pay, he says, "Before, I gave you pay, now I want to get married; you 'back' this."

Hai' are "brothers" and share interests in each other's sisters, and, therefore, like brothers, share claims on each other's wives. They also, for the same reason, relate to each other's children as "parents." Should a man inherit his hai' 's wife under the levirate, he would become the stepfather of her children, and might add them, especially the smaller ones, to his household.

The obligations and privileges consequent upon the "sibling-ship" of hai' can be traced, as can those of the junior levirate, in the kinship terms used between Ego and the affines of these "siblings." These turn out, in fact, to be the same terms in each case as are used with the affines of siblings; a man and his hai''s wife call each other sare; he calls her brothers and sisters baze and baze-we and her parents wąi and au. The terms are identical, in other words, with those used for elder brother's wife and her family. Baze who are related through one's hai' are called *hai' bare baze*. We have already glossed the term sare as "potential spouse under the levirate," and that is the case here, too. According to Daribi, this potential relationship is kept in mind by the father of his hai''s wife; when he receives wealth from his son-in-law, he thinks, "This man got his wealth from his hai'." He and his line relate to Ego and his brothers as wife-giving affines. Likewise, the husband of their female hai', together with his line, relate to Ego and his brothers as wife-taking affines. They call her husband and his brothers baze, his sisters ape ("sister," for they are wife-takers, and should not give these women to Ego and his zibi), and his parents wai' and auwa, "grandfather" and "grandmother." As "wife-takers" of Ego's hai', they give "pay" to the latter, who is obliged to give some of it, in turn, to Ego. Thus, by virtue of their "siblingship," hai' share the same affinal relatives and therefore share mutual obligations and rights with regard to them.

As the term hai' itself is reciprocal, so are the claims which hai' may make on each other. Insofar as they are "brothers," they are equal, regardless of the fact that each is linked to their common "parent" through a different kind of substance; a man is father's sister's son to a hai' who is his mother's brother's son. They are "brothers" by consanguinity, traced through two kinds of substance in a cross-substance tie. As we might expect, however, the "normative" system of claims traced through specific kinds of substance is also a factor here, for, as we have seen in our discussion of the pagebidi relationship, one hai' is always a pagebidi to the other. For this reason there is an "overlay" of attitudes and structural relationships resulting from the pagebidi relationship on that between hai'; a man will exercise more restraint toward his *awago ogwa*, his mother's brother's son, than toward his father's sister's son, who, of course, will regard him, in turn, as a pagebidi. Thus, father's sister's son is considered more of a "true hai' " than mother's brother's son, whom he calls "little pagebidi." Father's sister's son is said to be "the same as one's father"; mother's brother's son is "the same as one's mother." One's hai' pagebidi can, of course, curse one. The hai' relationship, on the other hand, is considered warm and friendly, yet every relationship between hai' will be "skewed" in these terms. According to Kagoiano, "a man's face is turned toward his *na'go ogwa* (father's sister's son), his back is turned toward his awago ogwa (mother's brother's son), for "we are a bit afraid of the pagebidi; na'go ogwa is closer." One hai' is always in a somewhat superior position, being a pagebidi of the other. If hai' are viewed as "the same as brothers," then the hai' pagebidi can be seen as analogous to an elder brother, who exercises authority over his younger brothers. Although this is not formally expressed as a "junior" leviratic succession in terms of affinal terminology, there is an instance in which such succession is enjoined among hai'. If a gominaibidi should die, his wife would not be inherited by his hai' pagebidi, "because he is very close to him, his mother came from there." This does not apply to his younger brothers. (A gominaibidi is considered "a bit closer" to his mother than the younger brothers; he is also obliged to be more careful about the strict observation of marriage rules than they, for he is in a position of authority and has the responsibility of arranging marriages for the zibi.) The hai' of a gominaibidi does not, for this reason, decline to give "pay" to him; it is given, just as with any other hai', but is refunded to him by the inheritor of the gominaibidi's wife. Otherwise, the pagebidi relationship does not interfere with that between hai'; a man gives more "pay" to his hai' pagebidi "because of his mother," and in the case of a gominaibidi may not leave his wife to him; but otherwise, in spite of this differentiation, the relationship between hai' is a two-way bond, with shared rights and obligations.

Like the pagebidi relationship with one's awa, the hai' relationship joins persons by consanguinity across clan boundaries; it is
also an aspect of the consanguineal alliance between groups. We
have already encountered this fact in our analysis of the levirate
between hai'; because hai' are members of different clans, their
obligations and rights in each other must be expressed in terms
of payments, and thus they must exchange wealth to validate
their leviratic claims in one another. As in the case of the pagebidi
relationship between mother's brother and sister's son, we have
here a symbolic relationship between groups, a set of roles which
may be filled by persons delegated to do so in each group. In the
chapter on the pagebidi we have seen how this is done in the case
of the awa mu and also how male cross-cousins may be paired off
as hai' mu of each other (Fig. 11). This is arranged between the
cross-cousins themselves, often under the guidance of a gominaibidi. A man's matrilateral hai' mu is the son of his awa mu if possible; likewise, his patrilateral hai' mu is someone to whom his
father is awa mu. Two men who are hai' mu to one another henceforth give whatever "pay" might be due to their hai' to one another, and they also transfer to each other those leviratic rights
which cross-cousins share. A man may thus have two hai' mu, a
patrilateral and a matrilateral cross-cousin who is his exchange
partner. It is conceivable that if a man died both of these hai'
might press claims for his wife (if he had only one), and in that
case his patrilateral hai' might have the stronger claim for reasons
outlined above, although Daribi stress that both kinds of hai' have
such rights.

Full cross-cousins other than the one with whom Ego stands in
the relationship of hai' mu can ask Ego for "pay" only once,
when they are marrying. When such a hai' dies, Ego goes to his
clan to mourn him and brings "pay" which is exchanged. In
spite of the differentiation between patrilateral and matrilateral
hai' discussed above, "closeness" to a hai' also depends on personal
factors; one is a particular friend to some hai', and not to others.
"If a man does not have any na'go hai', he will be close to his
awago hai', as it is the only hai' he has."

Hai' are thus "brothers" through consanguinity and share the
rights which Daribi associate with brotherhood, yet, because the

principle of consanguinity is made up of two contrasting kinds of substance tie, they are also linked through the pagebidi relationship, and one hai' is always the pagebidi of the other. The relationship between hai' is, therefore, a combination of the two key symbolic relationships which form the main themes, respectively, of the two preceding chapters, that of the pagebidi and that of the zibi. This, again, is a consequence of the fact that a man's sister's children as well as his own children are felt to be "his" offspring, and, consequently, that a child has two "fathers." His siblings through his father are brothers, ama'; those through his mother's brother are also "the same as brothers," hai'. Hai' are "brothers" who normatively belong to different clans, and, therefore, brothers through the pagebidi relationship, which symbolizes the substance ties between clans, and opposes ties of substance by reciprocity. Because they are "brothers," they share the rights of brothers in each other's sisters and wives; because they trace their brotherhood through the pagebidi relationship, they must fulfill these rights, the consequences of consanguinity, through the medium of exchange. Like the relationship between a mother's brother and his sister's children, theirs simultaneously includes two functions, alliance and definition; it allies the two clans through substance ties and also maintains the boundaries between the clans.

This, then, is the Daribi alliance bond, the result of the connection of mother's blood between two clans, which are related to each other by consanguinity and defined as against one another by the principle of exchange. The symbolic significance of the alliance bond is to make each person a member, either "real" or "token," of both his father's and his mother's clans. The extension of the rights of siblingship, the levirate, and the sharing of the bride price to these "brothers" in other clans is the formal expression of this alliance.

The two kinds of substance both equally "relate" people, they interrelate the members of a clan, and they relate each of these, in turn, to members of his mother's clan. Were this not true, we could not speak of hai' as consanguineals of one another. Taken separately, the two kinds of substance each allow certain kinds of "optional" claims to be made and certain kinds of "normative" alignment; yet, if these claims are not validated, if a child is aligned with its mother's clan, the relationship through substance still holds. A child is equally "related" to a clan whether his ties to it are through a man or a woman; he is a true member of the clan if he shares fully in its exchange activities, in its "pool" of vital wealth. Relationship, in the sense of consanguinity, equal relationship through both kinds of substance tie, is given by birth; clan alignment is determined by a number of "choices" which may be made by a person's father, mother, mother's brother, or by the person himself. It is only in the "normative" situation, when a father exercises his "optional" first priority in the possession of his children, that the claims made by virtue of maternal and paternal substance are in force; yet, as we have seen, Daribi fathers consider it desirable to retain their own children—this is a "norm" or value of Daribi culture. Hai' are thus "brothers," whether they belong to different clans or the same clan; if a man lives with his mother's clan, his "siblingship" with the members of that clan becomes clan siblingship, and he shares in their leviratic rights and mutual obligations as a full member.

Consanguinity

> This is the same as a tree; when it grows up
> and its fruit falls down, we can pick this up
> [Daribi saying *apropos* of hai' 's children].

The terminological distinction between brothers and hai', between siblings related through same-substance ties and those related through cross-substance ties, remains in effect for one generation only, for the children of hai' call each other "brother" and "sister" (and those of hai' of opposite sexes call each other hai'). Thus, by the second generation; the descendants of a marriage no longer distinguish between relationship through maternal substance and that through paternal substance. The distinction, in other words, relates to the pagebidi relationship alone and the opposition it implies between relationship and recruitment. Hai' are "brothers"; they are normatively members of different clans. But, in fact, they may or may not be so. In any case, it is they who may be recruited to one group or the other and to whom the pagebidi relationship between the two groups applies. The alliance between a man's group and that of his wife, which is realized in the conception of children embodying the substance of each group, is therefore embodied in their children. Yet, precisely because these children embody the substances of the two groups, thereby allying them, the claims of both, of their father as well as their mother's brothers, bear upon them. It is only where these claims have been settled, by recruitment to one group or the other, that consanguinity is not directly affected by recruitment claims, and this is in the generation of the children of hai'. They call their father's hai' "father" and "father's sister," their mother's hai' "mother" and "mother's brother," and the children of these are their classificatory "brothers," "sisters," and hai' (Fig. 12). As in the case of the levirate between brothers, that between hai' indicates channels along which children may be inherited. A man calls his hai' 's children "son" and "daughter" and may very well inherit them, especially small ones, together with his hai' 's wife. If this occurs, the children will be full consanguineals of their stepfather's clan, and will address and refer to them using the same terms as those used by his own children. Thus the "levirate" between hai', a consequence of their "siblingship," provides a final possibility for the recruitment of children

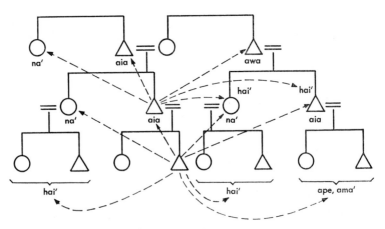

FIGURE 12.—*Closing of the alliance.*

to either group, though it is through siblingship in this case rather than through the pagebidi relationship, and the claims do not bear on the children directly, only on their mothers. These children, of course, have hai' and pagebidi of their own in other clans, and the pagebidi relationships of their parents do not affect them.

This marks the closing of the alliance; what began as a marriage between two "unrelated" lines has concluded in the recognition of full, equal consanguinity with both of them. The children of hai' should not marry, for they are the offspring of "brothers"; likewise, the children of parallel cousins should not marry, for they stand in the same consanguineal relationship. If the latter should happen to be members of different clans, they would be bound to one another by the same degree of relationship as obtains between the children of hai'; if a man joins the clan of his hai', he is thus still allied to that of his father, and his children are to the children of his clan brothers as they are to those of his hai'.

Just as the recognition of full consanguinity between the children of hai' and their lines marks the closing of the alliance bond, so it marks the beginning of the divergence of the two lines, for there are no longer any obligations here. Children of hai' may share the same man as father and stepfather and thus be members of the same clan, or, more likely, they may belong to separate clans, but they may not make claims on one another; there is no levirate between them as such. The consanguinity between children of hai' is a sort of residuum of the claims existing between their parents, yet it still "relates" them, and theirs is the last generation to feel the effects of these claims. Where there are no longer any such claims, the two clans cease to interact with one another in terms of the alliance; the relationship has become too distant, and must be renewed if the alliance is to continue. For this reason, although the children of hai' may not marry, their children may, and they may marry each other's children, thus renewing the alliance between the two clans. Such a marriage is, of course, a marriage between consanguineals, but their relationship is distant enough so that they may marry. Insofar as Daribi trace consanguinity through both parents, all members of the society could probably trace some sort of genealogical connec-

tion with one another, and the marriage rule as defined in terms
of consanguinity, or incest, is thus phrased in terms of genealogical distance. With the extinction of claims made through the
pagebidi relationship in the third generation following a marriage,
ties through one specific kind of substance, maternal or paternal,
are equated terminologically with cross-substance ties, for no special claims are made. Therefore, the rule of incest is expressed in
general, consanguineal terms, and not in those of some particular
substance.

The children of first cousins, who are in our terminology second cousins, thus stand at the limit of genealogical "closeness" as
regards incest. Their parents are related to each other as "children" of the same zibi, either full parallel or cross-cousins, and
they may marry each other's children, or marry their own children to these, without the union being considered incestuous.
This definition of incest in terms of distance constitutes the consanguineal aspect of the Daribi marriage rule (Fig. 13); it states
one of the limiting conditions for marriage. No two people who
are related consanguineally as second cousins or closer may marry.
People more distantly related than this may marry provided that
they are members of different clans. Taken together, these two
rules, those of incest and exogamy, representing, respectively, the
principles of consanguinity and exchange, constitute the Daribi

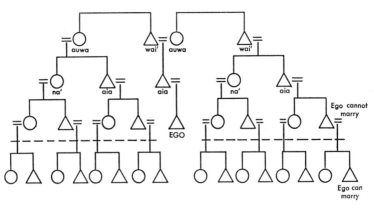

FIGURE 13.—*The limits of incest.*

marriage rule. In both aspects it is a negative marriage rule; that is, it indicates who may be married by specifying those categories of people whom one may not marry. It is because consanguinity does not recruit, or delimit groups, and because groups are defined by exchange, by exogamy, that the marriage rule is governed by two principles; it is because these two principles are combined in the normative system, and interlock to oppose (the pagebidi relationship) or reinforce each other (the zibi), providing idioms for relationship within and among units, forming discrete groups which both interrelate and intermarry with each other, that the marriage rule is "negative."

The idiom of incest is that of relationship, traced through "maternal" substance, "paternal" substance, or both. Those who marry within the limits defined by incest are marrying a "brother" or "sister" who is considered too closely related to permit marriage. If an alliance is formed between two lines, the marriage which is contracted should respect these limits. Thus my informants, Ţare of Kurube' and Kiru and his son Ogwane of Hagani, two clans which have in the past been allied, arranged for the eventual marriage of Ogwane's daughter Domuai to Ţare's son Semene. Semene's mother, Mori, is a hai' of Kiru, and their children should not intermarry, for they are the children of hai'; Semene, however, can marry Ogwane's daughter, for she is beyond the "second cousin" limit. Ţare himself made a similar marriage; his mother Mina and his wife Mori are the children of hai' and thus "sisters" at the limit of "close" consanguinity. Ţare is the child of Mori's "second cousin," and thus may marry her.

Incest, marrying within the consanguineal limits for marriage, is considered by Daribi to be reprehensible, "no good" (*duare*), and those who are guilty of it are condemned and often punished (see chapter 1, *Law and Political Organization*), the severity of punishment and condemnation depending on the situation. An incestuous marriage is "bad" corresponding to the degree of relationship between the partners; marriages between a full brother and sister, or between a parent and child, or sexual relations within these degrees of relationship, would be the most extreme degree of incest. I have no examples of such incest. Marriage or sexual relations between half-siblings or between first cousins is also highly reprehensible, and this occasionally occurs. The case of Panugiai's son and daughter at Masi offers an interesting example of the interaction of two ethical systems in culture contact. Sizi, the eldest son of Panugiai by his second wife, had a child by his half-sister Nouame, who was unmarried. What action the people of Masi took when this was discovered I was not told, but apparently Sizi was told he could expect punishment from the Administration, for his father Panugiai, who took his part, decided to ambush Patrol Officer Ernest Mitchell. Accordingly, he waited behind a tree when Mitchell next appeared on patrol, and confronted him with drawn bow. He was immediately disarmed by native constables, but he wriggled free of their grasp and assaulted Mitchell, who managed to subdue him. Sizi and Nouame were tried by the District Administration and given prison sentences, and Panugiai was given a detention sentence at Karimui for assaulting an Administration official. Another case of incest at Masi involved Sibunugiai, a Papuan "Humbert Humbert," who had sexual relations with his father's brother's daughter Magerame after "inheriting" her mother Maranugiai from his father's brother Baiare, a legitimate inheritance. Again in this case I was not told whether punishment was administered, but Panugiai significantly alluded to this as another instance of "no good" sexual conduct when discussing the incest of his own children. Because they usually belong to different clans, incestuous marriages sometimes take place between hai'. Such a marriage, although respecting the rules of exogamy, is nevertheless incestuous, for its unites a man and woman considered to be as "brother" and "sister." A wife, who was before marriage related to her husband as a close consanguineal, within the limits of incest, is referred to by a combination of the kinship term expressing her relationship with the word we, "wife." Thus, a man who has married his hai' refers to her as a *hai'-we*, a man who married his hai's daughter calls her *wegi-we*, a man who married the cousin of a parent calls her *ida-we* or *na'-we*, and a man who marries his second cousin calls her *ape-we* or *hai'-we*. All these marriages, although censured, have probably taken place at one time or another.

Informants remembered two instances of marriage with a hai'.

Pisamu of Maina married his hai', Moniwegi of Ogwanoma. "All the men of Maina came together and beat Pisamu, saying, 'Why did you marry your hai'?' " The marriage was not, however, dissolved. Similarly, Debia of Denege married his hai', Tawia of Hagani; his elder brother Aibe wanted to marry her, but Debia stood outside her house and cried, "She's *my* cross-cousin, I want to marry her," and he cried until the men decided to give her to him. The men of Hagani did not reproach him or attempt to punish him for this, for Hagani and Denege are allied by blood ties, and such action might bring a break in relations between them. (Making a pest of oneself is a means of getting one's way in this society, and there are certain personality types among the Daribi which seem to capitalize on this kind of interaction.)

Another kind of reprehensible marriage was made by Kanama, the younger brother of my informant Sạri of Kilibali, who married his mother's patrilateral parallel cousin. Kanama refers to his wife as an ida-we. I was unable to establish any evidence of condemnation or punishment in this case. Sạri's mother, Kege, arranged the betrothal of her daughter Kigi to Souw, the son of her father's matrilateral parallel cousin Yawi, still within the limits of incestuous marriage. This betrothal was objected to by the men of Kilibali, who told her, "This man is the same as your child, you can't give your daughter to him." But she insisted, saying, "She is my child, I would like to give her to this man," and the match was arranged. Upon the death of Souw, Kigi passed under the levirate to his brother Muabe. Since they are brothers-in-law to Sạri as well as "second cousins," close consanguineal "brothers," he calls Souw and Muabe ama'-baze, a combination of the terms "brother" and "brother-in-law" similar to the terms of reference used for consanguineal wives; ape-we, similarly, would be used by Souw and Muabe to refer to Kigi. Enebe's marriage to Usuanu, whom he "inherited" after the death of Pagarabu, a case which we encountered in our discussion of the junior levirate in the preceding chapter, was of a similar nature. Enebe's mother, Mina, is a patrilateral parallel cousin of Teaburu, Usuanu's father, so that Usuanu and Enebe are "second cousins" within the range restricted by the incest rule. This fact was ignored, probably because Usuanu is an older woman, and this was her fourth successive marriage (not counting her earlier adultery with Enebe).

The fact that incest between "closer" genealogical relatives is more reprehensible than that between those who are more distantly related, although, in fact, sanctions may or may not be applied due to varying political and social situations, and the fact that beyond a certain degree of genealogical distance marriage is permitted, is a manifestation of the fundamental nature of Daribi consanguinity: it is a measure of "relatedness," and persons may differ in relatedness only by degree. Consanguinity is, in turn, traced through two kinds of substance, paternal and maternal, and ties of relationship so distinguished differ in terms of "kind" or "type." Yet, since these are contrasts made within the principle of consanguinity, relationships traced through either one of the kinds of substance, or through both, also differ in terms of degree. Thus, a grandfather is not responsible for the recruitment of his grandchildren, a pagebidi cannot make claims on the children of his sister's children; the children of hai' are related through a cross-substance bond, and, although they may not marry, neither can they make leviratic claims on one another. Consanguinity and the claims made by virtue of consanguinity relate to specific individuals and through specific individuals, or to and through groups of siblings, zibi, which are as one person in terms of heredity.

Thus, every person or zibi is the center of a spreading, concentric network of relationships, which admit of claims and restrictions in proportion to genealogical "closeness." Where these relationships unite persons in different clans, those clans are related or allied to the extent of the relationship between those persons; where they unite persons within the same clan, they conform to the idiom of interrelationship of clan members. Because the claims and obligations of relationship diminish with consanguineal distance, only comparatively close relationships will provide effective bonds for either kind of attachment, for, where a relationship is distant, the individuals so related owe their primary obligations elsewhere, to more closely related kin. Thus, the contrast between relationships through specific kinds of substance, maternal and paternal, is generally significant only for close relationships, those to whom the normative claims directly apply. The distinctions are made terminologically only in these generations; i.e., Ego's own and the first ascending, where the pagebidi relationship is most significant, that is, where the opposition of consanguinity and exchange determines recruitment. Thus, one distinguishes one's father from one's mother's brother, and distinguishes parallel cousins from those related through cross-substance ties, one's "siblings" through the pagebidi relationship. By contrast, a man who is both father and pagebidi refers to both his own children and his sister's children as "sons" and "daughters," although they will call him, respectively, "father" and "mother's brother," and call each other hai'.

We can, then, view distinctions made through specific kinds of substance as part of the interaction of consanguinity and exchange which constitutes the pagebidi relationship. Male consanguineals in the first ascending generation are either "fathers" or "mother's brothers"; women are either "father's sisters" or "mothers." Consanguineals in one's own generation are either "siblings" or hai', which are "the same as" siblings. Even though these distinctions are made, they are drawn within the principle of consanguinity, and hence are distinctions between kinds of relationship; they indicate kinds of claims which can be made, but they do not determine whether the claims will be made or fulfilled, they merely relate people in specific ways. Consanguinity "relates," it only relates, and it alone relates. The definition of groups, and hence the recruitment of people to them, is accomplished in terms of the principle of exchange, which we shall discuss in the following chapter.

Consanguineal Kin Terminology

We have just seen how ties of consanguinity, those traced through substance, relate people. Such ties vary in "degree" of relatedness according to genealogical distance. Daribi kinship terminology does not express "degree" of relationship, although this is extremely important; this is instead determined by the actual tracing of genealogies. This is done usually by groups of men who have come together for some purpose, who can thus compare notes, and on these occasions certain individuals, such as Yapenugiai of Kurube' or Pini of Dobu, who are known for their abilities as genealogists, are consulted. Otherwise, degree of relatedness can only be expressed comparatively; a closer kinsman of a certain category can be distinguished as a "true" (*mu*) kinsman as opposed to a more distant one, who is an "other" (*me*) kinsman of that category. Thus, a full brother is an *ama' mu*, and a male second-cousin may be a *me ama'*. By the same token, a male first parallel cousin is an ama' mu in contrast to a male third cousin, who may be a me ama'. The terminology itself groups all those who fall into a certain category, whether "close" or "distant," under one term. What, then, is the basis for the distinctions between such categories?

As we have seen in the preceding section, certain categories of kin are distinguished by general consanguinity, irrespective of relationship through particular "kinds" of substance, whereas others are related through ties of "maternal" or "paternal" substance, or through cross-substance ties, for these correlate with the pagebidi relationship, with its normative mode of recruitment claims. Since the relationship ties involved in recruitment are those between the generation of the "parents" and that of the children, the categorization of kin is arranged along generational lines; since the pagebidi claims Ego as "his" child, but Ego normatively apprehends him as an "influence," he is distinguished from the father in the ascending generation, but the pagebidi does not distinguish Ego from his own children in the descending generation. Likewise, in his own generation Ego distinguishes those who are related to him through a pagebidi relationship, that is, through cross-substance ties, from those who are not. Terminological distinctions are therefore made on the basis of differential substance in those generations affected by Ego's pagebidi relationship; otherwise, relatives are grouped into categories irrespective of kinds of substance tie.

We may thus distinguish two general areas of consanguineal kin categorization (Fig. 14). In the first, that of generalized consanguinity, no distinctions are made on the basis of "kinds" of substance. All consanguineals of the second ascending generation and above are designated wai' if male, auwa if female. Very re-

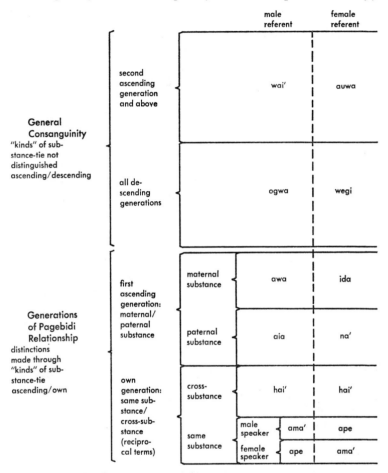

FIGURE 14.—*Daribi consanguineal kin categories.*

mote male ancestors may be referred to as *nu*. Similarly, all consanguineals of descending generations, the generation of one's children and below, are designated ogwa if male, wegi if female. The term wai', a reciprocal when used between grandfather and grandchild, may be used in a general way to refer to all of these. In the second area, that of the pagebidi relationship, distinctions are made in terms of "kinds" of substance. In the first ascending generation, relatives through paternal substance are designated aia if male (this term is also used as a reciprocal between father and child) and na' if female. Relatives through maternal substance are designated ida if female (this term is also used as a reciprocal between mother and child) and awa if male. In Ego's own generation, all terms are reciprocal, and relatives through same-substance ties are distinguished from those related through cross-substance ties. Relatives through cross-substance ties are designated hai', regardless of sex. Relatives through ties of one substance, either maternal or paternal, are categorized according to whether they are of the same sex as the speaker or of the opposite sex; such a relative who is of the same sex as the speaker is designated ama', and one of the opposite sex is designated ape. Thus, brothers call each other ama', sisters call each other ama', but brother and sister call each other ape.

Although these terms are the primary terms of reference and address and are used in formal situations and when tracing genealogies, the usual way of addressing or referring to adults in everyday situations, except where kinship is to be stressed, is by teknonymic terms. When a child is small, its mother and father call each other by the name of the child, or call each other "mother of . . ." or "father of . . ." the child, using its name. Thus, while walking through the bush with Sąri, I heard him call his wife repeatedly, and the name he shouted, Eri, was the name of his small son. Adult men and women will thus be called "mother of . . ." or "father of . . ." (naming any of their children) in preference to their given names. Hanari is called "father of Sezema" (Sezema agaia, "Sezema his father"). This holds for members of one's own clan as well as those of other clans. This is done to avoid the shame of familiarity; "because our mouths are heavy and we are ashamed" with members of the same sex, and because "she is not my wife, I do not want to call her by name" in the case of a man speaking of or to an adult woman. Another form is to give a man the name of his (deceased) father; thus Kagoiano is called Bapo, Ma is called Buruhuą. This may be done on the basis of a real or imagined physical resemblance to the father; Kagoiano and Ma are gominaibidi, but in the Sonozibi it is Hauba, a tomubidi, who is called Sono, rather than Hanari, who is the gominaibidi. Daribi say that those who have the same name (namesakes, or *sabi*) should look alike, and conversely those who look alike are thus often so named. Kagoiano also bears the name Suabe as a sort of secondary name, for he resembles his brother of the same name, and now he calls a more distant clan relative, also named Suabe, sabi.

Familiarity may also be correlated with the use of reciprocals within the nuclear family. The mother and father address each other using the name of one of their children, which thus becomes a reciprocal term of address. Father and child call each other aia, mother and child call each other ida, same-sex siblings call each other ama', those of opposite sexes call each other ape. Thus, every member of a nuclear family will address every other by a term which expresses their mutual interrelationship reciprocally and thus avoids distinctions which might connote authority. In this case the terminology emphasizes familiarity rather than avoiding it.

Consanguineal terms may be extended laterally to almost any degree; the children of those whom one's father calls ama' are designated ama' and ape, children of those whom he calls ape are designated hai'. Children of those whom one's mother calls ama' are designated ama' and ape, children of those whom she calls ape are designated hai'. The children of those whom one's mother and father, respectively, call hai' are designated ama' and ape if the hai' is of the same sex as the respective parent, and hai' if the parent's hai' is of the opposite sex. Distant relatives in the second generation are called wai' and auwa, according to the sex of the referent; distant relatives in all descending generations are called ogwa and wegi. Any of these extended terms will be automatically dropped and the corresponding affinal terms assumed if a marriage is made between distantly related kinsmen in such a way as to change them. This will be discussed at greater length in the following chapter. Where relationship is too distant to be traced, persons will be grouped roughly into generational categories on the basis of comparative age, and called ama', ape, aia, ida, ogwa, wegi, auwa, or wai', terms normatively used for members of one's own patriline. This is done on the basis of "idioms" of relationship, of the assumption of patrilateral interrelationship of clans within a phratry, and ultimately of the common descent of all members of the society, and of all mankind, for all men are the descendants of Souw. Let us now examine the basis of these idioms of relationship.

Idioms of Relationship

In our discussions of the pagebidi relationship and the zibi, we have seen that the Daribi system of recruitment can be described as "normatively patrilineal"; that is, although a child is a consanguineal of both his father's and his mother's groups and may be recruited to either, the father has first option to the recruitment of his children and may claim them, provided he "redeems" them by making recruitment payments to their pagebidi. That he should do this and want to do this is a "norm" of the culture; that is, it is considered part of his role as a father. Thus, a man should take the wealth offered to him as compensation for his sisters' children and use it to redeem his own, and we may speak of this system as "normatively patrilineal." We have also seen in this and the preceding chapters that ties of substance symbolize relationship for the Daribi and that they both interrelate the members of a clan and relate each of these, in turn, to members of other clans, providing ties of alliance with these. Daribi also distinguish two "kinds" of substance, maternal and paternal, and, although both "relate" people equally, and relationship can be traced through either or through both together, each by itself symbolizes a particular kind of relationship, as well as particular claims and obligations which may be made by virtue of that relationship. We have seen in the chapter on the pagebidi that mother's blood symbolizes the complex of sanctions and ties which constitute that relationship; normatively the tie of mother's blood interrelates members of different clans, forming the basis for the alliance between them and the "influence" on clan members exercised by their pagebidi. Mother's blood, then, serves as the idiom for the interrelationship of clans. By the same token, ties of paternal substance, which are normatively redeemed by payments made from the "pool" of vital wealth which serves to define the group, symbolize group membership and are the idiom for "normative patriliny." If all bride prices and recruitment payments are met, the members of a clan will all share in common the same paternal substance, which can be traced to a putative ancestor, and each member will in turn have a pagebidi linked to him by maternal substance in another clan, against whose claims his membership is defined. If, however, a child is recruited to his pagebidi's clan, he will be related to the paternal line of the latter's clan through a cross-substance tie (Fig. 8, number "3") through his mother and his awa. Thus, even members of a clan who are related to it through the tie of maternal substance can claim consanguineal relationship to its founder.

If normative claims are met by payments, the lines of paternal substance will be sustained by those payments within the same clan, whereas lines of maternal substance will pass across from clan to clan. Only in a situation where no wealth at all would be exchanged in marriage and recruitment payments, that is, where there would be a complete breakdown of the exchange system and hence of clans as Daribi define them, would maternal substance form unbroken lines. Thus, the idiom of relationship within the group is that of paternal substance, the idiom of relationship outside the group, to and through one's pagebidi, is that of mother's blood. In this respect the groups generated by normative patriliny resemble those in societies where recruitment is determined by descent, that is, from birth, although, in fact, patriliny in the Daribi system remains an idiom, for it is not a recruitment principle and does not determine group membership, but rather expresses a norm of group membership.

Thus, the genealogical links within a clan will be largely those of male substance, drawn through males, for every clan, to define itself at all, must make marriage and recruitment payments; the Daribi clan is by definition exogamous. As every clan maintains a "pool" of vital wealth, the consequences of its sisters and daughters having married out, so every clan will be able in some measure to sustain its male lines. This is but another example of the normative interlocking of the principles of exchange and consanguinity. The idiom of normative patriliny is an expression of the clan's definitional activity, like the "pool" of vital wealth which sustains it, and male substance lines are symbolic of the clan. Thus, regardless of whether a clan is differentiated from others through a male or a female ancestor, it will ultimately name a man as its ancestor, for he is the source of the substance line which symbolizes its membership. As an example of this, the three clans which live at Noru Rest House differentiate themselves as the descendants of Garo through his three wives, Poriame, Pobori, and Wazo, respectively, and designate themselves as the Poriamezibi, Poborizibi, and Wazozibi. Yet, each of these traces its paternal substance to Garo, as its male founder. This is one of the two standard Daribi ideologies of phratry relationship, representing the component clans of a phratry as the descendants of half-brothers, all of whom share the same father. The other ideology is exemplified by Para Phratry, where the component clans are represented as descended from a zibi of full brothers, the sons of Para. In either case it is male substance, embodied in each clan and traced to a common ancestor, that forms the link between the clans. As clans symbolize their membership by male substance, so they are related to the other clans of the phratry in this way. The ideologies of phratry interrelationship are, of course, symbolic and derive their significance from the idiom of normative patriliny; they constitute set, culturally uniform ideologies, into which the actual genealogical interrelationships of clans, the diverse results of segmentation, can be fitted.

I have chosen the terms "idiom" and "ideology" rather than "descent" to express the various specific types of relationship, that is, relationship through one kind of substance, because, as we have seen, these kinds of relationship are really subcategories, contrasts made within the principle of consanguinity. As such, they merely relate; they do not determine membership, but only possibilities for recruitment, and hence do not define groups. They form instead the means, the idioms, through which relationships within and among these groups are expressed. It is because of this fact, because they are basically ties of consanguinity, and can equally relate, that relationship can be traced through either kind of tie or through both together, as in crosssubstance ties. The same tie of relationship can at once serve to relate a person in a specific way, to his pagebidi, for instance, and also to relate him generally to a group of consanguineals through ties of same- and cross-substance; and it will also relate his children to the same group of consanguineals, although here the specific claims of the pagebidi relationship no longer hold. Consanguinity, ties of substance given by birth, relates people regardless of whether claims are satisfied or not. It is the principle by which persons are related to one another on the individual level, and it thus provides the idiom for the relationships between and among groups. Both of these aspects derive from the fact that consanguinity primarily relates. Exchange, the principle by which units are defined and group boundaries set, must necessarily oppose the claims of relationship on the individual level; and on the group level it aligns those who share the same exchange relations as against those whose claims are opposed by these. Let us now examine this principle of exchange, or reciprocity.

6
Exchange: The Principle of Definition

Daribi Reciprocity

Let us return for the moment to our earlier discussion of "influence" in the Daribi world view. We may recall that Daribi regard any kind of individual affliction, such as illness, madness, death, or even a seeming accident, as the result of purposive action on the part of an external agent. This often takes the form of an "influence" exercised on the individual by means of some sort of advantage which the external agent has over him. Where the agent is a ghost, the advantage is that of invisibility; where it is a sorcerer, it is secrecy coupled with the possession of personal substance, the leavings gathered by the sorcerer. The advantage of secrecy can be overcome by divination, by discovering the identity of the agent, and in the case of a ghost this suffices to dispel the influence. Where sorcery is concerned, however, divination only serves to identify the possessor of the sorcery material, who must then be paid so that he will remove it and thus remove the influence. The influence of a pagebidi is like that of a sorcerer, for it is based on substance, but in this case the substance is not composed of personal leavings, which may be discarded, but is, in fact, the very blood and vital organs of the individual, which are essential to his existence. Thus, the influence of the pagebidi can never be overcome, and he must be continually paid and satisfied so that he does not exert it. In cases where an influence cannot be overcome by divination alone or where the identity of the agent exerting the influence is known, the influence must be countered by reciprocity. On a symbolic level, an external influence, whether it is exerted by a supernatural being or by a kinsman, is nevertheless an influence, and it may be opposed by reciprocity in either case, by an offering made from a reserve of "vital" wealth representing the potential of the clan. In this respect we need not differentiate "religion" from "social structure," for both share as a "common denominator" the same symbol system. On this level, then, reciprocity opposes external influences on the individual; in terms of kinship, where such influence serves as a sanction for the claims made through blood ties, it discharges these claims and thus averts the sanctions.

We may thus list certain characteristics which govern the operation of reciprocity in Daribi society and which, in turn, derive from its symbolic role:

1. Reciprocity consists in the substitution of items of wealth for living persons, under circumstances where an external influence or claim bears on these persons (i.e., a "hold" on the soul or a claim made through blood ties). This wealth constitutes a special category, sizibage (see chapter 1, "Land and Property"), and, insofar as it may be substituted for persons, represents the self-perpetuating potential of the clan. I have termed it "vital" wealth.

2. Reciprocity, therefore, is a means of settling claims; it discharges obligations and acts to bring matters to a state of equilibrium, rather than setting up self-perpetuating, ongoing relationships. The exchange cycles contracted between clans in marriage will, therefore, oppose counter-prestation to prestation in such a way as to eventually close and settle all claims between them.

3. The factor which provides the ongoing element in marriage and recruitment exchanges is the principle of consanguinity; payments given to a pagebidi do not cancel his relationship to his sister and her children, but merely discharge claims made by virtue of that relationship. Ties of relationship continue to bind individuals for the duration of their lives and may justify the making of further claims and further payments. Wife-givers are thus in a position of advantage over wife-takers, for they may

press continual claims by virtue of the blood ties with their sisters and the children of the latter.

4. In order to counter this advantage, so that one clan does not stand in a perpetual relationship of disadvantage to another, every marriage should be "backed" or reciprocated at the clan level by the giving of a wife in the opposite direction. Thus, a state of equilibrium with respect to such advantage is reached between clans. Insofar as a clan relates as such to the component zibi of another, such a state of equilibrium must also be reached.

5. In addition, every prestation of "male goods" (pigs, pearl shells, axes) should be reciprocated at the same time by a (smaller) counter-prestation, consisting wholly or in part of "female" goods (net bags, bark cloaks). This has the effect of "settling" the exchange itself, of discharging any obligations which might arise from the presentation per se. Thus, every prestation is actually an exchanging of goods between the two groups concerned.

The obligations incurred in a marriage exchange are discharged in three ways. First, the wife-giver's claims to the wife (and her children) made by virtue of consanguinity are satisfied by the substitution of wealth for the individuals themselves. This is the opposition of consanguinity by exchange which plays such an important part in Daribi social structure as a whole. Second, women themselves are exchanged; a marriage is reciprocated by another marriage in the opposite direction to offset the advantageous position of the clan which has given the first woman. Third, each payment is itself reciprocated at the time it is made, to counter any obligations arising from the payment itself. Thus, each obligation or advantage arising from an exchange must be balanced off and "settled" by a transference in the opposite direction.

Insofar as they oppose or cancel the claims made by virtue of certain ties of relationship, whereas they "redeem" or validate others, exchanges effectively arbitrate between the claims of a father on one hand and those of the mother's brother on the other, or, in the case of marriage, between the claims of a woman's husband and her brother. They allocate a child to the clan of its father by substituting wealth for its presence in the clan of its mother's brother and likewise satisfy the wife's brother by substituting wealth for his sister. In so doing, they determine clan boundaries, for they cancel the claims of relationship to one clan, while validating those of relationship to another. Thus, every person in a clan has normatively one or more consanguineal pagebidi who belong to another clan and who must be paid to validate his membership in his own clan, and he has a group of consanguineals within his own clan who share the responsibility for contributing to these payments. Seen in terms of the clan as a whole, its membership is defined by the cancelling of the relationship claims on its members by other clans, and it defines itself as a group in terms of the exchanges which set these boundaries. Every zibi in a clan has its own pagebidi, and the pagebidi relationship affects only the zibi itself; its pagebidi cannot claim or curse others in the clan. Yet, all adult members of the clan are obliged to contribute to the payments made by the zibi to its pagebidi.

Thus, the principle by which clans are defined is that of exchange; members of a zibi share consanguineal ties in common, those of a clan share exchange functions. The criterion of clan membership is that of sharing wealth, as opposed to exchanging wealth. This is symbolized by the sharing or giving of meat; members of a clan "eat meat together," while those of other clans "give meat" or "are given meat." A man cannot marry the sister or daughter of someone with whom he shares meat, for meat is sizibage, currency; marriage within the clan would necessitate an exchange of wealth among those who normally share such wealth anyway and thus would be senseless. A clan is, therefore, necessarily exogamous, for marriage is a form of exchange, and clan members by definition share exchange relationships; that is, they contribute to each other's bride prices and share in the distribution of the wealth received through exchange by one another.

Daribi restrictions regarding the eating of deceased relatives may be interpreted in the light of the symbolism of "eating meat together" and "giving meat." Normally, young persons, children, and those who have not yet married are not allowed to partake of human flesh, and when they die, are not eaten. Daribi say they "are afraid of bodily decomposition, and the juices" (relatives were mourned for a period of up to ten days before being eaten). It is true, however, that those who have not married have not yet shared in bride price distributions or contributions and hence are not yet members of the exchange system. Only adults and aged persons are eaten, and may eat the dead. Members of the nuclear family do not normally eat one another either, for the relationship is too close. Thus, parents will not eat their offspring, and vice versa. It is necessary to obtain the permission of such a close relative before eating a deceased clan member; if Sezema were to die, Paro, Tạre, and others would have to receive permission from his father, Hanari, before doing so. When Hanari's mother died and the men were cutting up her body, Hanari became enraged and rushed at them with his bow drawn, shouting that they had killed her, and they became frightened and ran away. With the exception of hai', only members of one's own clan may be eaten. A person may eat his father's brothers, their wives, and their children, and also his own brothers and their children. He should not eat his wife or his brothers' wives (who are potential wives under the levirate). Those whom one calls awa or baze may not be eaten "for shame." Hai' are "sometimes eaten," but, as we have seen, hai' share bridewealth and leviratic rights as "brothers," token members of each other's clans. Thus, a person may eat the flesh of those with whom he "shares meat" and may not eat the flesh of those to whom he "gives meat" or from whom he receives it. We may correlate the eating of the flesh of clan members with the sharing of "vital wealth" among them in bridewealth contributions and distributions; as this wealth, which includes meat, may be substituted for persons in marriage and recruitment payments and may be used to "buy" wives and redeem children, it represents the potential manpower of the clan. As this is also represented by the people themselves, their bodies may be consumed just as the pork which is received in substitution for the clan's sisters and daughters.

The member clans of a community may also share meat, as well as wealth, with one another. This is either because such clans are in the final stages of segmentation and still considered to be "one clan" to an extent, or because they have become so interlinked through alliance that further marriage is impossible between them, and they share meat and wealth as hai'. The former is the case between Kurube' and Noruai, the latter between each of these and Kilibali. In the instance mentioned above, where Hanari's mother was to be eaten, both Kurube' and Daie, which were allied, had come together to do this. Where the victims of warfare are to be eaten, the restrictions on age are relaxed; young men and women are eaten as well as adults. At a massacre at Dobu Clan in 1960–61, when about thirty people were killed by a force composed of representatives from all the other Daribi clans, the victims were eaten by the enemy force, which subdivided into groups of men according to community to do this.

The definition of clans is based on the principle of exchange; clans are defined by the boundaries set by exchange, and marriages may not be made within these boundaries regardless of genealogical distance. When a child is claimed by its mother's brother and joins his clan, this is done through default of an expected payment, when the normative exchanges have broken down. Such a child becomes a member of his mother's brother's clan and shares in their exchange relations and may no longer share in those of his father's clan. The basis of both claims, that of the father and that of the mother's brother, is, of course, consanguinity, and it is consanguinity that relates the child to both of their clans; yet, precisely because it relates him equally to both and diminishes with distance, consanguinity cannot form group boundaries. It merely relates, and it justifies claims made by virtue of relationship. Thus, all the members of a clan are related to one another, for either alternative of recruitment aligns a child to a group of his relatives. Rercruitment involves both consanguinity and exchange and is the result of the interaction of these two principles. The idiom of "normative patriliny" and the pagebidi relationship are the results of this interaction when the normative obligations are fulfilled. What, then, is the relationship of this "normative" system of obligations to the two basic principles themselves?

The Normative System

As we have seen in our discussion of consanguinity, the Daribi marriage rule is the result of two kinds of prohibition; one derives from consanguinity and specifies the degrees of closeness of relationship within which a marriage would be incestuous, and the other derives from exchange and relates to a unit within which marriage would violate the rule of exogamy. The dual aspect of this marriage rule reflects the two basic principles of Daribi social structure, one of which forms a concentric network around each individual, while the other defines the boundaries of groups. Since units are made up of individuals, social structure must necessarily involve the interaction of these two principles; that is, the members of a unit will always have relatives both within and outside of the unit, and individuals will always, therefore, distinguish some of their relatives, who belong to the same unit as they, from others who do not. The specific functions in which the two principles interact, then, are those of alliance, the relationship of persons to consanguineals outside the clan, and recruitment, the allocation of persons to one unit of consanguineals or another. The normative system prescribes the mode of interaction between the principles of consanguinity and exchange; it expresses unit membership in terms of relationship and gives norms of differential unit membership for specific kin categories. Thus, in terms of recruitment, a child should normatively be recruited to its father's unit (normative patriliny), while its mother's line remains external to that group (pagebidi relationship). This kind of normative distinction of relationship through one "kind" of substance is necessary if one mode of recruitment is to be enjoined as against another, and the differentiation of "kinds" of substance is, therefore, a function of the normative system. Paternal substance is normatively correlated with the sharing of meat and wealth, that is, with relationships within the clan, and this gives rise to the idiom of normative patriliny. Maternal substance is normatively correlated with the giving of meat and wealth to maternal relatives outside the clan and symbolizes the pagebidi relationship. In terms of alliance, both the fact of relationship in one unit and that of relationship with members of other units must be taken into account; relationships are traced across unit boundaries. Thus, the two substance ties are combined in the alliance relationship; it is traced through cross-substance ties. This can be correlated with the combined obligations of sharing and exchanging between hai', who are "brothers" belonging to different clans. Hai' may share wealth and wives as brothers, but, because they are members of different clans, their leviratic privileges must be validated by exchanges.

Recruitment and alliance, the functions in which consanguinity and exchange interact, are thus governed by preferred "norms" of interaction; that is to say, a person should normatively be recruited to his father's clan, pay his pagebidi in his mother's clan, and be related across clan boundaries to his hai'. With respect to these functions, distinctions are drawn according to "kinds" of substance (see Figure 14), and exchange roles are distinguished according to whether meat and wealth are shared between relatives or exchanged between them. In areas where the two principles do not interact, normative prescriptions are not necessary, as the operation of one principle has no implications in terms of the other. Thus, in terms of the integration, or grouping of people, consanguinity always relates, exchange always defines; a zibi is always a "nuclear unit" of kinship, for its members share all possible substance ties; a clan is always defined in terms of exchange, regardless of the relationships of its members. In terms of marriage, account must be taken of both the genealogical "closeness" of individuals and their clan membership. In these areas, terminological distinctions are not made on the basis of "kinds" of substance; all ties relate equally, and incest is reckoned equally through both kinds of substance. Clan membership and exogamy are likewise determined without reference to relationship. The area of interaction between the two principles, where normative distinctions apply, is represented schematically in Figure 15.

The normative system is not a principle of Daribi social structure, but merely a series of norms governing the interaction of the two principles. If the norms are not followed, the principles still apply; should a child be recruited to his mother's brother's clan, that is, if the norm of recruitment is not followed, he will

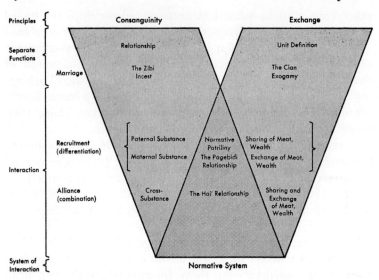

FIGURE 15.—*The normative system.*

still be related to both his patrilateral and his matrilateral kinsmen, and he will still be a member of a clan and participate in its exchanges. The system of normative reationships will not, however, apply, for he will neither be a member of his father's clan, pay his pagebidi, nor relate to his hai' across clan boundaries (he will also pass out of the pagebidi relationship through his father with his patrilateral hai'). Thus, the normative system can break down in the case of an individual, and his relationships as an individual, those of consanguinity and zibi membership, as well as his membership in a clan, still apply.

The Clan: Units in Marriage

The exogamous unit in Daribi society, which is, therefore, the basic unit of marriage contraction, is the clan. By definition, a clan is that group of people within which marriage may not be contracted, and which shares in the contributions to a bride price raised by one of its members and, therefore, shares in the wealth given in exchange for its members who have married out. It is also the unit of recruitment, and may likewise be defined as that group which shares in the contributions to recruitment payments made for its members and in the distribution of recruitment payments given to any of its members. It participates in these two functions insofar as the principle of exchange is concerned, and thus the clan is defined in terms of the exchange principle. Where individuals interact with members of other clans, they must do so in terms of the exchange of wealth (viz., the exchanges between hai' by virtue of their "brotherhood"), regardless of the fact of their relationship to them, for it is through this kind of exchange that clan boundaries are maintained. The wealth which is thus exchanged is therefore shared among clan members, and, because it is used in the definitive functions of marriage and recruitment, it symbolizes the unity and potential of the clan.

The Daribi term for clan is *hane* or *bidihane*. This term may or may not be of Daribi origin, for a very similar word, *kane*, is used to denote "clan" among the speakers of Chimbu dialects in the Gumine area to the north and also by the Chimbu–Daribi-speakers in the Bomai Census Division (speakers of Chimbu dialects substitute "k" for "h" when pronouncing Daribi words). The clan is also the basic social and residential group in Daribi society, and, as we have seen, it is the unit of land tenure. It is also a basic jural unit; feuds within a clan should not be settled with bows or axes, but with sticks (lengths of cane, *kanda* in Pidgin, *kerua* in Daribi). A clan is the largest group which may share the same house, and, in time of warfare or when moving to a new location, the whole clan will occupy a single sigibe', or two-story longhouse. For this reason a clan is sometimes referred to as a *be'*, or house, and the clanmates of a person are called his *be'bidi* ("house-people"). A clan may, however, inhabit several houses, or be divided into several residence groups, each living at a separate locality, and still retain its unity. Two or more (but seldom more than four) allied clans may live adjacently within the same territory (which is usually subdivided among them) to form a community. Member clans of a community are closely knit by ties of relationship, usually so much so that marriage between them is impossible, and they share wealth through these ties, and to some extent share jural functions. The member clans act in certain respects as "one" clan, and this is, of course, the object of alliance. To differentiate clans in such a community, the idiom of patriliny is often referred to, relating them to their respective phratries. Thus when Sogo, Kurube', and Noruai formed a community together at Waramaru, the first-named clan was referred to as Noru, naming the phratry of its affiliation. Thus, also, when I asked Kagoiano what the affiliations of Karu-wabu Clan, which lives in community with Ḥaubidi, are, he answered, "Their fathers came from Masi, their mothers from Ḥaubidi." Alternatively, a clan may be divided between two communities; thus, part of Sogo lives at Oragamaru with Di'be' Clan, and the other at Waramaru, where it formerly lived in community with Kurube'-Noruai. A clan may also live by itself, as does Hagani, or, presently, part of Sogo. Shifts in place of residence are not uncommon among clans, and this may be done for a number of reasons, including especially warfare and disputes with other members of the community.

Because it is defined by exchange, the functions of reciprocity in marriage are all performed at the level of the clan. This, then, is the unit of marriage reciprocity. As we may recall from the opening section of this chapter, the obligations incurred in marriage exchanges are discharged in three ways. Bridewealth is given in exchange for the bride herself; women themselves are exchanged, so that each marriage is reciprocated by another; and finally each prestation of wealth must itself be reciprocated by a smaller payment at the time of giving. Each kind of exchange takes place at the clan level. The bride price is raised by contributions from all members of the clan of the wife-takers and distributed to all members of the clan of wife-givers. A sister given in marriage by a zibi of one clan may be reciprocated by the giving of a woman to that zibi by the clan of the recipients. The counter-prestation made to the wife-takers at the time of their presentation of the marriage payment is likewise raised by all members of the clan of the wife-givers.

Because all members of a clan contribute to the bride prices raised by its members and all share in the wealth which comes in through the marriages of its sisters and daughters, a woman who marries into a clan is to some extent a "wife" of the clan.

By the same token, children recruited to a clan through recruitment payments are to an extent "children" of the clan. The situation is the same as in the case of the zibi (see chapter 4, "The Zibi"), with the exception that the claims of zibi members to such wives and children are stronger, for they are made by virtue of close consanguinity as well as exchange. Yet, there is also a clan levirate, as well as adoption of orphaned children of clan brothers by others in the clan. A man calls the wives of his clan brothers, in addition to those of his elder brothers, sare, "potential spouse under the levirate," and may inherit them if no stronger claims are made. Likewise, he may inherit the wives of his father (other than his mother or foster mother), as well as those of his father's brothers, or of other clan members of ascending generations. A man calls his mother's co-wives *paba*, and he may also apply this term to the wives of his father's brothers or to his mother's sisters, who would be wives of his father under the preferred practice of sororal polygyny. A man may inherit as a wife anyone he calls paba (although marriage to his mother's sister would be incestuous, and it is probable that another claimant would be found in such a case). A man's younger brothers have priority over his sons in inheriting his wife. If, however, no stronger claims are made, a son will inherit his mother's co-wife. Elder brothers have first prority in such inheritance. If a man marries his paba, he refers to her as a *paba-we*, while she refers to him as an *ogwa-bidi* (she would otherwise call him ogwa). This type of inheritance, of a man's wife by his son, can only take place if the father dies; a man cannot simply transfer his wife to his son. Such inheritance occurs frequently, although I have not recorded any instances of a man marrying his mother's sister.

Otherwise, however, women may be given by one clan brother to another without the husband dying, just as an elder brother may give a wife to a younger within the zibi. In the case of clan brothers, the recipient of a wife ought to pay the giver, for the true brothers of the latter have the strongest interests in her and made the greatest contributions to her bride price. Payment is not always demanded, however, for the giver's brothers may waive their claims, and he himself may simply grow tired of the wife and give her away as a gesture. At Kurube', Kaite did not like being married to two women, and he gave one of his wives to Kiape in return for "pay." Later, Kiape had a child by this woman, and Kaite thought, "I could have had that child," and asked Kiape for more "pay." Hauba had a quarrel with his wife Ebai, or Doromo, and gave her to Kiape without asking for payment. Later "he thought of her" and asked Kiape to pay him. Eventually Kiape himself fell out with her and decided to give her to Buni, who has withered legs. When a man wants to give his wife to another, he makes an appointment to meet the latter in the bush. He takes the wife along with him, and at the appointed place he tells her to go with the recipient. In this case Kiape held the (apparently reluctant) woman down while Buni had intercourse with her. The men of Kurube' expected trouble with Peria, the woman's clan of origin, because of this incident, but nothing came of it. The payment given in return for such transfer of a wife usually amounts to one pig.

As the clan is the unit of marriage reciprocity, so the zibi, the nuclear unit of kinship, is the basic unit of relationship in marriage. As we have seen in our discussion of the zibi, all men of a zibi are equally related to their sisters, and hence they are all equally brothers-in-law to the man who marries one of them and equally pagebidi to his children (unless and until a pairing off with awa mu occurs). Because of this common claim on their sisters and sisters' children, and hence on the wealth brought in by virtue of them, zibi members share a primary claim on the inheritance of each other's wives, expressed through the junior levirate. Whereas the clan levirate is based on a sharing of exchange functions, the junior levirate, that of the zibi, is based on consanguinity, on the common siblingship of a group of brothers with their sisters, and the claims of the latter are stronger; a man's true brothers have priority over his clan brothers in the inheritance of his wives. Because of their close relationship to one another and to their sisters, zibi members share both affinal and consanguineal ties resulting from marriage. Thus, these relationships, including affinal relationships between brothers-in-law as well as the pagebidi relationship with the children of sisters, and the hai' relationships between children of the zibi and its sisters' children, all concern the zibi involved, and all are to an extent relationships between zibi.

Marriages are preferentially contracted in such a way as to respect the functions of both the clan and the zibi. Thus, the marriage will be made on the level of clan exogamy, so that the resultant exchanges will occur between clans, and individuals to be married will be chosen in such a way that their respective zibi will remain related in one way with regard to the giving and receiving of wives; in other words, so that no one zibi will be related as both wife-giver and wife-taker to another.

Thus, although the clan is the unit of reciprocity, the zibi, because it is the unit of relationship in marriage, is the unit of wife-giving and wife-taking. Each zibi will relate to some zibi of another clan as wife-giver and to others as wife-taker. Insofar as it relates to the affinal clan as a clan, however, each zibi should reciprocate the marriage of each woman given to it by giving a woman to another zibi of that clan, and each zibi expects a woman of the other clan to be given to it in exchange for a woman it has given to that clan. Each clan, in other words, should relate to every zibi of an affinally related clan both as wife-giver and wife-taker, its component zibi performing complementary functions in this. Applying our observation that Daribi reciprocity operates in such a way as to settle accounts, or bring things to a state of equilibrium, we can see that a total of four separate marriages is necessary to effect this and to close the cycle initiated by the giving of a woman in marriage between two clans previously in a state of equilibrium. This is depicted schematically in Figure 16; if zibi A of Clan I gives a sister to zibi B of Clan II (1), zibi B should reciprocate by giving a sister to Clan I, and she is given to zibi C (2), for zibi A are wife-givers. Thus, zibi B has discharged its obligation with regard to Clan I. Zibi A, however, has given a sister who had not been reciprocated, and zibi C has received a wife and must reciprocate by giving one to Clan II. It does this by giving its sister to zibi D (3) of the latter clan, for zibi B are its wife-givers, and thus discharges its obligation to Clan II. Now zibi D has received a wife from Clan I, and it discharges its obligation by giving a sister to zibi A (4), thereby

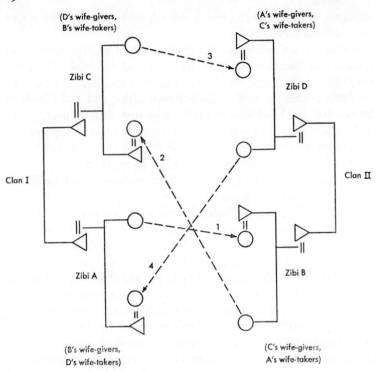

(D's wife-givers, B's wife-takers)

(A's wife-givers, C's wife-takers)

Zibi C

Zibi D

Clan I

Clan II

3

2

1

4

Zibi A

Zibi B

(B's wife-givers, D's wife-takers)

(C's wife-givers, A's wife-takers)

FIGURE 16.—*Clan and zibi reciprocity.*

discharging the obligation of Clan II to zibi A, which began the cycle. Insofar as the two clans themselves are concerned, the obligation created by marriage 1 is reciprocated by marriage 2, but where the respective zibi are concerned, two additional obligations remain; for zibi A has given a wife without receiving one, and zibi C has received a wife without giving one. This must be balanced off by two additional marriages to bring matters to a state of equilibrium, and thus zibi C gives a wife to D, and D reciprocates by giving a wife to A. Because of the interaction of clan and zibi, therefore, two exchanges of women are necessary to achieve equilibrium, a total of four marriages.

These marriages need not, of course, be made in the order indicated in Figure 16, nor are sisters always given to discharge such obligations; a daughter may be betrothed instead. There may be a considerable time lapse between a marriage and the one which reciprocates it, and, in fact, a marriage may never be reciprocated due to warfare or some other cause. Again, the marriages might be made as compensation for loss in warfare, or to discharge some other kind of debt, and thus would not require reciprocation. What I have presented here is an idealized model, to which a real situation may more or less approximate.

Returning to our idealized model for the reciprocating of marriages (Fig. 16), it is obvious that wife-givers will be pagebidi of the children of their wife-takers; thus zibi A will be pagebidi to the children of B, B will be pagebidi to the children of C, C to the children of D, and D, in turn, will be pagebidi to A's children. Pagebidi, of course, cannot marry their sisters' children, since these are in a sense their "own"; and cross-cousins, the children of two zibi related by marriage, cannot marry, for they are also consanguineals, hai'. Wife-givers, in other words, may not marry the daughters of their wife-takers, nor may the children of two zibi related as wife-giver and wife-taker marry. Wife-takers, on the other hand, are not consanguineally related to the children of their wife-givers, although their children are, for, unlike wife-givers, they have not given any of their substance to the other zibi. They may, therefore, continue to take wives from the patri-line of their wife-givers, including their children and grand-children.

Let us, then, examine the possibilities for continuing marriage between two zibi related as wife-giver and wife-taker. Once a marriage has been made, the members of a zibi can continue to take the sisters of their wife-givers, whom they call baze-we, as wives (Fig. 17). They can also take the sisters of their father-in-law (wai), whom they call wai-we. They may marry the daughters of their wife-giving baze, whom they call *yage*, and also the daughters of his son (yage), whom they call *yame*, in the second descending generation. For this reason, the wife of a wife-giving baze, as well as the wife of his son (yage), is called au, "mother-in-law." The wife of Ego's male yame is also called au, indicating possible further marriage into the patriline; however, informants were unable to supply kinship terms for this yame's

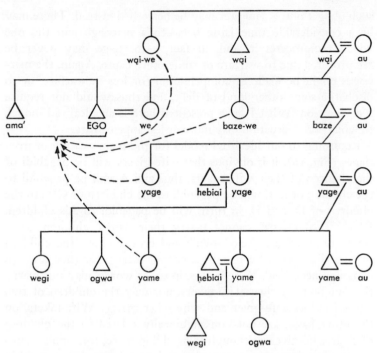

FIGURE 17.—*Possibilities for continuing marriage with wife-givers.*

children. The husband of a female yage or yame is called *hebiai*
("husband of potential wife"), and their children are called ogwa
and wegi, "son" and "daughter," for they may well be children of
Ego's brothers or clanmates.

A zibi, then, may continue to take wives from a zibi related
to it as wife-givers and from its patriline in the ascending and
descending generations, although its children may not, for these
are their pagebidi. A man may, in other words, marry his son's
matrilateral female hai', or, conversely, a woman may be given in
marriage to her father's sister's husband. A generational distinction
is therefore made among wife-takers; sisters, father's sisters,
daughters, and granddaughters may marry into the zibi with
which the first marriage was made, but not into those of its offspring. Thus, a zibi may give its sisters to its father's wife-takers

and to its grandfather's wife-takers, but not to the offspring of these. The term yage is a reciprocal, used between wife-takers in the first ascending generation and their wife-givers in the first descending generation (Fig. 18), and the term yame, also a reciprocal, is used between wife-takers in the second ascending generation and their wife-givers in the second descending generation (Fig. 19). The term wąi (see Figure 17) is used as a reciprocal between wife-takers in the first descending generation and wife-givers in the first ascending generation.

Our idealized model of reciprocity between zibi and the set of continuing marriage possibilities and terminological distinctions elaborated upon it, are all predicated upon the premise that a zibi, as the basic unit of relationship, should not be simultaneously wife-giver and wife-taker to another zibi. There are certain ways, however, in which this system can be "short-circuited" and obligations satisfied by direct reciprocity between zibi. The first of these is a sister-daughter exchange between zibi, where a man who marries the sister of another man will reciprocate by giving

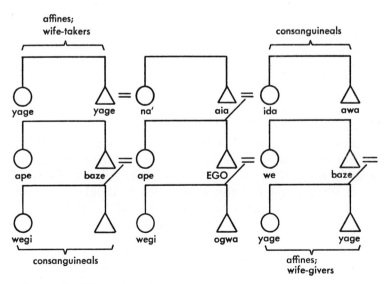

FIGURE 18.—*The reciprocal yage.*

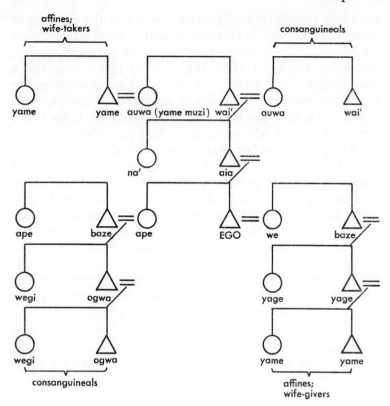

FIGURE 19.—*The reciprocal yame.*

his daughter by another wife to the latter (Fig. 20). In this situation, zibi B calls zibi A its *baze-soro*, wife-takers, stressing the fact that it has given its sister to them, in order to claim payment for her. Zibi A, however, calls zibi B its *wai-soro*, also wife-takers, stressing the fact that it has given its daughter to them, likewise in order to claim payment. Thus zibi A and its sons of zibi C take alternative roles with regard to zibi B; zibi A are wife-takers, zibi C wife-givers. Continuing marrages may be made along lines of the original exchange, but zibi A should not give sisters to B, nor should B give daughters to A. Zibi D cannot intermarry with either B or E because they are its pagebidi, and,

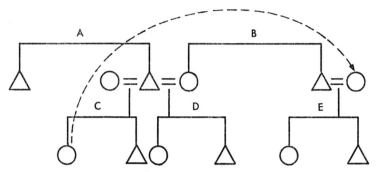

Figure 20.—*Sister-daughter exchange between zibi.*

similarly, zibi C are the pagebidi of zibi E. Thus, following such a sister-daughter exchange the possibilities for continuing intermarriage with the patriline of wife-givers are nullified.

A more direct way of "short-circuiting" the system by discharging obligations is through sister exchange. This brings the added benefit that the two men who have exchanged sisters need not give as much "pay" to each other as wife-givers as they would otherwise, for the wealth they exchange is intended for each other's brothers, who are entitled to a share in their sisters' bridewealth and have not been compensated by the giving of a wife (see chapter 4, "The Zibi"). Men who have few relatives close enough to make large contributions to the bride price they are raising may, therefore, resort to sister exchange. According to Daribi, "If a man's parents die, he will think, 'Who will help me with the bride price,' and he will arrange a sister exchange." The arrangement of a sister exchange is up to the man to whom the first sister is offered:

when I have given my sister to a man, I call this man's sister ape ("sister")—she is not my true sister, but a woman of another clan. If I should marry her, I would not call her "sister" any longer. It would be possible for me to marry her, but I could not ask her brother for her. If he wants to, he can say, "I married your sister, you can marry mine if you want to." I could marry her, but it is up to him.

No betrothal is made where a sister exchange is to take place; the sisters are exchanged simultaneously, and the matter is contracted solely by the brothers of the women concerned (and not by their fathers). No exchange of bride price takes place, although later each party will pay the brothers and father of the other. One party to a sister exchange may choose to give two sisters to the other, and "if a man has given two sisters in a sister exchange and received only one in return, he is entitled to 'pay' in addition." Such was the case at Soridai, where Bibi of Sora' gave his two

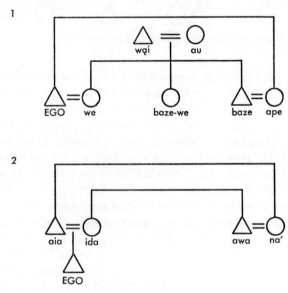

FIGURE 21.—*Terminology in sister exchange.*

sisters, Sizi and Awi, to Nawi of Soridai in exchange for Nawi's sister Buruwe. Each party to a sister exchange speaks of the other as a wife-taker (*ape sai bidi,* literally "sister-taker"), although the kinship terms used between them are those for wife-givers (Fig. 21, number 1). Continuing marriages along the lines of the original sister exchange are thus possible. Two men who have exchanged sisters are pagebidi to each other's children, and a child calls his father's sister's husband awa in this case, rather than the affinal term usually used for na' 's husband, yage (Fig. 2, number 2). The effect of this is to put each zibi in a position to make demands on the other and also to render impossible any further intermarriage between the two lines in descending generations, for a man's wife's brother's children are here his sister's children, to whom he is pagebidi, and not yage. In addition to the exchange between Bibi and Nawi, I was able to record two other examples of sister exchange. Pusi of Hwaio gave his sister to Inoai of Wenaio in exchange for the latter's sister, among the Tųdawe. Siazabo of Sogo and Sezema of Kilibali exchanged matrilateral half-sisters, and it is significant in the light of Daribi consanguinity that informants classed this together with the other examples of sister exchange.

Sister exchange, and to a lesser extent sister-daughter exchange, is always considered somewhat reprehensible by Daribi, although all of my informants agreed that both are quite permissible. What they considered objectionable was the cancelling of bride price payments between the participants, for it is the sharing of contributions to and dividends from bridewealth which symbolizes clan membership. The deadlock reached in sister exchange, where two zibi are simultaneously wife-giver and wife-taker to each other and pagebidi to each other's children, precludes the standard Daribi system of obligations in exchange, whereby the demands made upon a zibi by its wife-givers, the pagebidi of its children, are balanced off by the demands it can make in turn on its wife-takers and their children. The system of clan and zibi reciprocity which we have discussed above is thereby short-circuited, for, whereas ordinarily a zibi balances off the functions of wife-giver and wife-taker among several zibi in the affinal clan and thus allows a complementary functioning of the zibi of one clan *vis-à-vis* that of another, sister exchange requires only two zibi to close the system. Thus, we can distinguish two ways in which sister exchange obviates the necessity of interaction by clan members as a group in marriage. First, since there is no bride price, but only compensatory payment to members of the two zibi who do not receive wives in the exchange, members of the two clans other than those of the two zibi involved do not share in the contributions to or the dividends from bridewealth exchange by virtue of the marriage. Second, since the two marriages themselves reciprocate each other, other zibi of the two clans are not involved in the satisfaction of obligations incurred in the exchange, and two zibi of a clan do not share functions *vis-à-vis* a zibi of another clan. In both of these points, the two zibi involved in a sister exchange thereby isolate themselves respectively from the rest of their clans, for they take upon themselves the functions normally shared among clan members.

We have seen above that the clan is normally the unit of reciprocity in marriage; by ruling out both means by which the separate units of a clan interact in such reciprocity, sister exchange thus relegates to the zibi the functions of both relationship and reciprocity in marriage. Because the interaction with their respective clans is comparatively weak, while their lines are allied by a reduplicated alliance bond, the parties to a sister exchange come to depend more upon each other than upon their clan brothers, and it is, therefore, not surprising to find that both instances of sister exchange that I recorded among the Daribi (two out of three at Karimui) involved the co-residence of the exchangers; that is, one party went to live with his wife's clan of origin (and sister's clan of marriage). Bibi and Bizimani of Sora' now live at Soridai with Nawi, their sisters' husband, and Siazabo of Sogo lives at Kilibali with his exchange partner Sezema.

The theme of sister exchange is treated allegorically in the following story, which again deals with the role of payments in marriage and alliance.

A man was living with his sister. One day a dugumaru bat caused a big wind (*mazhuku*) to shake their house. The man then killed a pig and left a piece for the dugumaru. As the dugumaru came to take it, a big wind accompanied him, and when he brought it to his house, it had turned into a great deal of meat. Later, another big wind came and shook the man's house, and he put his sister out for the dugumaru. The latter came and took her, and again he was accompanied by a big wind. The man did not know where his sister had gone to. After a long time he set out to find her. He walked and walked and finally arrived at the home of the dugumaru, where he found his sister. The dugumaru was away. The man's sister said to him, "You shouldn't stay here; my husband is always speaking ill of you. He has a very long penis, and he stands way over there and thrusts it into me and it goes in all the way up to my neck. I'm sick of him. Look at all my children running around here. If you want to stay somewhere, go and stay with your cross-cousins. Let them get water for you; don't get it from the lake." She said this, and then the dugumaru arrived and said to her brother, "Go away. Do you want to stay and watch me copulate with your sister?" With that he inserted his penis into her while her brother was watching. The man's sister told him to go, and he left and went to the house of his cross-cousins. At sunset he was thirsty, and his cross-cousins told him, "You go along this road; you will pass a lake and then come to a man's house, and after that you will come to some water." The man went along the road, passed the lake, and came to the house. A beautiful woman lived in the house, and she was sitting on the veranda making a net bag. She invited him in, gave him food and water, and asked him where he had come from. He told her what had happened to him, and she said, "Don't stay with your cross-cousins; stay here with me." She made a bed for him and asked him, "Didn't you get pay in return for your sister?" He replied that he hadn't, and she said, "If your cross-cousins ask you where you slept, tell them 'with a man.' If the dugumaru should give you, as his baze, a pig, it will become many pigs; if he should give you one item of pay, it will become a great deal of pay. Don't accept this, however; tell him that you want to take a boy, one of your sister's children. Ask for the second child." The man heard this and left, and his cross-cousins asked him, "Are you going to ask for pay?" and he said that he would, and they went with him. He came to the dugumaru and asked for payment, and the dugumaru gave him a pig, which turned into many pigs, and a piece of pay, which turned into much pay. Then the man said, "I already have enough pigs and pay." The dugumaru said, "What do you want, then?" and the man said, "I want to take one of my sister's sons," and all of his sister's children came together. The man said, "I'll take the second child," and the dugumaru said, "No, I will give you more pay," and he brought more pigs and pay. The man, however, said, "No, I'll take the child," and he took him, and together they left. They went on and passed a mountain, and then the child of the dugumaru ran back to its father and the beautiful woman appeared. She told him, "You don't have to do any work. I'll do all your work for you, cut your garden, build your house. All you have to do is cook the food." Then they arrived at a spot, and the woman made a house for him. Down below the house she made a lake and said, "This is my house." She made a garden and took care of the pigs and said to the man, "You live in this house, I'll live in the lake; if you want to see me or have intercourse with me, come to the lake." When they were first married, the man cooked food regularly. They had two sons and two daughters, and these lived in the lake with their mother. One day the man was lazy and didn't cook the food on time—later he cooked a little with some dirt and took it to the woman. She said, "I treated you well, and did your work for you, and now you are lazy," and refused the food. Later he cooked some more and cooked it well and took it to her, but she said, "I spoke to you about this before," and the man was disgusted. The woman said, "You don't like me; I'll go back now. You are getting rid of me; I'll give you to another woman." He saw another woman there, and he went up to her and she was ugly, a *toro* woman. Then his first wife took his pigs one by one and gave them to the father's brothers of the toro woman in order to "buy" her and then took all her possessions and her children and went back to her father and said, "I lived with this man, and he took all my pigs to buy another wife with," and then her father went to the clan of the toro woman and killed all the men. The man then went to the dugumaru, who asked him why he had come. The man said, "I'm just walking around." The dugumaru said, "Do you want to copulate with your sister?" The man's sister then said, "You didn't follow my instructions. You got a good wife and didn't take care of her." The man went back to his house, and later the dugumaru came to kill him. The man asked what he was doing, and the dugumaru said, "You didn't follow instructions; I will kill you." The man said, "All the wind came, and I gave you my sister, and you treated me badly." The dugumaru replied, "I gave you my sister and you didn't take good care of her." Then the dugumaru made a great deal of wind and shook the house; he shook it and shook it so that the man couldn't sleep, and his wife left him. One night the wind awoke the man, who had been wondering what he should do, and he cried out, "I would like to turn into a dugumaru; can you do it for me?" but the wind just blew. The man was sick of the wind, and he turned into a bird-of-paradise and stayed inside the house. Then a great deal of wind came, and he came outside of the house, and the wind caught him and took him away.

This story is complicated by the fact that one of the characters, the dugumaru (together with his sister) is a supernatural and has supernatural powers. He is able to cause strong winds, which are greatly feared by Daribi, and he possesses "magical" pigs and pearl shells, capable of multiplying themselves, as well as the power to cause wealth to multiply. His sister lives in a lake, like a ghost or an izara-we.

The story begins with the giving of his sister by the hero to the dugumaru in order to conciliate him as an "influence" so that he will stop shaking the house with winds. The dugumaru treats his sister badly and further insults him by copulating with his sister in his presence (although ordinarily the very mention of sex in the presence of a wife's brother will make a man feel shame). His sister tells him to stay with his cross-cousins and says explicitly that he should not get water from the lake. He goes to his cross-cousins, and in going for water passes the lake and comes to the house of a woman who is in reality the sister of the dugumaru. She gives him food and shelter and proposes to him that he refuse payment for his sister and claim instead one of her sons, as their pagebidi. She is, in fact, proposing that he accept her, the dugumaru's sister, in exchange for his own sister, and it is significant that she makes the proposition. He, accordingly, goes to the dugumaru and refuses the "magical" wealth, despite the latter's protests, and takes his sister's second child. On the way home the child disappears, and the dugumaru's sister appears in his place. She, however, plays an inverted role; she does man's work, although a woman, and forces her husband to do woman's work. She had, in fact, proposed the marriage to begin with, which is usually a man's responsibility. The fact that she plays a man's role, although a woman, places her in the category of "strange" or supernatural women, and she lives in a lake, as do other types of supernatural beings. When the hero tires of doing woman's work, he lets this be known in characteristic woman's fashion, by not preparing the food well, whereupon his wife, in anger, buys him an ugly, monstrous toro wife with her pigs and lies to her father, who, misled by her words, wipes out the line of the toro woman. When the hero comes again to the dugumaru, he is shamed again, and his sister reproaches him, first, for not following her instructions, and, second, for mistreating his wife. The man goes home, and when the dugumaru comes to kill him, they confront each other with the fact that each has mistreated the other.

Finally the hero meets his doom, the same that he originally tried to counteract by giving his sister to the dugumaru. He makes two mistakes; he gives his sister to an inhuman, supernatural being, who mistreats him, and, instead of reaping the rewards of this by taking the magical wealth, he compounds his mistake by marrying the sister of the dugumaru, who is herself supernatural. As a sister of the hero's wife-taker, she is also a wife-taker, and thus she makes a "wife" of the hero, who is unable to stand this. Now, however, he is trapped by the fact that he has entered into a relationship of mutual reciprocity with a supernatural being, and, as he refuses to be a "wife" to the sister of the latter, is confronted by him for "mistreating" his sister. The substitutions in this story represent the kinds of payment a man can expect in return for his sister: "magical" wealth (for the "pay" which one receives in a marriage exchange can be lent out and increased), a sister's child (as its pagebidi), a sister of the brother-in-law (who is represented here as a "man" to emphasize the conflict of wife-giving and wife-taking functions in sister exchange), and, as a substitute for the masculine wife, an ugly, monstrous woman, who is disagreeable in another way.

Daribi Marriage

Daribi say they marry women belonging to lines "with whom we do not eat meat." A sort of myth is usually quoted in connection with the subject of incest and exogamy:

Once there was a man who lived with his sister; their parents had died. One day his sister went to a different place, where there were pigs. She said, "My brother is at home and doesn't have anyone to marry." The people there betrothed her to one of their men and sent her brother two pigs, one of which he was to eat and the other he was to use in purchasing a wife elsewhere.

Daribi say that if the man in the story had married his sister, they would marry their sisters.

Daribi girls are often betrothed or "marked" to men as future wives when they are infants, and few girls reach the age of ten or so without being betrothed. The future husband may be himself a child, or he may be a young man, or one of quite advanced age. If he were to die before the child attained marriageable age, a brother or hai' would inherit her under the levirate. "Marking" a child by making payments for her is called *noma' sabo,* "taking the soul." By the time they have reached puberty, all Daribi girls have been thus bespoken, and there are no "courting parties" or prearranged liaisons between young people at Karimui as there are in the Highlands, or even at Lake Kutubu.

The father or mother of a girl can "mark" her; if one of them decides to betroth her to a certain man, the consent of the other must be obtained. If they have taken the initiative in this way and have chosen a man, they will send a messenger of the latter's clan to ask him if he will consider the betrothal. If a man would like to marry the daughter of another man, he will send a man of the girl's clan as intermediary to ask if she has been "marked" yet. If not, he asks whether they would like to "mark" her to the man who sent him; if they agree to this, the "marking" proceeds.

A girl may be "marked" because her parents would like to have a certain man as a son-in-law (often because he is wealthy or a good worker), to reciprocate for a woman previously given to their clan, because a previous daughter "marked" to the same man has died and they would like to keep him as a son-in-law, or because he has proven a good, generous son-in-law in the past, and they consider him a good investment for future marriages. Daughters may also be "marked" to fulfill an outstanding obligation (such as to make up for a killing), to cement an alliance, or in peacemaking. When an epidemic of meningitis struck Di'be', women were married to Telabacul (in the Bomai Census Division) to counteract the "sorcery" being practiced. A man of Noruai "marked" his daughter to Kagoiano to compensate for the accidental killing of the latter's brother Sizigwa, who was shot in the back while eating pork at Iogoramaru, being mistaken for a Iogoramaru man by a man of Kilibali, which was at that time living at Noruai. This is the first marriage to be contracted between Noruai and Kurube', which have formerly been regarded as one clan, Weriai. If the older men of Kurube' and Noruai allow the marriage to take place (and some, notably Kai of Noruai, have spoken against it), it will mark the formal splitting of Weriai into two clans.

When the parents have decided to "mark" their daughter to a certain man, and the arrangements have been made, he will start to assemble "male" goods for the bride price, and they will assemble "female" goods, bark cloaks and net bags. The future husband makes an initial payment of some pearl shells (about four) and some other jewelry (a shell headdress and perhaps a string of cowrie shells), as well as a pig (which may not be given immediately), and receives in return a few net bags and a bark cloak or two. After this, the girl has been "marked," and her future husband is obliged to bring her parents gifts of meat which he has obtained in hunting at odd intervals. These gifts are reciprocated with bark cloaks and net bags. The girl stays at her parents' clan until puberty. At some time when she is about eight or ten, she goes to stay for about three or four days in the women's quarters of her future husband's house with his mother and returns to tell her parents that her future husband is accumulating the bride price. No sexual activity takes place at this time.

The marriage itself takes place when the girl reaches puberty. She may not have intercourse with her husband until she has menstruated for the first time. If her breasts have begun to swell and she is married at this time, she will stay with her husband's mother in the women's quarters of his house until the flow of her menses, and his mother will continue to prepare food for him until then. On the evening before the ceremony, a songfest is held in the women's quarters of the bride's parents' house, and all male and female members of the community who wish to attend do so. The groom's relatives should also attend, but in my experience they have always elected to remain in the men's quarters of the bride's house during this ceremony. During this event, the girl's people tell her of her obligations to her future husband, and the groom's people, if present, tell the groom of his obligations to his future wife. A recent innovation is the interruption of the songfest by a dramatic interlude, in which transvestite women pretend to try and kidnap the bride. This has been introduced from the Mengino area within living memory, and is by no means always done; Daribi have no explanation for it.

The ceremony takes place at about one o'clock the following afternoon. The groom and four or five men of his clan cover their bodies with soot, place cassowary plumes in their hair, decorate themselves with shells, and stand at attention in single file before the ladder of the bride's house. This is the Daribi "guard of honor." Each holds a bow and arrows in his left hand and part of the bride price in his right. The bride, who has remained in the women's quarters until this time, is then led out by her sister or father. She is decorated with paint, decorative leaves, shells, a headdress of feathers, and perhaps marsupial fur. She walks down the line formed by the "guard of honor," taking the bridewealth from each one as she passes him. As he hands her the shells, the man shifts an arrow to his right hand and resumes his stiff posture. When the bride has collected the bridewealth, she gives it to her father, then goes and stands behind the groom. Then the groom's party go back to their house together, and the bride follows in the charge of the groom's mother.

In addition to the bride price, a final payment of a pig is given to terminate the period of "marking." If this payment is not made, the clan of the girl will tie up a tree trunk like a pig and carry it to the wedding, placing it next to the "guard of honor." When the ceremony is over, they get an ax and "kill" the tree trunk, thus shaming the groom, who will bring his gift of a pig shortly to wipe out the stigma.

After the ceremony, bride and groom stay at the latter's house, with the woman secluded in the care of his mother, for five or six days. Then both go on a hunting trip in the bush for a similar period, during which the man shoots marsupials and smokes them over the fire. After this, they return to the groom's house for one night, then take the meat to the bride's father. It is only after this, and if the bride has passed her first menstrual flow, that the marriage may be consummated.

The bride price itself includes two kinds of payment; *were oromawai* ("given without return for the woman") and *we pona siare* ("woman buying finished"), the wealth which has been reciprocated ("finished") by the return payment of "female" goods. If, as in the case of Maruwe of Kurube', the bride price must be returned later because of the death or divorce of the

woman, only the first payment (were oromawai) will be returned. Knots are made on a cord, or small pieces of stick are
broken, to serve as a record of the wealth exchanged. An additional payment equal to about one-tenth of the bride price is
made by the bride's clan to her pagebidi. If the bride has been
"marked" to another man previously, a payment is made to him
at this time also. A typical marriage exchange, between Nekapo
and Kilibali, is recorded in Table 1.

TABLE 1

EXCHANGE OF BRIDEWEALTH BETWEEN NEKAPO AND KILIBALI

Bride price (given by Nekapo to Kilibali):

were oromawai	*we pona siare*
10 pearl-shell ornaments	14 pearl-shell ornaments
2 one-pound notes	1 one-pound note
2 shell headdresses	2 blankets
3 shell disk ornaments	6 lengths of trade cloth
1 beaded headpiece	
1 beaded belt	
19 shillings	
1 linked shell bracelet	
2 pig-tusk nosepieces	
3 axes	
1 bushknife	

"Dowry" (counter-prestation given by Kilibali to Nekapo):

8 net bags	5 pearl-shell ornaments
2 bark cloaks	7 lengths of trade cloth
1 one-pound note	

Payment given by Kilibali to the bride's pagebidi:

2 pearl-shell ornaments	1 ax
1 shell headdress	1 length of trade cloth

Payment given by Kilibali to a man to whom the bride was formerly betrothed:

4 pearl-shell ornaments	2 lengths of trade cloth
2 net bags	1 noosed rope as pledge for pig

Postmarital residence is very largely virilocal, the only exceptions occurring in cases where a man has been driven out by his
clanmates, or has no father or brothers to give him support in his
own clan, so that he is driven to seek the support of his brother-
in-law. We have seen above how sister exchange strengthens the

bond between brothers-in-law at the expense of that between clan members, so that one of the parties to a sister exchange frequently moves in with the other. This is not solely uxorilocal residence however, for the man in this case has also taken up residence in his sister's clan of marriage. Daribi prefer living with their married sisters to living with their wives' people, for wife-givers are treated with deference. Thus, if he is unable to take up residence with his hai' or some other consanguineals, a man's first choice for a new home is that of his sister's husband.

A man asks his wife, "Should we go and live with your clan or with my sister's people?" She says, "Your clan is always angry with you; let's go and live with my parents." He replies, "I have given my sister to ——— clan; let's go and live there."

Failing this, they will go to live with the wife's clan. Thus, if Ṭạre, who has no full sisters, were to be evicted by Kurube', he would go to live with his wife's people at Sogo. If his daughters were married, he would prefer living at their clan of marriage, but they are still small, and "if a man's daughters are not yet married, but just 'marked,' he cannot go and live with the clan they will marry into."

When a man goes to live in another clan, he no longer shares in the contributions to or distribution of bridewealth within his original clan, but takes part in those of his new clan.

Affinal terms are used between a man and his future in-laws from the time of the "marking" onward. A marriage initiates a series of exchanges between wife-takers and wife-givers which lasts throughout its duration. In addition, it establishes the relationships of wife-giver and wife-taker, which should be respected in the contraction of further marriages.

Affinal Kin Terminology

> To look at one's mother-in-law is like looking at the sun
> [Daribi saying].

Daribi affinal terms designate a series of relationships consequent upon marriage; each marriage generates a set of such relationships between relatives of the two parties concerned. We have observed earlier that affinity among the Daribi is in some sense a function of consanguinity; that is, marriage consists in the "buying" of a woman from her consanguineals, and the relationships of affinity thus oppose Ego to various persons who have claims and interests in, or at least relationship to, a woman who has been exchanged. These relationships, like that between baze, for instance, can be said to arbitrate or control the kinds of interaction which should take place between the parties concerned, whether these be of avoidance or potential marriage. The fact of connection through marriage establishes such affinal relationships; in addition, some affinal relationships indicate the degree or kind of consanguinity through which the tie is traced.

We may, therefore, distinguish two basic subdivisions of affinal relationships: those traced through marriage links alone (as with husband and wife) and those which include a factor of consanguineal relationship in addition to the affinal link, the consanguineals of affines, and the affines of consanguineals. Since affinal terms are almost wholly reciprocal, denoting the relationship itself which exists between two persons, the terms themselves do not distinguish affines of consanguineals from consanguineals of affines, but rather one term will be used reciprocally by a person of the former category for one of the latter, and vice versa. Thus, Ego calls his father's sister's husband, the affine of a consanguineal, yage, and the latter calls Ego, the consanguineal of an affine, the same thing. Insofar as zibi are the units of relationship in marriage, such affinal terms are used between members of zibi which are connected by marriage, and we can distinguish a set of relationships between "close" affines, those whose zibi are connected by marriage, from more distant affines. Among these "close" affinal relationships, between members of two zibi connected by marriage, and those of their parents, we can distinguish a set of relationships between affines whose interests conflict in the pagebidi relationship. We can also distinguish certain relationships which permit marriage. A schematic representation of these distinctions is given in Figure 22.

The strongest consanguineal claims on a woman are those of her parents and brothers; the strongest affinal claims on her are

	Wife-Takers	Relationships	Wife-givers
"PAGEBIDI" AFFINES	DaHu, DaHuBr	wqi	WiFa, WiFaBr
	DaHu, DaHuBr	au	wimo, wimoz
	ZHu, ZHuBr	baze	WiBr, BrWiBr
"NON-PAGEBIDI" AFFINES	HuFa, ZHuFa, HueBr (f. sp.)	wai'	sowi, SoWiBr, sowiz, ybrwi (m. sp.)
	humo, zhumo, hufaz, zhufaz	auwa/wai'	sowi, SoWiBr, sowiz, brsowi, BrSoWiBr (f. sp.)
	zhuz (m. sp.)	ape	BrWiBr (f. sp.)
	zhuz (f. sp.)	ama'	brwiz (f. sp.)
	brwi (f. sp.)	mene	huz
MARRIAGEABLE	BrDaHu	wqi/wqi-we	wifaz
	ZHu, ZHuBr	baze/baze-we	wiz
	HuyBr	sare	ebrwi
	HuSo, HuBrSo	ogwa-paba	fawi, fabrwi
DISTANT AFFINES	FaZHu, FaZHuBr, fazhuz, FaZSoDa FaZDaDaHu, MoBrSoDaHu, MoBrDaDaHu	yage	WiBrSo, wibrda, WiFaMoBrSo, WiMoMoBrSo WiFaFaZSo, WiMoFaZSo.
	FaFaZHu, FaFaZHuBr, fafahuz, DaHuFa, dahumo, SoDaHu, DaDaHu, HuFaFa-mo, HuMoFa-mo	yame	WiBrSoSo, wibrsoda, BrWiBrSoSo-da, SoWiFa-mo, WiFaFa-mo, WiMoFa-mo, sosowi, dasowi.
TRACED THROUGH AFFINITY ALONE	WiZHu, WiBrDaHu	hebiai	WiZHu, WiFaZHu
	huwi	abere	huwi
	Hu	bidi/we	wi

Left-margin bracket labels: RELATIONSHIPS TRACED THROUGH SERIAL LINKS OF AFFINITY AND CONSANGUINITY; TRACED THROUGH AFFINITY ALONE; CLOSE AFFINES; DISTANT AFFINES; UNMARRIAGEABLE; MARRIAGEABLE.

FIGURE 22.—*Daribi affinal terms.*

those of her husband and his brothers. In addition, the strongest claims on a man's children are those of their pagebidi, who are, again, his wife's parents and brothers. Thus, the three most strictly controlled affinal relationships are those between a man and his siblings and his wife's father, mother, and brothers, respectively. Since these are the pagebidi of his wife and children, we can speak of these most strained affinal relationships as those of the pagebidi relationship (Fig. 22).

A man and his siblings, and his father-in-law and his brothers, call each other wąi. Wąi may speak to each other, but "should not talk much." In the presence of his father-in-law, a man should "speak carefully, and not joke, because we are ashamed in his presence—he is the father of my wife." Wąi may not speak each other's names. These restrictions may be relaxed somewhat between wąi who are not directly related as father-in-law-son-in-law, but are always observed otherwise.

A man and his siblings, and his mother-in-law and her sisters, call each other au (her brothers are classificatory wąi). Total avoidance is practiced between au; they may not see each other, speak each other's names, or hear them spoken. "To look at one's au is like looking at the sun." It is common at Karimui to see women pulling off the road, turning their backs, and pulling their bark cloaks over their faces to avoid setting eyes on an au. If they cannot avoid this, the man is obliged to make restitution to his au in the form of payment; an ax or a pearl-shell ornament is said to be sufficient. The woman is obliged to reciprocate later by giving him a net bag and a bark cloak. Au may speak while the goods are being exchanged. A person is said to feel shame (*hare*) before his au and wąi; he would feel this if he looked at his au, or joked with his wąi. If a man should encounter a classificatory au and unknowingly speak to her, he would feel shame afterwards. If he should go to his wąi's house and observe the latter fighting with his wife, he would feel shame. "If a man's au came to live with his clan, and the other men of his clan spoke badly of him, he would feel shame before his au and go and fight them." F. E. Williams has recorded an almost identical relationship between mother-in-law and son-in-law at Lake Kutubu.[1]

A man and his brothers, and his wife's brothers, call each other baze. Baze should not call each other by name, but use the term baze. There are no tabus on talking or looking, and baze may joke with one another. They should exchange "pay" whenever

[1] F. E. Williams, *Natives of Lake Kutubu, Papua*, Oceania Monograph No. 6 (Sydney: The Australian National Research Council, 1940), pp. 60–61.

they visit each other; "a man jokes with his baze, then gives him 'pay'." The groom-to-be visits the brother of his future wife, brings him a marsupial, and sleeps at his house. Later, when the couple are married, her brother will come to visit her. When a man dies, his baze come to lament and to build the exposure-coffin (kų), or to dig the hole in which he is buried. The relationship between baze is somewhat strained, and the wife's brother has a clear advantage over his sister's husband; as pagebidi of the latter's wife and children, he can press claims on them. Where restraint occurs in this relationship, it is directed to the wife's brother, and this is the side of the relationship one informant had in mind when he told me that one should not joke with one's baze.

As opposed to a man's relationships with the pagebidi of his wife and children, his relationships with the parents and sisters of his sister's husband do not involve any conflict of interests, and he and his siblings use consanguineal terms for them, and vice versa. They call his sister's husband's father and his brothers wai' ("grandfather"), and he and his brothers call them the same ("grandchild" in this case). There are no restrictions on joking, talking, or looking between wai', although persons who use this term between them should not marry or have sexual relations. The sister of a sister's father-in-law is called auwa, "grandmother," and she calls Ego and his siblings wai'. Ego and his siblings call his sister's husband's mother and her sisters auwa (she calls them wai') and her brothers wai'. Ego and his brothers, and their sister's husband's sister, call each other ape ("cross-sex sibling"), and should not marry (although they do in sister exchange; see above). Ego's sisters (apart from the ones through whom the bond is traced) call their sister's husband's sister ama' ("same-sex sibling"), and this is reciprocal. Children of such ama' and ape are called ogwa and wegi. These terms are all used by the women through whom the bond is traced, except that she calls her husband bidi and his sisters *mene*, which is reciprocal. As we have seen in our discussion of the junior levirate (chapter 4), a man and his younger brother's wife call each other wai'.

Certain cross-sex relationships among "close" affines allow the possibility of marriage. A man and his brothers call his wife's sisters baze-we, and they, in turn, call him and his brothers baze. Marriage is permitted between a man and his baze-we, and a certain avoidance is practiced between them. Likewise, a man and his brothers call his wife's father's sister wąi-we, and she calls them wąi. Marriage is permitted between these relatives, and there are no avoidance restrictions. A man and his elder brother's wife call each other sare; they may not joke or call each other by name, but otherwise there are no restrictions between them. Sare may marry if the woman passes on to her husband's younger brother, either through his volition or his death. A man and his siblings call their mother's co-wives paba and use consanguineal (matrilateral) terms for her relatives; she calls them ogwa and wegi. There are no restrictions here save those on sexual contacts, and a man may inherit his paba on the death of his father.

Beyond the range of "close" affinal relationships are those which are traced through more distant consanguineal ties in addition to the link of affinity. Ego and his siblings, and their father's wife-takers, call each other yage, as do Ego and his siblings and his hai' 's children's wife-takers. The term yage indicates potential marriage connecting those who use it; thus, Ego's father's sister's husband and his brothers are his potential baze, wife-takers, for they may marry his sister, although Ego should not marry theirs (for they are wife-takers). Similarly, Ego may marry his wife's brother's daughter, in which case the roles are reversed. Ego's hai' 's children's wife-takers may marry his sisters, for they are wife-takers to his hai' 's children, who are his consanguineals, but he should not marry theirs. Otherwise, there are no particular restrictions between yage. The term yame is used for more distant affinal relationships. Ego and his siblings, and his paternal grandfather's sister's husband and the latter's siblings, call each other yame, and the relationship is again one of potential connection through marriage. A man's paternal grandfather's wife-takers may marry his sisters, and so become his baze, although he should not marry theirs. This role is reversed in the case of Ego's wife's brother's son's children, for he can marry their sisters. The term yame is also used between Ego and his grandchildren's spouses and between the men and women whose children have married, although here it is not used to indicate potential marriage, but merely distant affinal relationship. The term yame carries no particular avoidances or restrictions.

Certain terms are used between those linked through affinal ties alone, whose relationship is not traced through ties of consanguinity as well. Thus a man calls his wife we; she calls him bidi. The term hebiai is used between men who marry sisters or between Ego and a man who marries some other potential wife. Women who are married to the same man or to brothers call each other abere. None of these terms carries any restrictions whatsoever.

7
The Processes of Clan Formation and Alliance

> Only that which has no history is capable
> of being defined.
> —Friedrich W. Nietzsche

Complementary Processes

In the preceding chapters we have been concerned with the analysis of Daribi social structure in terms of relationships and groups, and principles of relationship and grouping, that is, in terms of abstract rules and distinctions which govern the operation of Daribi social structure and hold true as a synchronic system. These principles and relationships remain constant in time, for the functions which they regulate, such as recruitment, marriage, and alliance, are, in fact, techniques for containing the life processes, the birth, reproduction, and dying of individuals within the framework of a given system. Insofar as they are unchanging aspects of a system which is continually in a state of flux, we can look upon these principles and relationships as timeless determinants of a phenomenon which must necessarily exist in time, like the laws which govern the trajectory of a moving object. We can, also, to continue the analogy, describe the motion of an object by an equation, and, similarly, we can analyze a social system in terms of its operation over a period of time and see the principles and relationships which govern it as factors in an ongoing process. Such an approach is often a necessary complement to that of deriving the principles by which a society is organized, for, in fact, human social systems must always exist with relation to ongoing processes, and the ways in which their elements interact over a period of time may not always be obvious. Some aspects of a given society may indeed be described more coherently and parsimoniously in this way. I will distinguish this approach as that of process.

We have heretofore touched only in passing on those changes which occur in units over a period of time, such as the growth and the changes in composition of a man's family as he grows older or the serial maturing of a group of brothers and the effects of this both on the zibi itself and on the clan of which it is a component. Because social units are made up of living human beings, who are born, mature, marry, and die severally and who proliferate variably but often with great success, these units are always in a state of flux with regard to composition and effective membership and often in the process of merging across or subdividing within boundaries previously defined. We have seen earlier how certain features of the social system, such as the organization of the zibi and the levirate, effectively accommodate some of the consequences of differential maturing and death rates. What remains to be seen is how the social system functions, in terms of its principles, as an ongoing process.

As treated here, process is simply an extension or working-out in time of the principles of social structure. It is, therefore, as much a part of the social system as the kin relationships we have analyzed, for it is, in fact, merely another way of conceptualizing these relationships. We can differentiate process, as the logical consequence of a given social system, from incident, which I will define as the effects on a social process of other processes, biological, meteorological, geological, or historical, which are not functions of the social system. Thus, for instance, a man and wife being blessed with twenty-four daughters, or a zibi being wiped out by a windstorm or massacred by a party of Chimbus, is an incident. The history of a people or a clan is always an interplay of social process and incident; the details of human life, the necessities of eating and sleeping, the facts of reproduction and its differential results, are all ordered to some extent by social process, and they also have their effect on the working-out of the process. This is true of all history; the emergence of urban life in the high cultures, for instance, can be seen as a process, but wherever this has taken place it has involved interaction with all sorts of phenomena, individuals, events, and pressures, which are not part of the process. Insofar as human life participates in a vast matrix of processes, which intersect and interact with one another, we can never really isolate a social process as a closed system. We can only create idealized models that serve to identify those elements in the history of a group which are functions of the social system and show the extent to which and the means by which social process participates in the history of the group. A group at any given time, the assortment of individuals encountered by the anthropologist, an assemblage of men sitting and smoking, of women preparing food or working in the garden, of children running about and doing nothing in particular, is participating in any number of individual processes, and any number of processes impinge upon it; some of these are social processes, while others may be classified for our purposes as incident. The census or genealogy of such a group records the result of many processes, some of which are controlled by the principles of social structure, while others are not. Thus we distinguish the "people on the ground" from the abstractions of a model, and a group from a unit.

Because units are defined and interrelated by the principles of social structure, they are formed and merged through processes governed by these principles. Thus, what remains the same over a period of time is the set of principles and the processes which they govern, for the units themselves are constantly changing, interacting in terms of these. We cannot define a clan insofar as it "has a history," for that history is one of sucessive redefinitions. What is now Kurube' Clan was once part of a group called Pina; before that, its ancestor(s) probably belonged to a group called Para, which is now the name of a phratry. Yet, all of these groups, as units, were defined by the principle of exchange and related to others through consanguinity and were formed by the same processes as Kurube' has been.

What, then, are these processes? We have seen that a unit defines itself in terms of exchange and traces relationship to other units in terms of the consanguineal links between its members and those of the other units. Both of these functions, definition and relationship, are ongoing ones with regard to time; children are continually being born, in each case linking two units through ties of substance, and payments are continually being made, defin-

Figure 23.—*A Daribi meditative position.*

ing the members of a unit against the claims of external relatives. Every marriage or payment given for the recruitment of a child is an act of definition of the clan; every child which is born in a clan forms a link with some other clan. We can speak of a process by which people are continually being related, and a process by which units are continually being defined. Because people belong to units, and units are made up of people, that is, because there is an intersection of the principles of exchange and consanguinity, these two processes must necessarily interact with one another.

Consanguinity governs both relationships within units and those between units; exchange defines the unit boundaries within which and between which relationship is traced. People can only become related, and units come to have memberships, as the result of the conception of children consequent upon a marriage, which must be made between units. Relationships can only come into existence as the result of the intermarriage of units; units can only be defined by opposing, or satisfying, claims made by virtue of relationship. The contraction of marriage, initiating an alliance, and the subsequent birth of children, which must be recruited, thus effects both the definition of the units involved and their interrelationship.

Because relationship is reckoned according to genealogical distance, whereas unit membership is determined only by a boundary established by exchange, the interaction of relationship and definition as processes involves further consequences for the units generated by them. The members of a unit are linked together by ties of substance, and their allegiance to one another is to a large extent determined by the closeness of such ties (i.e., zibi membership); persons belonging to different units who are related by ties of substance can make certain claims on each other (i.e., through the hai' relationship) which can also be made by virtue of unit membership. Thus, relationship has consequences for the process of definition, and definition has consequences for that of relationship. The definition of a group of people as a unit places a moratorium on the creation of further relationships among their lines, and it necessitates the creation of relationships with external units. In the process of relating themselves to external units, the component lines of a clan become progressively less closely related to each other; in the process of defining itself, a unit becomes related to others.

As the component lines of a clan become more and more distantly related to each other with the passage of time and the unit itself becomes larger, the claims a man can make on more distantly related clan members become less viable, and the weakness of the bonds is further aggravated by the differential relationship of lines within the clan to various external units and the tendency of people to subdivide on the basis of relationship in politico-legal disputes. In order to reestablish ties of close relationship between such lines, a marriage must be made between them. Marriage, however, involves definition as well as relationship, and the groups which thus intermarry thereby define themselves as separate units. Thus, through the ongoing effects of relationship, the process of unit definition operates continually to contract or restrict the units being defined. This process is one of exchange and involves the subdividing or segmenting of units in terms of the symbolic principles of sharing and exchanging wealth.

Coincident with the process of definition is that of relationship, by which lines, whose consanguineal relationship has become distant with the passage of time, are continually being rerelated by the conception of children embodying the substance of each. This process operates to form ties of close consanguinity between lines which define themselves through exchanges as against one another. As the relationship between allied clans becomes distant with the passage of time, further marriages will be made between them in order to rerelate them in succeeding generations. Insofar as the blood ties thus formed extend claims on clan wealth to those in other clans (through the hai' relationship), the process of relationship has the effect of extending clan privileges to persons outside the clan, and we have defined this extension earlier as the Daribi alliance bond.

The processes of definition and relationship are therefore, in their interaction, processes, respectively, of segmentation and alliance. The former, in the distinctions it draws between sharers and exchangers of wealth, is restrictive; it draws distinctions between persons who are related by consanguineal ties. Unit definition therefore always operates to restrict. In the case of marriage, a woman is separated from her brother by a redefinition of her group membership through the exchange of wealth; in that of recruitment, a child is separated from its matrilateral relatives in the same way. Segmentation merely involves the same process as it occurs within what was formerly a unit; persons related by consanguinity are grouped into, restricted to, different units. The process of clan formation is the same as that by which clan boundaries are maintained; units are simply redefined, as they are redefined every time a woman is given in marriage by one clan to another or a child is born and recruited to the clan.

The process of relationship, by contrast, is extensive; it extends ties of relationship to both lines involved in a marriage and extends privileges of sharing wealth to cross-cousins who belong to different clans (the Daribi alliance bond). The effect of relationship is continually to bind together those who define themselves as members of different units. Ties of relationship and of sharing among hai' serve to create bonds similar to those of clan membership between members of different clans, and this process is selective. Where a strong alliance is to be made between two clans, many marriages will be contracted, and the result, in the following generation, will be a closeness of relationship and of obligation in sharing wealth among the members of the two units. Two or more clans which have become interrelated in this way, whose members are all interknit through the obligations of sharing among hai', may take up residence together as a community. In the community a unit of a sort is created which to all intents and purposes functions as a clan does; members of a community share wealth in bride price exchanges, are usually too closely related to marry each other's sisters and daughters, form a unit in warfare, and formerly would often share a communal garden. The component clans of such a community, however, maintain their boundaries through the payments exchanged between hai' by virtue of the pagebidi relationship and in return for leviratic rights. As the member clans of a community become less closely related with the passing of generations, further marriages may be made between them in order to bring them into closer relationship again, and the continued exchange of definition payments in marriage and recruitment follows as a matter of course.

This process of continuing an alliance through the making of further marriages between allied clans as the relationship between them weakens is, of course, identical with that by which segmentation occurs, for in the latter case the marriage which effects redefinition of the component lines initiates their alliance through the birth of children. In both cases a group of people who formerly could not marry, either because of membership in the same clan or because of the blood ties between member clans of a community, have become more distantly related with the passing of generations, and the making of a marriage among them at once defines them or sustains their definition as separate units and also initiates closer consanguineal ties between them. The effect of both processes, segmentation and alliance, is to produce a set of more or less interrelated (depending on the number of bonds between them), differentially defined clans. It follows that there are really two ways in which the clans of a community can be linked, one of which is the prelude to segmentation, wherein the component segments of a clan, which have diverged because of distance of relationship between them, have not yet defined themselves as separate units by intermarrying and still consider themselves to be "one clan." Such segments act for the most part as separate clans, but trace their connection to one another through patrilateral ties (i.e., the idiom of normative patriliny). In this way they bear the same relationship to one another as do clans linked through cross-substance ties as a result of marriage, which we have discussed above, for in each case the individual clans are parts of a larger whole and may not intermarry. When a marriage between such patrilaterally joined lines does take place, and segmentation is completed, their relationship becomes that of allied clans, linked by cross-substance ties.

The interaction of definition and relationship as processes can be seen most clearly within the community, for here the process of alliance is most completely carried out through the making of marriages and proliferation of substance-ties among clans. Member clans of a community remain distinct units through the exchanges which must precede and follow upon the marriages whose issue unites them or which effect their segmentation; groups which have not yet segmented may be considered distinct when they, as "proto-clans," no longer take full responsibility in raising contributions for each other's bride prices and other exchange payments. In either case, just preceding segmentation or when the units have already intermarried, the boundaries are drawn by exchange functions. In both cases, as we have seen, the separate units are linked together as one by the ties of consanguinity extending between them and the obligations of sharing wealth which accompany these ties. Proto-clans, which have not yet segmented, are linked by their common ancestor and by that residiuum of their clan status which obliges them to share, however incompletely, in each other's exchange payments; clans already defined as such vis-à-vis one another by marriage are linked by the bonds of consanguinity which connect a woman with her brothers, her children with their pagebidi, and a man to his hai'. A community is in this way continually being bound together by the process of relationship and at the same time being subdivided into component units by the process of definition.

The former process, as an *extensive* one, thus acts within the community to create the larger whole; the latter, as a *restrictive* process, acts to subdivide this whole.[1] Yet, as we have seen above, the two processes are completely interdependent; neither could exist without the other. They are, in fact, two specific aspects of a single system. Because each depends upon the other, although they operate, so to speak, in opposite directions, I will refer to them as "complementary processes." They complement one another, and their interaction generates the units and the relationships between units which make up the Daribi social system.

It is possible to draw an analogy between relationship and definition in their interaction as complementary processes within the Daribi social system and two similar processes which govern word formation within the Daribi language. We can identify these latter processes for our present purposes as agglutination

[1] An ethnographic note: in societies characterized by moieties, such as the Dani of the Baliem Valley in West Irian, or the Tlingit of the American northwest coast, the functions of consanguinity and exchange with regard to relationship and definition (extensive and restrictive principles) are the inverse of those among the Daribi. Hence, in such societies the unit which is analogous to the Daribi community, the Dani set of linked clans, or the Tlingit village, is bound together by the *exchange* functions of its components, local representatives of the moieties, which are defined in opposition to each other by consanguinity, in the form of unilineal descent.

and contraction. Much as in German or English, a new word is formed in the Daribi language by stringing together a series of modifiers, followed by a concluding noun or verb, which is thus given a new or more precise denotation. Thus the word for "shaman" in Daribi is *sogoyezibidi*, "tobacco-spirit," made up of the word *sogo*, "tobacco," and the combining form of "ghost" (*izibidi*), *yezibidi*. "Wise man" in Daribi is *duagiai-korizaga-iai-bidi*, a "good-thought-making-man." Likewise, the original word for "bamboo tobacco pipe," now seldom used, was *sogo-genage*, literally "tobacco-bamboo."

When Daribi refer to a bamboo pipe, they will at present call it a *sogonage* or perhaps a *sogane*. These terms illustrate the operation of the second process, that of contraction, in which syllables are dropped to shorten a word in constant use. In the first, the middle syllable has been dropped; in the second, an *o* and a *g* have been dropped in a further transformation. A suggestion of the probable result of continued operation of this process is given by the prevalance of monosyllabic terms for "basic," everyday things, for instance; "ground" is *to*, "water" is *we*, "road" is *tu*, "tree" is *ni*, "house" is *be'*, "bird" is *ba'*, "stream" is *ai*, "sago" is *o*, and "garden" is *gi*. These terms are, of course, recombined with others again in the agglutinative process to yield new words; thus, we have forms like *sigibe'* ("arrow-house"), Suguai ("Fish-Stream"), and *wiliba'* ("wild bird," a bird of prey).

The interaction of both these processes regulates the formation of words. The word for "bamboo pipe" was a combination of two words referring to other things (tobacco, bamboo), joined through agglutination; later contraction operated to reduce it and thereby change it further to *sogonage* and finally *sogane*. Verbs may likewise be formed in this way; informants will often explain that a present tense form like *aga posogobo*, "he is hot," is short for *aga posogo-ebo*, "he hot-makes."

This analogy, which can never be more than an analogy, provides another example of how complementary processes, in their interaction, can determine the resultant configuration of a phenomenon.

Clan Formation

We have seen above how the complementary processes of relationship and definition interact to determine and maintain Daribi social structure as an ongoing system. We have also seen, in previous chapters, that consanguinity and exchange, the principles of which these processes are merely an extension into the dimension of time, interact according to a mode prescribed by the normative system, giving rise to what we have called "normative patriliny" and the pagebidi relationship. It follows from this that the normative system will also serve as the mode of interaction between our complementary processes.

It is a cultural norm for Daribi that a father should recruit his children to his own clan by giving wealth to their pagebidi to compensate the latter for his claims on them. Thus a clan, insofar as it combines the common exchange interests of many such fathers, should act in recruitment to incorporate its own lines of paternal substance. In our discussion of "idioms of relationship" in chapter 5, it has been shown that the paternal substance which is "redeemed" by recruitment payments in this way is an expression of clan solidarity, much as the pool of "vital wealth" from which clan members may draw to meet the payments which define the unit.

Turning once again to the mechanics of interaction between relationship and definition as processes, wherein consanguineal ties between component lines within a clan become more and more distant as the process of relationship progresses, for new relationships can only be formed between differentially defined units, and the definition of new units, or segmentation, results from the attempt to rerelate, or ally, such component lines as a consequence of marriage, it becomes apparent that the "patrilineal" idiom of clan membership represents a prescribed outcome of this interaction. If the norm for recruitment is followed, the consanguineal links which clan members share in common will be those of paternal substance, while those which connect them with external units will be traced through maternal substance. As time passes, and the clan continues to define itself as a unit vis-à-vis external units, thereby forming external relationships, it is the connections of paternal substance among its component lines which will become more distant, and when redefinition, or segmentation, occurs, it will take place among patrilaterally related lines. Thus the normative mode of clan formation among the Daribi is one of segmentation between lines related by patrilateral ties.

I have called the ideology by which a clan identifies itself with a certain line of paternal substance, traced to an original ancestor, the idiom of normative patriliny. It remains an *idiom*, and not, for instance, a *principle*, for it is invoked regardless of the genealogical relationships involved. Most of the men of Hagani Clan, for instance, trace their ultimate connection to the "core" Hagani line through a link of maternal substance; yet, the clan conceives of itself as being related as a whole to the other clans of Noru Phratry. The selection of male "common ancestors" and of ties of paternal substance as the significant ones linking member clans of a phratry constitutes the ideological expression, or idiom, of normative patriliny.

The ideology by which Daribi formalize the relationship of clans within a phratry is a result of this idiom. The clans are regarded as the descendants of a group of brothers, the sons of one man, who is represented as the founder of the phratry. The founders of the various clans are seen as his sons, either by one wife or by a number of wives. In this form, the founders of the various clans of a phratry can be seen as a zibi from which the phratry itself sprung, the founder of the phratry being the father of the zibi; thus, the group of men alleged to have founded the member clans of Para Phratry would be called the Parazibi. The existence of such a formula for the phratry can be traced to the fact that, given the operation of the processes of relationship and definition within the normative system, segmentation will occur among patrilaterally related lines. The phratry constitutes the form in which Daribi represent and record the facts of segmentation; it schematizes the point, external and previous to all existent clans, where their lines of paternal substance converge and meet. The phratry has no unity and no leaders, it does not under any circumstances convene as a body, nor does it especially "venerate" its founder (though the lines descended from Sugage share a common curse). Member clans of a phratry may intermarry and war with each other. It is highly improbable that any of the phratry ideologies now held by the Daribi give an accurate rendition of the segmentations which they represent, for they are specimens of a cultural model, or format, into which the facts are fitted and in terms of which they are manipulated. As with an origin myth, there are in each case many versions of a phratry ideology, all differing as to details, and this, in fact, is precisely the function fulfilled by a phratry—that of an origin myth.

The ideological scheme of a Daribi phratry gives an account of what has allegedly happened; our theoretical model of the processes gives a description of possibilities for what can happen. Where the Daribi formula disregards generalities altogether, our model misses completely the specific, the world of incident. What actually did happen lies somewhere between these two areas. Clans, which from time to time segment, live in a world of names, events, and personalities, of malaria and wife-stealing. The processes of social structure which we can trace intersect "on the ground" with the countless other processes involved in the life of man, and it is in this world of incident that segmentation takes place. Out of this ever changing macrocosm, the Daribi abstract patrilines; we abstract principles and processes.

One of the considerations which lie outside the scope of our study is that of differential fertility and survival. Yet the processes which determine these, as well as other processes, interact with the processes of relationship and definition to produce the actual situations in which clans segment or form alliances. In a clan where the fertility and survival rates are low, for instance, and, correspondingly, the rate of population increase is very slow, the financial strain on members to help with each other's exchange commitments will not be nearly so great as where a clan quickly outgrows a convenient size, and segmentation may not come for a long time.

Although the Daribi ideology assumes segmentation among lines which trace patrilateral connection, this need not always be the case. A line which is incorporated into a clan to which it traces matrilateral relationship may later increase and define itself as against that clan by contracting marriages with it, and thus relate to it simply as another allied clan within the community.

The process here would be identical with what occurs in segmentation otherwise, except that it would not be "normative";
the two clans resulting from the segmentation would not share
a common line of paternal substance. This seems to be happening
in the Kurube'–Noruai–Kilibali community. Eranabo and his
brothers went to live at Noruai, the clan of their mother, as a
result of dissension between them and the men of Nekapo, the
clan of their father. Now their descendants, called Kilibali, have
contracted marriages with Kurube' and Noruai and are assum-
ing the status of a separate clan, tracing its patriline to Nekapo.
Kilibali has also intermarried with Nekapo. The very numerous
Dobu line at Hagani, the ancestor of which, Kiru's grandfather
Wiribe, traces connection to the main Hagani line through his
mother Si, could likewise split from Hagani in a similar manner,
but thus far it has not done so.

   Another alternative is for the line which comes to live with a
clan not to merge with it, but to continue to intermarry, defining
itself as a separate unit within the community from the outset. This
is exemplified by the Genabi line at Dobu. When Pini's father
came to Dobu, probably to live with his affines, intermarriage
with Dobu did not cease, and a total of nine marriages with the
various units within the community were made. On the other
hand, the excellent genealogy given to me by Pini records no
marriages between this line and Genabi Clan itself, and we can
therefore regard the Genabi line at Dobu as simply a component
of the main clan which has associated itself with the Dobu community.

   In spite of the exceptions we have been discussing, segmentation, in the majority of instances that I have recorded, takes
place among patrilaterally related lines. As examples of such
segmentation, let us examine some genealogical material collected
in the Dobu community. The ideology of Dobu Phratry indicates
five sons of the immediate founder, Duabo, as the founders, respectively, of the Huzabe and Hwere lines at the Dobu community itself, of a line said to be extinct but actually traceable to
the Dobu line at Hagani, of Yamani Clan, and of a line living at
Masi (Fig. 24). Of these five, only the first two lines live at the
Dobu community. Among the members of these lines, two seg-

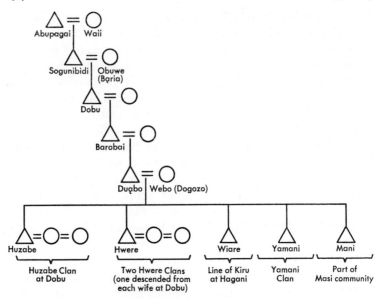

Figure 24.—*Dobu Phratry ideology.*

mentations seem to have occurred, both in what appears in the genealogy to be the third descending generation from that of Huzabe and Hwere (though this does not necessarily indicate that they were contemporaneous). The first segmentation occurred between the lines of Huzabe and Hwere, and I have recorded six marriages made between them in this generation (Fig. 25). This segmentation is represented in the phratry ideology, for Huzabe and Hwere are given as sons of the phratry's founder, Duąbo. The second segmentation is between the two major genealogical subdivisions of the Hwere line, represented as the descendants of Hwere by his first (Hou) and second (Komi) wives, respectively, and is not represented in the ideology, perhaps because of the recency and genealogical preeminence of the first split. I have recorded three marriages between the two Hwere lines (not shown). Upon consulting the complete Dobu genealogy, a contributing cause for this quick succession (or perhaps simultaneity) of segmentations becomes apparent; I

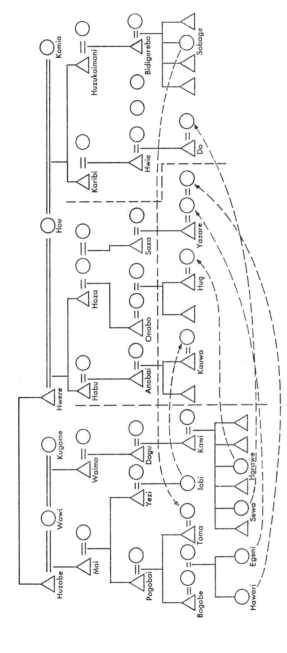

FIGURE 25.—*Segmentation between the Huzabe and Hwere lines.*

counted a total of fourteen male members born to the Huzabe line in the third descending generation from its founder, as against forty-four males of the Hwere line in the same generation. Even considering the high death rate at Karimui, forty-four males is far too unwieldy a number of men to function efficiently as a single Daribi exchange unit.

The "generations" counted here are, of course, abstractions, taken from a genealogical chart, but they do provide a quick, effective measure of the numerical strengths of the lines involved. Both segmentations are quite recent, occurring in the generation of the fathers of the present generation at Dobu. It will be noted that all the marriages recorded respect the limits of incest discussed in chapter 5.

The clans formed in the segmentations we have just examined all remained within the same community, which, together with the other components, the Gęnabi line and perhaps Kalibai Clan, remains a large and powerful one (despite the massacre staged there by the other Daribi clans acting in concert, *ca.* 1960). This pattern has been characteristic of Dobu, Masi, and Tiligi Phratries. Other phratries, Para, Di'be', and the Noru complex, have spread widely over the Daribi area. These phratries are perhaps somewhat older, and their scattered components have subdivided further within their respective areas. Let us examine the evidence for Para Phratry.

The founder of Para Phratry is given as a man named Bupariga, or Pariga, of which "Para" is probably a shortened version. Para is linked with Mese, the founder of the Masi Phratry, in all genealogies, and this probably refers to an earlier connection or even segmentation between the ancestral groups. Many of the versions I collected at Kurube' give Para as the father of Mese; others give Mese as the father of Para. According to the traditional account of the origin of the phratry, however, Mese adopted a boy (Waburu) and girl who had come along the Bore River "from the Urubidi." When the two grew up, Waburu copulated with his sister, and Mese was angry and said, "I took care of you, you were brother and sister; I wanted to marry the girl off elsewhere and get meat and 'pay'," and he threw the two out. Waburu and the girl went to Boromaru, and there they had a child,

Bupariga. When Bupariga, or Para, grew up, he married Koro-bame of Sora', and their sons were the founders of the various clans of Para Phratry.

Side by side with this legend, and the phratry ideology of which it forms a part, a certain amount of evidence exists for the gradual increase of the phratry through the formation of new clans. When I asked an informant whether the constituent clans of Para Phratry ever ate pork or initiated their youths together, he said, "We did when we all lived at Boromaru." At that time, however, Para was not yet a phratry, but merely a community, and it probably consisted of three clans living together. When the ancestors of Kurube' and Noruai moved to Waramaru, they no longer took part in such activities at Boromaru, and today Kurube', Noruai, and Kilibali share these activities.

I was told that Para had three sigibe's when it lived at Boro-maru, belonging, respectively, to Kurube'–Noruai, Sizi, and Yo-gobo. At this time, it was said, Sizi, Kurube'–Noruai, and so on, "were small." Subsequently, a part of Para moved to Waramaru, and consisted, according to my informant, of two sigibe's, one belonging to Kurube'–Noruai (which was at that time called Pina) and the other to the ancestors of Daie and Waime Clans. Both of these descriptions are probably reminiscences of stages in a series of segmentations, in which members of the original community living at Boromaru went elsewhere to settle, and in their turn formed new communities. The original community had very likely been formed by segmentation within a clan called Para, which had perhaps even earlier been formed by splitting off from the line of the Masi people, as is suggested in the tale of the phratry's origin.

We can picture, then, a series of splits within the Boromaru community, beginning perhaps with the first separation of a new clan from that called Para, the ancestral line of the clans tracing their lineage to Mare. Following this, another split must have oc-curred, forming the three clans mentioned by my informant. I was given a legendary account of how the Kurube'–Noruai line, that of Weriai, left Boromaru. An expedition was formed at Boromaru for the purpose of trading stone axes to the Kewa' people to the southwest in return for shell neckpieces. The line of

Weriai sent a good ax, Yogobo sent a bad one; the Kewa' people, accordingly, sent Weriai a good neckpiece in return, and sent Yogobo a bad one. Yogobo, however, switched neckpieces and gave the bad one to Weriai, keeping the good one for themselves. The two lines fought over this, and Yogobo shot Weriai in the eye, blinding him, hence his name (*weriai* means "blind," and is an adjectival form of *weria*, "belt"; a man who is blind has his view "fastened"—cf. Pidgin, *ai i pas*). After this the line of Weriai left Boromaru.

Weriai went to Waramaru, and Yogobo—perhaps afterward—moved to its present location below Nekapo. At Waramaru further segmentation must have occurred, the line splitting into "Pina" (Weriai) Clan and that of the ancestors of Daie and Waime Clans. At some time after this, perhaps, the latter group moved to Iogoramaru, where it split into the present Daie and Waime Clans. Close involvement as well as antagonism seems to have persisted between Weriai and Daie–Waime until the contact period, for Kagoiano's brother was shot while eating pork at Iogoramaru, and warfare with the Iogoramaru clans was given as a reason for the move of Weriai to Baianabo. The segmentation between Kurube' and Noruai, begun at Waramaru, was in its final stages in 1965. At Nekapo, Yogobo probably segmented further, perhaps giving rise to Wio Clan.

Segmentation also occurred within the line that remained at Waramaru, identified as that of Mare. Part of it, identified presently as Sizi Clan, migrated piecemeal at some time in the not-too-distant past to Bosiamaru, to live in community with affines at Soboro. Those remaining at Boromaru have since split into Warai and Ogwanoma Clans and live in community with Maina. Although the name Para may be used, especially by those outside the phratry, with reference to any of the clans in Para Phratry, the name is used most often—particularly by phratry members—to designate the three clans (Sizi, Warai, Ogwanoma) of the Mare line. This may be because the ancestral line remained at the location of the original settlement, as a sort of "rump" segment from which the others budded off, and continued to identify itself as Para Clan, or it may be that this line had some closer connection to the man named Para than the others.

The clans identified as descending from Hunai (Maia), Hwanai (Maza), and Yao at Iogoramaru, and Wio (Buibage) at Boromaru may perhaps have resulted from further segmentations of the Daie–Waime or Yogobo lines, but I was unable to gather sufficent data to establish a connection. The segmentations we have traced here are represented in Figure 26. The size and spatial extent of Para Phratry, which contrasts with the smaller Dobu, Masi, and Tiligi Phratries, is perhaps the result of age as well as of the availability of the broad, fertile Karimui Plateau as an area into which expansion was possible. Dobu Phratry has been limited to a "two-dimensional" realm by its location in a narrow valley, and, with some exceptions, the clans budding off of the Noru complex at Unamaru have moved westward, as Hagani and other

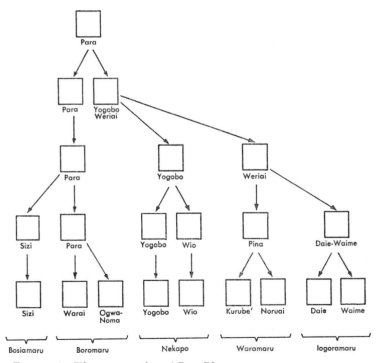

FIGURE 26.—*The segmentation of Para Phratry.*

Noru lines have recently, up the central valley within the Mac-Gregor Peaks. Masi, to the south, has claimed land on the southern slopes of Mount Karimui, but here it has been hampered by warfare with the Tudawe of the Pio River.

In this brief reconstruction of the history of Para Phratry, we have seen something of the dynamic, ongoing process of clan formation. The results of this process are registered ideologically by the Daribi in terms of the standardized formula identifying the founders of various clans of a phratry as the sons of one man. As the process continues, and more and more clans are formed, an increasing number of "sons" is attributed to the founder of the phratry through the telescoping of genealogies, as perhaps happened in the case of Daie and Waime (above), and the phratry becomes a large one indeed. Para Phratry, with a maximum of eight or nine sons so recorded, is the largest I have encountered. In some cases, as with Kurube'–Noruai and Sizi–Warai–Ogwanoma, additional "sons" are not added to the list, and divisions are recognized below those of the phratry ideology.

Eventually, if the process continues long enough, the list of "brother" clans becomes too unwieldy to manage, and some clans no doubt become too remote to matter, while at the same time the more recent segmentations below the ideological line of connection become more and more the focus of attention. This situation is met, gradually perhaps, by the abbreviation of the original list of fraternal founders, by the identification of a new set of such founders a generation or so below the original set, by the fusion of such sets, or by a combination of these practices. The result of this activity of genealogical editing is the formation of new phratries, that is, of new ideological constructs. Just as clan formation may be seen as a continually active process, so the genealogical tailoring of phratry ideologies is probably always in operation. Some genealogical material which I collected at Hagani might furnish examples of how this editing takes place.

Phratry Formation

Conventionally, only one fraternal set of clan founders is given for each phratry ideology, although, as we have seen in the case of Para Phratry, other kinds of genealogical connection with external units may be recognized at higher levels. Some accounts of the Noru Phratry, however, show two sets of fraternal clan founders, occurring in different generations. I will distinguish these two proliferations of clan founders, an elder and a younger, respectively, as the "senior" and "junior" phratries. The senior phratry includes groups (Maina, Tubia—the latter, at least, is a phratry in its own right) which are not generally recognized as being related to the Noru people; these are given as descendants of the brothers of Garo, founder of the Noru Phratry. The junior phratry, on the other hand, includes clans which are normally referred to as Noru, and these are seen as descendants of Garo by his various wives.

This "unfused" version, showing two phratry proliferations, was given to me by Yapenugiai, a genealogist with an unusually retentive memory, who was born and raised in Hagani but later moved to Kurube' (Fig. 27a). Several of the lines mentioned here (Nekapo, Hawasare) have moved to the Bomai Census Division, at Mount Suaru, and are now effectively removed from the Daribi society at Mount Karimui. Yapenugiai has given, in

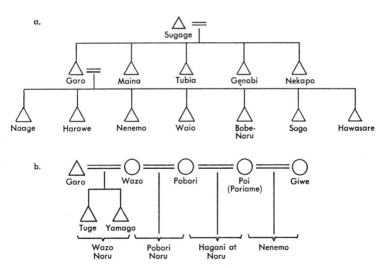

FIGURE 27.—*Noru Phratry, unfused version.*

addition, a more detailed account of the relationships within the junior phratry (Fig. 27*b*), which differs in some points with accounts collected at Noru. (Giwe, otherwise identified as the mother of Garo, is here given as his wife.) Earlier, in tracing his own genealogy, Yapenugiai had identified Dazubidi, the traditional founder of Hagani and a patrilateral ancestor of Yapenugiai, as a son of Garo by his wife Wazo. This is at a variance with the account represented in Figure 27*b*.

Another genealogical account of Noru Phratry was given to me at Hagani, which, however, included the junior phratry alone. In this version, the first two wives of Garo, Poriame and Pobori (Fig. 27*b*), are merged into one person, "Poboriame." A founder of Hagani named "Hagani" was mentioned as the son of Garo by this person, and Dazubidi was identified as Garo's son by Wazo, as in Yapenugiai's version. This version perhaps represents an attempt to distinguish the several "Hagani" lines within the phratry (another lives at Noru Rest House).

Several times during late 1964 and early 1965 I attempted to obtain versions of the Noru Phratry ideology. A group of men at Ogwane's house gave me the version represented in Figure 28*a*, which fuses the senior and junior phratries into one set of brothers, identifying the members of the senior phratry as older

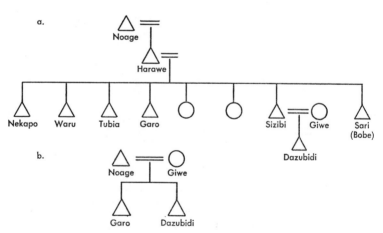

FIGURE 28.—*Noru Phratry, fused version.*

brothers of Garo and those of the junior phratry as his younger brothers. This version dissociates Dazubidi from the line of Garo by identifying him as the son of Sizibi, founder of Sogo Clan, in a collateral line.

While collecting a genealogy of Hagani Clan as a whole in February, 1965, I asked a large gathering of men at Waro's house whether Dazubidi had been the son or the brother of Garo; they answered that he was Garo's brother, a son of Noạge (Fig. 28*b*).

Each of the versions cited here represents a distinct, equally "valid" attempt to represent the genealogical connection of Hagani Clan to other clans in terms of the standardized Daribi phratry ideology. Figures 27*a* and 28*b* are, respectively, extended and telescoped representations of a tradition within an ideology. In some cases, notably Yapenugiai's genealogy and the "Poboriame" genealogy from Hagani, Garo, founder of the Noru clans, is identified as a direct ancestor of the Hagani line; otherwise, as in Figure 28*a* and *b*, Dazubidi, its founder, is shown to be either a brother of Garo or a brother's son. Such attempts to derive Hagani from a collateral line may well represent a kind of "charter" of segmentation.

Two main themes run through the series of examples we have just examined, that of the integration of two sets, or proliferations, of phratry founders and that of the relationship of Hagani Clan to the other clans of the phratry. Both of these themes are dealt with in terms of the standard Daribi phratry ideology, and in both cases an attempt is being made to formulate a history of clan formation, of budding off or segmentation, in such terms. The confusions and discrepancies evident in our examples are the consequences of trying to contain an ongoing process within a static paradigm of relationships and thus of the necessity continually to revise such a paradigm.

All of the clans mentioned in the senior and junior phratry proliferations are probably the results of segmentation among a group of people who have settled the valley within the hollow limestone ridge known to Daribi as Hoyabi. The senior phratry is a conventionalized account of a series of earlier segmentations, the resulting clans of which have now developed into phratries in their own right. Members of Sora' Clan, of the Tubia Phratry, with whom I spoke, claimed that their ancestors used to live at Unamaru, the location of the present Noru clans. This earlier series of segmentations probably filled the valley with clans, and certain clans which separated afterward from the Garo line (Bobe, Sogo) settled elsewhere, outside of the valley. Two clans belonging to the Tubia Phratry, Ozi and Taiare, were massacred by the Daribi clans acting together during the time of the fathers of the present generation, and, after this, clans resulting from more recent segmentations at Unamaru began moving westward again. Hagaini Clan is known to have separated from the people living at Noru Rest House (Unamaru) a few decades ago. Another clan known as Hagani, said to have descended from Garo by his wife Poriame, remains at Unamaru. The later segmentations, including those of Bobe, Sogo, Hagani, and the Noru clans, are formalized in the junior phratry. The segmentation and westward movement of groups continues today; the latest examples are a group of Noru people situated between Hagani and Soridai and the Hagani people at the "new garden" (*gezi gi*) between Noru and Hagani. Locations of the clans mentioned here are given in Map 4.

The effort to integrate the junior and senior phratries represents an attempt to dovetail two phratry traditions, one much older than the other, in a synthetic way. The senior phratry was allegedly founded by Sugage, who lived at Bumaru, on the Tua, a legendary home of the ancestors of the Daribi. His sons are given as Garo ("Pirigaro" or "Moni"—"big"—Garo), founder of the junior phratry, Maina, perhaps the founder of Maina Clan, and Tubia, founder of the Tubia Phratry. Tubia's three sons, Sora', Soridai, and Genabi, founded the clans of those names, though Genabi is sometimes given as a son of Sugage (Ozi and Taiare are also linked to the Tubia group); Waru, founder of the now extinct Waru Clan, is sometimes mentioned, as is Nekapo, founder of a line by that name which moved to the region of Mount Suaru. The tradition of Sugage includes a myth and a curse, the use of which is restricted to his descendants. These are linked in the story which follows.

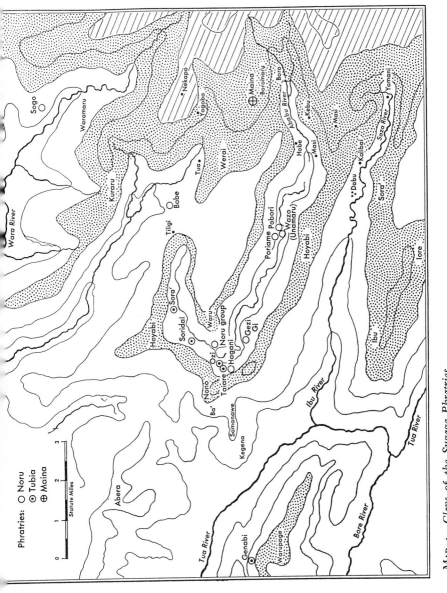

MAP 4.—*Clans of the Sugage Phratries.*

Phratries: ○ Noru ⊙ Tubia ⊕ Maina

Sugage was living at Bṵmaru. His sister's son Marauwa came to live with him there, and died at Bṵmaru. His body was put onto the exposure-coffin (dripping-pit, or *kṵ*). While the body was lying there, the young boys went out at night to hunt for frogs in the nearby streams. Marauwa got up out of the dripping-pit and followed them and caught and ate some of them. The next day, some of the children did not return, and the feet of some of the missing children were seen protruding from the body lying on the rack. Sugage collected firewood and brush and piled them around the kṵ, after which he set it afire. As the corpse burned, the skull burst open with the heat and flew to the stream Kawia Togonizi, a tributary of the Tua, and the eyeballs burst and flew to the top of the mountain Yamano. The ghost of Marauwa told the line of Sugage, "If you give your sisters and daughters to another clan, and they don't reciprocate with 'pay,' don't curse them with leprosy (in any other way), just mention the name of Yamano." Now when the people of Noru do not receive payment, they speak the names "Yamano" and "Kawia Togonizi," and their debtors are afflicted with leprosy.

Certain traditions are associated with the junior phratry also; the Bạria (the Wiru people of Pangia) are said to have killed all the line of Garo except Garo himself and his four wives; they are also said to have killed all the children of Sogo except two, who escaped and started the line. Sari, or Bobenoru, founder of Bobe Clan, acquired his name because of the long tanget leaf he is said to have worn tucked in the back of his belt (*bobe* means "long").

We have seen here an attempt to relate the junior phratry filially to the senior (Fig. 27*a*), giving rise to a phratry within a phratry, and recognizing two phratry-like proliferations, as well as an attempt to fuse the two phratries, tracing connection through a number of intermediaries to Sugage. Those of the senior phratry in this case are represented as Garo's older brothers; those of the junior, elsewhere his sons, are given as his younger brothers. The former attempt demonstrates operationally how a new phratry can grow up within an older one; the latter demonstrates a fusion by which a "new," syncretic phratry is formed, incorporating old and new in one standardized group of brothers. Both of these formulations exemplify techniques which figure prominently in the formation of phratries.

The relationship of Hagani Clan to the Noru clans involves the issue of segmentation as well as the fact that Hagani has now moved away from the Noru community at Unamaru. All the genealogies show Hagani to be closely related to the Noru clans; the Hagani line at Noru is said to be descended from Garo's first wife Poriame, yet the separate Hagani line at which this material has been collected traces its lineage to Dazubidi, who is variously identified as a son of Garo's third wife Wazo (by Yapenugiai) or a brother of Garo ("official" version, Waro's house). The tendency to remove Garo to a collateral line, or make him a brother rather than a son of Garo, may be seen as a genealogical confirmation of Hagani's status as a clan separate from the Noru community.

Alliance and the Community

The phratry, as we have made explicit, is a conceptual construct, part of an ideology, and not a viable social unit. There is no occasion upon which all the member clans of a phratry come together, nor are there any privileges or considerations shown to members of one's phratry as opposed to nonmembers. The Daribi phratry ideology is a result of the idiom of normative patriliny, of the plotting of paternal substance lines beyond the limits of existing clans. It is, if you will, a schematized residuum of clan formation. Our discussion of the phratry in the preceding pages was undertaken, first, to use the lines of paternal substance as "trace elements" in reconstructing a history of clan formation and, second, to show how Daribi formulate and conceptualize the process of clan formation.

The actual relations between clans, as opposed to the mere tracing of common origins conceptualized in the phratry, are carried on in terms of alliance and hostility, and the maximal viable social unit in this respect is the community. A community is made up of clans which are allied through close substance ties, or are in the process of becoming allied in this way; it can include clans which have intermarried widely as well as clans in the process of segmentation, which, since it is effected by marriage between the segmenting groups, has the same result as intermarriage between two previously "unrelated" clans. Although both the phratry and the community are based on consanguineal ties traced outside the unit, the bonds connecting member clans of a community are ties of "close" consanguinity, traced normally through maternal substance and carrying the powerful obligations of the pagebidi and hai' relationships, whereas the links which interconnect clans of a phratry are of necessity "distant," for such ties—ideally of paternal substance—must have grown weak enough to be ineffectual for the segmentation to have occurred at all. The phratry is a mere ideology precisely because the ties on which it is based are removed from the interaction of exchange and consanguinity; they trace the genealogical skeleton of segmentations which have occurred in the past. The ties which interconnect clans of a community are, by contrast, closely involved in the interaction of exchange and consanguinity; they comprise the links of maternal substance associated in the normative system with obligations of exchanging wealth, and their counterparts are the ties of paternal substance, normatively associated with the sharing of wealth, which interrelate members of a clan.

As basic social units, the clan and the community are results of the interaction of our principles of consanguinity and exchange. In terms of our "complementary processes," wherein these principles are seen as processes respectively of relationship and definition operating over a period of time, their operation and interaction can be shown to determine the alliance and the formation of clans. Since neither principle could exist in the social system without the other, consanguinity and exchange are dependent upon one another and must of necessity interact; translated into the dimension of time as processes, relationship and definition, they become necessarily complementary ones. A clan cannot proceed to define itself without thereby becoming related to other clans; it cannot become related to other clans without thereby defining itself. Clan formation and alliance are further consequences of the interaction of these complementary processes; the ties of consanguinity within a clan become more distant as exogamy (the result of definition) forces its members to forge close ties outside of the group, until finally the diverging lines are rerelated through marriage—which effectively defines them as separate units. The ties of consanguinity which connect clans give rise to cross-substance ties, the hai' relationship, which carries obligations of sharing as well as exchange between members of different clans, and thus extends privileges of clan membership through the alliance tie.

Because the processes of clan formation, or definition, and alliance are complementary in this way, every clan must of necessity be connected to external clans by ties of substance, by alliance bonds, in fact. It is against these bonds that the clan defines its own membership, and it is also by virtue of them that it makes claims on other clans. Yet, although the existence of such bonds is automatic, given the existence of the clan, the particular external clans to which such bonds are to be extended, and the distribution of bonds among such clans, are not predetermined by the system. Such considerations are a matter of choice and are at the disposal of the parties concerned. The placement and distribution of a clan's alliance ties depend on the contraction and distribution of marriages, for the making of a marriage initiates both a sequence of definitional exchanges and the establishment of substance ties between brothers and their out-marrying sisters, and it is also a preliminary to the conception of children embodying the substances of the two allying clans.

The distribution and concentration of its marriages, and therefore of its alliances, is an important factor in the interaction of a clan with other, similar units in the society. Alliance, like hostility, is, in a sense, optative; a clan can, if it chooses, concentrate its marriages, both in the giving and the taking of wives, very heavily on a few external clans, assuring a maximum of alliance bonds with them. It can also take up residence near one or more other clans, for the ecological situation places few restraints on a clan in this respect. Alliances between clans can vary a great deal with respect to strength; an alliance can be based on only one marriage and set of "common" offspring, it can have as a basis a few or a great many marriages, and it can, in addition, be strengthened by the co-residence of the parties. The community represents the maximal degree of alliance between clans; it constitutes a "unit," a kind of superclan, built up on the basis of a great many consanguineal ties among its component clans, often to the point where further intermarriage among these clans must be postponed for a generation or two because of their consanguineal closeness.

Thus, unlike the clan, the community as such is not a necessary result of the operation of the complementary processes, although the alliance ties which form the basis of the community are. A community is built up of such ties, and, since these ties are "extensive," since cross-cousins share privileges of membership in each other's clans, the concentration of alliance ties among a number of clans can eventually produce a situation in which members of each claim rights in the sharing of wealth with the others, through the "brotherhood" extended in the hai' relationship. The result is a kind of structural alter ego of the clan, a pseudo-unit built up around the ties of consanguinity which extend between clans. Such a community, as remarked in the first section of this chapter, constitutes a self-contained microcosm of the processes which form and ally clans in Daribi society: the extensive process of relationship encompasses the community and interrelates it into a whole, while simultaneously the restrictive process of definition maintains the boundaries of its component clans.

The concentration of marriages necessary to produce a strong alliance or a tightly integrated community has some drawbacks; as in the cases of sister exchange noted in the previous chapter, where two men who exchange sisters in marriage become increasingly dependent upon each other and correspondingly isolated from others, so two clans which intermarry heavily thereby multiply the bonds of dependency upon one another and diminish the extent of their interaction with other clans. Every marriage which is made within a community diminishes by two the number of potential marriages which could connect the community with external units, for a woman, who could be married off elsewhere, is given to an already allied clan in return for a bride price which could otherwise be given to bring in a wife from somewhere else. On the other hand, the making of only one or two marriages between two clans may prove insufficient, in terms of the alliance bonds engendered as a result, to ensure any kind of solidary cooperation between them.

The kind of reciprocity cycle described in the preceding

chapter, wherein the contraction of a single marriage ideally initiates a succession of four marriages in a scheme of delayed, serial reciprocity, tends to encourage the concentration of marriages. In addition, such a cycle creates a pattern of staggered pagebidi obligations among the various zibi of the clans which have taken part in it, so that, whereas one zibi of a clan may be pagebidi of the children of some zibi of another, and have other zibi of that clan as pagebidi of its own, a second zibi of the first clan will be pagebidi of the children of those who are pagebidi to the children of the first zibi, and so on. The children of the zibi so interknit will, of course, all be cross-cousins of each other.

Apart from such considerations, the matter of the exogamy pattern, or how a clan distributes its marriages among other clans in the society, lies beyond the scope of the kind of model with which we have been concerned. Our model yields certain possibilities, in the form of alliance ties, which can be manipulated or concentrated in a number of ways; one such possibility implicit in the conception of the alliance bond is that of the creation of a community through the close concentration of bonds between two or more clans. Thus, the form in which alliances are made is given by the social system; the actual exploitation of the possibilities is a matter left to the initiative of the concrete group "on the ground," subject to the simultaneous pressures and influences of a great many external processes.

Nevertheless, the community is a fact of Daribi social structure; if its existence is not demanded or determined absolutely by the processes that have emerged from our analysis, but only rendered possible by them, it remains, nevertheless, a widespread and popular tactic of clan interaction and deserves our attention as an example of the social system in operation. Given the social structure as we have described it, a clan could choose, if it wished, to distribute its marriages evenly and widely, preparing the way for a large number of fairly weak alliances, or it could concentrate many marriages in one or two external clans, thus assuring the alliance of at least a few such units. The former procedure has certain obvious drawbacks; if the two or three marriages allotted to a particular clan should fail to produce issue, the alliance would break down, for it is based on substance ties—concentration of marriages assures that some, at least, will bear fruit. Another weakness in the widespread scattering of marriages would be the difficulty in pressing strong claims; any clan would be so reinforced by its many ties with other units that it could comfortably refuse any plea for assistance from one of them. Such a system would yield no allegiances, only excuses. Only concentration of marriages, and the consequent formation of strong alliances, will produce sufficiently widespread proliferations of obligations to be of use to the clan as a whole in its demands for assistance. The most complete concentration of alliance ties, and hence the strongest of alliances, is that occurring within the community.

To what extent do Daribi clans, in fact, concentrate their marriages? Let us examine some statistical material collected at Kurube', Hagani, and Dobu. First, we shall consider the marriage distributions of a sample of three clans, taken from a total of perhaps forty-five such units. In each case the figures were taken from genealogical material, including the present generation and going back four to six generations. When the earliest marriages recorded in such genealogies were made, the clans to which those genealogies correspond were perhaps not yet in existence, but the marriages are nevertheless significant, for they record alliances and directions of alliance which influenced the descendants of those involved. I have not subdivided the data according to generation, as generations frequently overlap in any case and the distinction becomes a purely arbitrary one. Instead, I have chosen to present aggregates representing the total distribution of marriages over a number of generations in each case.

Of the 102 marriages recalled by my Kurube' informants, fifty-two, or 50.9 per cent, are concentrated in eight clans (20.5 per cent of a total of thirty-nine clans). Among these, twenty-six, or 25.4 per cent of the total, are concentrated among three clans, Hagani, Sora', and Sogo (Table 2). This is actually a comparatively low concentration, and it can be explained by the fact that intermarriage between Kurube' and the Noruai–Kilibali group, from which it has been slowly separating, has been impossible until very recently, and is still largely in the stage of negotiation. Kurube' has been free to distribute its marriages

TABLE 2
KURUBE' CLAN MARRIAGE DISTRIBUTION

	Number of Clans	Number of Marriages with Kurube' Clan	Percentage of Total Kurube' Marriages
Hagani		9	9
Sora'		9	9
Sogo		8	8
Dobu	8	6	6
Peria		6	6
Iuro		5	5
Moi		5	5
Hobe		4	4
Total	8	52	51
Other clans	31	50 (1–3 each)	49 (1–3% each)
Grand total	39	102	99

among clans outside of its community and has relatively high concentrations in three of these, Hagani, Sora', and Sogo, the latter of which lived in community with Kurube' at Waramaru.

At Hagani, of 116 marriages, eighty, or 68.8 per cent, are concentrated among eight clans (30.7 per cent of a total of twenty-six clans). Of these, sixty-two, or 53.3 per cent of the total, are concentrated in five clans, Pobori (Noru), Wazo (Noru), Sora', Tane (Hagani at Noru), and Hobe (Table 3). A total of 36.9 per cent of the marriages are with clans living in the community at Noru Rest House, and, although Hagani is not living in community with these clans, it had been until a few decades ago, and it probably "split off" from this complex in the period covered by the genealogy. Sora' Clan, which also shows a high concentration of marriages, is adjacent to Hagani in the Hoyabi Valley, to the north.

Huzabe, one of the newly formed component clans of the community at Dobu Rest House, has a total of fifty-eight recorded marriages, of which twelve, 20.7 per cent, are concentrated among the other three units of the community. In addition, nineteen marriages, 32.8 per cent of the total, are concentrated among three other clans, Hagani, Sora', and Kalibai—formerly, and perhaps still, a part of the Dobu community (Table 4). Kalibai Clan allied with Yamani in 1960–61 to attack the clans at

TABLE 3
HAGANI CLAN MARRIAGE DISTRIBUTION

	Number of Clans	Number of Marriages with Hagani Clan	Percentage of Total Hagani Marriages
Pobori (Noru)		21	18
Wazo (Noru)		12	10
Sora'		11	10
Tane (Noru)	8	10	9
Hobe		8	7
Dobu		8	7
Yamani		5	4
Denege		5	4
Total	8	80	69
Other clans*	18	36 (1–4 each)	31 (1–3% each)
Grand total	26	116	100

*Only four of the nine marriages known to Kurube' could be cross-checked with Hagani.

Dobu Rest House, and, on the grounds that the latter were a center of kebidibidi activities, initiated a massacre in which twenty-eight people are known to have been killed, and all the Daribi clans took part. It is therefore difficult to assess the present relationship between Dobu and Kalibai.

Each of the clans in our sample shows a high concentration of marriages (50 to 69 per cent) among seven or eight clans. In each case, three or four of these have a concentration in the neighborhood of 10 per cent or above in each, and a small range

TABLE 4
HUZABE CLAN MARRIAGE DISTRIBUTION

	Number of Clans	Number of Marriages with Huzabe Clan	Percentage of Total Huzabe Marriages
Clans at Dobu	3	12	21
Hagani		7	12
Sora'		6	10
Kalibai	4	6	10
Waru		4	6
Total	7	35	59
Other Clans	16	23 (1–3 each)	40 (2–4% each)
Grand total	23	58	99

show a concentration of between eight and three per cent, while the large majority of clans (67 to 80 per cent) have concentrations of below three per cent in each. Thus, the tendency here is to distribute marriages unevenly, concentrating them on perhaps three to five clans, some of which may be community members, in the interests of obtaining a strong alliance. The remaining marriages can be attributed to considerations which are not directly aligned with clan policy.

The distribution of marriages for a community as a whole shows the same pattern as that for an individual clan (Table 5).

TABLE 5
DOBU COMMUNITY MARRIAGE DISTRIBUTION

	Number of Clans	Number of Marriages with Dobu Clans	Percentage of Total Dobu Marriages
Clans at Dobu	4	39	19
Kalibai		33	16
Hagani*		28	13
Sora'		13	6
Waru	6	10	5
Masi		9	4
Mabere		8	4
Total	10	140	67
Other clans	24	69 (1–7 each)	33 (0.5–3% each)
Grand total	34	209	100

* Several units grouped.

As both the giving of a woman and the taking of a woman constitute marriages as these are recorded here, for both give rise to alliance bonds, a marriage made within the community is counted twice in our figures—and, in fact, such a marriage replaces what would otherwise provide opportunities for two marriages with external units. (The odd number of marriages recorded within the community in Table 5 thus represents an inconsistency in the data.) As it is, 18.7 of the marriages involving the Dobu community were made within the community. The extensive concentration of marriages with Kalibai Clan argues for a strong alliance here and perhaps for the community membership of Kalibai. Together with the marriages made with three other clans, Kalibai, Hagani, and Sora', the marriages made within the community constitute 53.9 per cent of all those made by the member clans of the community at Dobu Rest House.

The concentration of marriages to form a strong alliance and the decisions of several clans to live together in community are the manifestations of a deliberate policy on the part of the natives. Such alliance constitutes a kind of total involvement, based as it is on ties which carry obligations for support and help in the face of almost all conceivable situations. Insofar as the "extensive" principle of Daribi social structure, which holds together the community, is that of consanguinity, the Daribi frequently describe the joining of one clan by another in this way in terms of "going to live with one's sisters." With reference to the binding together of the units in community, I have heard Daribi use the phrase "making one of two." Clans living in community would often cooperate in horticultural activities and frequently would share one large, communal garden.

As elsewhere in New Guinea, however, the proliferation of ties between units, their close involvement, can also lead to expectations which may not always be fulfilled, and the results of close living can lead to squabbles within the community. Communities frequently dissolve, temporarily as well as permanently; the warfare between Kalibai and the Dobu Clans, disastrous as it was, may have been only a temporary dissociation of these closely allied groups. The community, and, in fact, close alliance in general, is not an infallible insurance against anything, but merely the best way which can be provided under the circumstances of strengthening a unit against adversity. The strengthening and the adversity are both significant to the natives in quite general, nonspecific terms.

Warfare, therefore, is not the "function" of the community, anymore than it is the function of the clan, the bride price, or the mother-child bond. That fighting may exist on an intercommunity level is a consequence of the whole Daribi social system. As much as it meets certain needs or requirements, a social system imposes needs and requirements of its own onto the situation, for it is only in terms of the social system that the situation can be apprehended or dealt with. Daribi rely upon their alliance patterns to facilitate living in a Daribi world. The alliance bond is a structural feature, which exists in connection with other structural features; the uses to which it is put (the "functions" that it "fulfills") are a matter of *tactics*. An analogy may be drawn with language, distinguishing in a similar way the features of the grammatical structure from the expressive *uses* to which such features are put, the tactics or their use. The Daribi language contains an extensive paradigm of "hortative" forms, present and future, negative and positive. A non-Daribi-speaker, coming across this fact in a university library, might conclude that, because the forms are identified as hortatives, they are used largely or solely for issuing commands. This kind of assumption, attempting to reconstruct the use of a word from its classificatory label, is encouraged by systems which classify on the basis of (assumed) function. The Daribi "hortative" forms are structural features, and are used with a great deal of flexibility. They can convey suggestion, command, or advice, or can be used ironically: *aga nai tumainau*, "let him eat (and see what happens to *him*)," or even to shame someone: "go ahead, shoot (since that's the kind of person you are)." The grammatical form itself is a structural phenomenon; its use involves syntax, idiom, and rhetoric.

Similarly, the Daribi social system, with its multifunctional units and the possibilities it offers for their interaction, is a factor in all kinds of activities, which we distinguish as political, legal, domestic, ecological, and so on, yet, neither in its entirety nor in its several component elements is it specifically oriented toward any particiular one of them; it provides, instead, a general-purpose matrix in terms of which the organization of such activities is structured. Likewise, language provides a structure for utterances regardless of their semantic content or of the nuances of expression.

The Context of Alliance

In the course of this and the preceding chapters we have seen how the Daribi social system, which is, in fact, an application of the symbolic principles of exchange and consanguinity to the relationships among people and their organization into units, provides a general-purpose structure for the ordering of affairs within the society. Exchange and consanguinity, however, take their places within the total range of Daribi symbols, including or generating some as subcategories, and overlapping with others, as in the case of "influence." Such symbols, implicit as well as explicit, constitute a complete microcosm of cultural referents, which oppose (contrast with) or contain each other (as in systems of classification; we "define" a word by placing it within the overlapping ranges of several broader, containing words). They are the conceptual elements through which Daribi deal with each other and their environment by a process of "closing the system," of articulating and comprehending the events in the world of incident in terms of the limited range of symbols proper to their culture. It is this "translation of the world," this setting into meaningful context, which Rilke equates with man's being "turned about" to apprehend things "backward" in terms of patterning and which is the basis of the Daribi (and every other culture's) system of "projective causality." It was the curse of Souw, according to Daribi, which gave man this treacherous world of symbols, which made him see life in terms of that prime symbol, death,[2] and thus "reversed" his vision.

When Daribi conceive of, discuss, or work within their social structure, they do so within this symbolic framework; yet, every other concern or relationship of theirs is similarly circumscribed. That which emerges as "social structure," the consequence of particular applications of certain symbols which is yet manipulated in terms of those symbols, exists in a world whose realities are no less symbolic. Clans, obligations, and mother's blood are all subsumed within the Daribi world view, along with ghosts, death, the izara-we, and the kebidibidi, and have a place within the cosmological scheme. Thus it is that the notion of "influence" is applicable both to social structure and religion.

Analogous to the structure which results from the application

---

[2] The powerful symbol of death, which lends force and meaning to the concepts of sickness, ghosts, and the "other world" of souls, also reflects upon the "life" symbols: those of food and sex, which are bound up with the notion of exchange, and the symbolic notion of consanguinity, of the continuance of life through the passing on of bodily substance.

and interaction of exchange and consanguinity is a set of beliefs and practices, of relationships conceptualized in terms of the "world of souls," grounded on certain symbolic axioms of the world view, which we might interpret as the Daribi religious system. Like the social structure, this "system" emerges in the light of our analysis as a structuring or disposition of symbolic elements in terms of certain criteria introduced by the analyst. In the preceding section we have distinguished the social system as a structure from the tactics of its use, including the concentration of alliance bonds and the formation of communities. Similarly, we can distinguish the structuring (or is it not perhaps a "restructuring"—of the same symbols) apprehended by our analysis as a "religious system" from the manipulation of its component elements and relationships in the politics of interpersonal and interunit activity. The term "social control" has come to be applied to such involvements of a religious system.

We have reviewed the Daribi world view as a logical complex of thought and action organized according to certain basic conceptions, such as the world of souls and the notion of influence, in chapter 2. Daribi "social control" usages simply reflect the fact that all human activities and situations are seen in the context of these basic conceptions. Ghosts, sorcerers, kebidibidi, and the various divination practices are all conceived in the light of such axioms, which effectively restrict all causation in the world to human or supernatural agencies and thus relegate it to the realm of human social interaction.

Just as the existence of units and of bonds of alliance between units is given by the social structure, but the issue of which concrete groups are to be allied with which others is a matter for individual decision and manipulation, so the existence of ghosts, sorcery, and the kebidibidi and the notions of "influence" and the world of souls are given by the religious system, but the identification of specific instances of spirit or sorcery activity, and the determination of the causal sequences involved in each case, is likewise left up to the individual. Alliance, the choice of one's friends or allies, and divination, the ascertaining of one's enemies, are thus both open to manipulation.

The identification of ghost activity, and the divination or admission of sorcery or kebidibidi activities, provides, like warfare, a culturally recognized relationship, subject to negotiation, which can exist between individuals or clans. When a case of sorcery is traced to another clan, compensation is demanded, with the threat of retribution by warfare or kebidibidi activities as a sanction; when a clan or a person admits to sorcery, either a willingness to compensate or pacify the clan of the victim is thereby expressed or a more fundamental grievance against the victim's clan, the motive for the sorcery, is indicated. In both cases the issue of sorcery provides an idiom for the political interaction of the groups involved, with several alternatives open to each side.

The "social control" elements, as well as warfare, provide a context of accusation, negotiation, and possible sanctions between clans within which the political applications of the structural phenomenon which we have called alliance become meaningful. Individuals and clans may admit to sorcery that was never attempted; persons may attempt sorcery only to be discovered, yet manage to air their grievances in process; accusations and admissions of sorcery may take place merely to concretize or narrow down and "exorcise" the tensions between groups. All of these are tactics for the political "use" of a structural phenomenon, just as the concentration of alliance bonds and the community are.

Such a system of intergroup and interpersonal relations is necessarily predicated upon a great deal of assumption, investigation, and innuendo on the part of individuals. Daribi are forever examining motives and drawing conclusions on the basis of various kinds of evidence, attempting to "close the system." In one case, a man of Sogo had died, and it was suspected that the person responsible might have been from Maina. A man of Maina came silently to the grave and began whistling. A Sogo man in the house saw him and said, "Baze, you come." He replied, "Yes, I have come." The men of Sogo called him to the house, and, when he came, one man seized him and another dispatched him with an ax. Affines of Maina at Nekapo heard the subsequent jubilation (*hai po*, Pidgin *bikmaus*) at Sogo, and word eventually got to Maina, members of which subsequently recovered the body and planned and executed revenge (in the form of a raiding party, which attacked the Sogo men in a garden and cut off and killed a man who pursued them into the bush).

In another case, five men of Kurube' had died, and kebidibidi activities were suspected. A Di'be' man, baze of Ozobidi of Kurube', came stealthily down the path used by the Kurube' women for sanitary purposes and shoved an owl he had shot up through a hole in the firebox and into the women's quarters. This was taken by Kurube' as good reason to suspect him, and, the next time he came, he was seized, tied to a house-post, and killed the following morning. His guilt was accepted by members of his own clan, which did not undertake retribution.

Of course, the total context of alliance is not solely political, for it includes the total range of activities in which the multifunctional units of Daribi society participate. A community is a kind of superclan, and, therefore, may function as a unit in whatever kinds of activities a clan may, including religious ceremonial, gardening, hunting, food-processing, house-building, and the clearing of land. Nevertheless, the political relations between units is perhaps the most influential variable here.

8

Conclusion

Symbol and Model

The relationships we have been discussing have all been referred, however obliquely, to native Daribi symbolizations of the ways in which people may be grouped and the kinds of connections that can exist among them, and I submit that such considerations are relevant to the formation of models by the anthropologist for the purpose of understanding and describing a society. Specifically, there is an extent to which social structure and the relationships within it are consciously manipulated and dealt with by members of the society, and this intersects with the symbolic system of the culture. Insofar as it suffices for the maintenance of the social structure among the people themselves, for, in fact, it determines the structure, a description of this symbolic system would suffice as an analysis of the social system.

Social anthropology, however, is concerned with the comparison of societies in terms of certain generalized criteria: the relationships between people, the definition and interaction of units, and the relationship of people to units; and, insofar as the analysis of a society is to be relevant to social anthropology as a whole, these functions must be dealt with. Further, since societies differ in the ways in which these functions are carried out, and have different symbols for group membership, for instance, or differ in the ways in which alliances may be contracted between groups, we can distinguish certain principles in terms of which a given society may be contrasted with others in this respect. Such principles are the result of the anthropologist's application of native symbolic principles of relationship and grouping to the generalized criteria in terms of which societies are compared (unit definition and alliance). Thus, we are dealing here with a complex of concepts and relationships seen in two different perspectives, that of the native symbolic system, in terms of which the social system operates, and that of analysis, in terms of which the consequences of the application of this basic symbol system to kin and group relationships are understood. Both native and anthropologist are concerned with the native symbolic principles, and each also recognizes analytical distinctions; the former area I shall designate as "symbol," the latter I shall designate as "model."

Although both the native's and the anthropologist's views may be seen as ways of expressing or articulating the details of the social structure, there is a significant difference between them. The native view is that of someone within the society, and it abstracts categories and relationships which are significant in terms of the ways in which people interact with one another, but it need not generalize. The anthropologist, on the other hand, must generalize, that is, construct models on a higher level of abstraction, for he is interested in comparing whole societies with one another. Thus, for example, Daribi do not recognize general principles such as consanguinity or exchange, for the exigencies of their social existence do not require them to draw distinctions on that level, yet they do recognize and differentiate such principles as connection through paternal substance, connection through maternal substance, sharing of meat, etc. Further, they apply these principles to kinship relationships in certain culturally prescribed ways; thus, one exchanges wealth with relatives through maternal substance (the pagebidi relationship) and shares wealth with relatives through paternal substance (normative patriliny). Consanguinity is a concept which is implicit in the Daribi symbolic world, for Daribi social structure is based on relationships in which connections traced through substance are contrasted with distinctions based on the principle of exchange, yet Daribi need not make it explicit, simply because their culture need not deal with abstractions on that level. It is made explicit by the anthropologist, however, because he is concerned with the ways in which social structure is organized and conceptualized in the various cultures.

Thus, the constructs and distinctions of the anthropologist fall wholly within the area of "model," for they are made in terms of his comparative, analytical interest. We may distinguish two areas within the range of concepts introduced by the anthropologist. One comprises generalized criteria, unit definition and alliance, which are purely comparative, introduced for the purpose of comparing societies, and do not vary from one culture to another. For this reason, such criteria do not express native symbolic categories, but are rather imposed from the outside as cross-cultural constants, and they are not contingent upon the area of "symbol." The other area includes principles derived by the anthropologist from native symbolic categories, relating these to the criteria of comparison between societies. Thus, the implicit categories of consanguinity and exchange are abstracted as principles governing the functions of alliance and definition. The notion of "influence" discussed in chapter 2 also belongs in this area, for it has been abstracted from the Daribi conceptual world, and is an implicit symbolic category. Influence is a broad category, embracing all external forces, supernatural as well as human, which bear upon the individual, and it can, under certain circumstances, include kin relationships. These principles are contingent upon both the area of "symbol," for they express implicit native symbolic principles, and that of "model," for they are derived with reference to the generalized criteria introduced by the anthropologist.

The natives' view of their own social structure falls wholly within the area of "symbol," for this is the medium of their formulation and understanding of it. Here, too, we may distinguish two areas, that of the native symbolic principles in terms of which relationship and group membership are conceived and that of the actual relationships in which these principles interact. The former area comprises the kinds of symbolic distinctions explicitly recognized by the natives, including connection through paternal substance, connection through maternal substance, the sharing of wealth, and the exchange of wealth. As symbolic constructs of Daribi culture, these principles are not contingent upon the area of "model," for they are not in themselves analytic constructs, but rather part of the native symbol system. The latter area, however, is contingent upon that of "model," for the kin relationships which constitute it, those of the pagebidi, hai', father-son, and so forth, are, in fact, native analytic constructs, which deal with social structure(as opposed to symbolic differentiation) in terms of the native symbolism.

Although the native's view of the social structure is wholly contained in the area of "symbol," and the anthropologist's is wholly within that of "model," a distinction is drawn in each case between an area which is included both in the area of "symbol" and in that of "model" and another which is contained in one but excluded by the other. Thus, the native principles of grouping and relationship fall within the area of "symbol," for they are, in fact, purely native categories of thought, but they do not fall within that of "model," for they are not the result of analysis. By contrast, the kin relationships recognized by the natives fall into both the areas of "symbol" and "model," for they constitute the native model, based on the interaction of symbolic principles. Likewise, the principles derived by the anthropologist for the description of the social system fall within both areas, for they apply the native symbolic categories to the criteria introduced for the comparison of societies. These principles, the anthropologist's model, are, in turn, distinguished from the criteria themselves, which as introduced constructs do not fall within the area of "symbol." For the native view, one section is contained only in the area of "symbol," the other in both "symbol" and "model." For the anthropologist's view, one section is contained in both the area of "symbol" and that of "model," the other only in the area of "model."

In each case, the distinction drawn is meaningful in terms of another set of distinctions, which cross-cuts that of the native's versus the anthropologist's view. This is the distinction between the principles of social structure and its details. The former exist on a higher level of abstraction than the latter and provide a set of symbolic categories in terms of which they are organized. Thus, the native symbolic categories are used by the natives to explain the kin relationships, which are in themselves symbolic, but also analytic in that they deal with the combinations and interactions of other symbols. The principles derived by the anthropologist are abstracted from the native symbol system, but are also analytic in that they are derived with respect to the generalized criteria for the comparison of societies. Thus, in speaking of kin relationships (details), the native refers to the native symbolic principles; in speaking of the criteria of comparison, within which unit definition and alliance serve to order the interaction of such functions as recruitment, marriage, and the kinds of relationship which can exist between people and groups, that is, the details of comparison, the anthropologist refers to the principles of social structure he has abstracted from the native categories.

The relationship between these areas is schematicized in Figure 29. The area of "symbol" is superimposed on that of "model." Where these areas overlap (darker shading), the two sections corresponding to social structure, the natives' (kin categories) and the anthropologist's models are generated. The two sections where they do not overlap, that of native symbolic categories, which are wholly symbol, and that of the anthropologist's general functional criteria, which are wholly model, do not correspond to social structure, but rather to the symbolic categories of its organization and the criteria by which it is analyzed respectively. The diagram charts the organization of concepts in terms of the three kinds of distinction we have been discussing, that drawn between the native viewpoint and that of the anthropologist, that of the principles of social structure as opposed to its details, and that of analytic model as opposed to the native symbol system.

Let us review once again the contents of these categories. The native symbolic categories, as we have seen, consist in certain kinds of substance ties, which link individuals through bodily substance given at conception, and certain criteria for unit membership, based on the sharing and exchange of wealth. Mother's blood and father's semen are given by Daribi as the substances necessary for the formation of a child, and the consequences of their transmission, resulting in substance lines and cross-substance bonds, form the basis of Daribi consanguineal kinship. The distinction between paternal and maternal substance is significant in

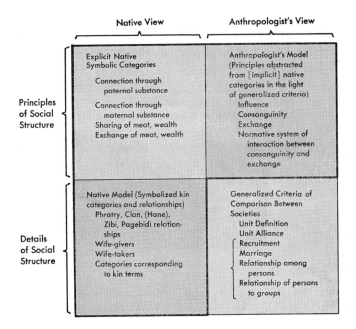

	Native View	Anthropologist's View
Principles of Social Structure	Explicit Native Symbolic Categories Connection through paternal substance Connection through maternal substance Sharing of meat, wealth Exchange of meat, wealth	Anthropologist's Model (Principles abstracted from [implicit] native categories in the light of generalized criteria) Influence Consanguinity Exchange Normative system of interaction between consanguinity and exchange
Details of Social Structure	Native Model (Symbolized kin categories and relationships) Phratry, Clan, (Hane), Zibi, Pagebidi relationships Wife-givers Wife-takers Categories corresponding to kin terms	Generalized Criteria of Comparison Between Societies Unit Definition Unit Alliance Recruitment Marriage Relationship among persons Relationship of persons to groups

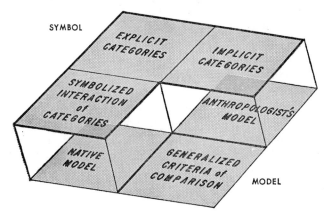

SYMBOL

EXPLICIT CATEGORIES

IMPLICIT CATEGORIES

SYMBOLIZED INTERACTION of CATEGORIES

ANTHROPOLOGIST'S MODEL

NATIVE MODEL

GENERALIZED CRITERIA of COMPARISON

MODEL

FIGURE 29.—*Symbol and model.*

terms of the normative system and coincides with the pagebidi relationship and the idiom of normative patriliny. The criteria for unit membership, the sharing or exchanging of wealth, are combined with relationships based on substance ties to generate the series of kin categories and relationships which constitutes the Daribi model of their own social structure.

The Daribi paradigm of kin categories includes general, inclusive categories as well as specific kin categories and relationships corresponding to kinship terms. Thus, there is the category pagebidi, which includes the mother's brothers (awa), mother's brothers' sons (hai'), mother's father (wai'), and mother's mother (auwa) of a male or an unmarried girl, and the brothers (ape) of a married woman. Ego's pagebidi are his relatives through maternal substance to whom wealth must be given if he is to retain membership in his father's clan (or, for a married woman, her brothers, from whom her membership in her husband's clan is to be redeemed). The categories "wife-givers" (*we mawai bidi* or *we bidi buru*) and "wife-takers" (*we sai bidi*) similarly include a number of specific kin relationships, in this case affinal. The phratry, the clan (hane), and the zibi may likewise be seen as such categories.

The categories corresponding to individual kin terms are more elaborately subdivided. Consanguineal kin relationships are traced by means of connection through maternal or paternal substance, or both. Specific categories are determined by generation and kind of substance tie. Affinal kin relationships are determined by the existence of an affinal link and are usually traced through consanguineal links as well; they may indicate generation, kind of affinal link, and, indirectly, the kinds of substance tie separating Ego and the referent from the affinal link. Certain normative obligations based on exchange functions are associated with some relationships; thus, one should exchange "pay" with a baze or an awa, share "pay" with an ama' or an aia, and both share and exchange it with a hai'.

Through the analysis of these kin categories on the basis of our generalized functions of group definition and alliance, we have derived certain principles based on distinctions implicit in the Daribi symbolic system. The first of these is that of influence, the notion of control or dominance exerted upon an individual by an external agent. Influence can be exerted upon an individual either by human or by supernatural beings, and is countered by discovering the identity of the agent, reciprocity, or both of these means in succession. The notion of influence intersects with the kinship system in the pagebidi relationship, where the influence exerted through maternal substance is countered by reciprocity in the form of recruitment payments given to a person's pagebidi. This opposition of substance and exchange, based as it is on the substitution of wealth for persons, gives the key to the interrelationship of the two main principles in the Daribi social system. These principles, consanguinity and exchange, like that of influence, have been made explicit by the anthropologist. Consanguinity is the principle by which people are related to each other through substance and in terms of which alliances are made connecting units; exchange is the principle by which units are defined. Because units are made up of people, and people belong to units, these two principles intersect in certain normative modes, and this gives rise to yet another construct of the anthropologist, the normative system, which describes the prescribed interaction of the principles. The set of these principles, together with, the normative system, constitute the anthropologist's model of the Daribi social system.

This model has, in turn, been derived with reference to certain generalized criteria relating to the definition and alliance of groups and through these functions to various other comparative functions. These criteria stand outside the native symbolic system, for they are, in fact, criteria in terms of which the models derived for different societies may be contrasted. The function of definition refers to the way in which unit boundaries are established and maintained and involves the function of recruitment as well as the marriage rule. I have used the term "alliance" to designate the function by which units are interrelated, or linked to one another. The usage here may not be etymologically correct, for the term "alliance" originates among the so-called "alliance theorists," yet I have found no standard term on this level of abstraction which refers to such a function. Both functions, definition and alliance, refer generally to the ways in which units are bounded and interrelated, respectively, within a given society and involve, therefore, the ways in which recruitment, marriage, and individual relationship are effected. The interrelationship of all these functions within one kind of model has been well characterized by Schneider: "to take marriage apart from the classification of kinsmen, or the mode of descent apart from the relationship between the segments, or the 'corporateness' of the segments apart from the way in which they are related to each other is simply to distort and deny their meaning." [1] I have selected unit definition and alliance as the essential comparative criteria, insofar as they generalize the social system as a whole which results from the interaction of such functions as recruitment, marriage, and individual relationship.

Insofar as such functions as marriage, recruitment, and so on will be fulfilled differently in different societies, they will vary in their position within the total system from one model to another, and this variation implies the existence of organizational principles which govern such total systems. Since all the societies with which we are concerned are characterized by units (segments), our comparative criteria, unit definition and alliance, are sufficiently general to accommodate the kind of comparison which we would like to undertake. In Daribi society, for example, marriage and recruitment are subsumed under the function of unit definition, while individual relationship fulfills the function of unit alliance. In another system, unit definition and alliance might subsume these functions in a different way.

General Conclusions

As anthropologists, let us, then, compare the model we have derived for Daribi social structure with models developed for other societies. Comparison will be in terms of the generalized criteria of unit definition and alliance.

We have seen in the preceding chapters that functions pertaining to the definition of the unit among the Daribi, marriage

---

[1] David M. Schneider, "Some Muddles in the Models: or, How the System Really Works," in *The Relevance of Models for Social Anthropology*, A.S.A. Monograph No. 1 (London: Tavistock Publications; New York: Frederick A. Praeger, 1965), p. 57.

and recruitment, are fulfilled by the substitution of "vital" wealth (sizibage) for living persons, thus opposing the claims made on them through ties of consanguinity by persons outside the unit. Persons in the latter category, the mother's brother, his parents, and his sons, of a child or grown man, the brother of a married woman, are Ego's pagebidi, and the relationship through which exchange is thus opposed to consanguinity is the pagebidi relationship. Definition of a person's group membership against the claims of his pagebidi, whether in marriage or recruitment, is effected by the payments which are made to counter them, and a unit may be defined as those persons among whom such exchanges are not made. Thus, Daribi speak of members of a clan as those who "share meat" or "share wealth," whereas those of other clans "give wealth" or "receive wealth." Unit boundaries are always defined in this way, regardless of the interrelationship of persons within the unit, although the fact that the persons recruited to a clan, either through the giving of payments, or through default of such payments on the part of others, will be either children or sister's children of its male members, and thus clan members will also be interrelated. We can thus speak of a principle of exchange, which is capable of forming units in its own terms, although it necessarily interacts with the principle of consanguinity.

Because the wealth which is substituted for persons in the pagebidi relationship does not cancel ties of consanguinity (indeed it cannot, for these are based on the bodily substance of the persons concerned), but only claims based on consanguinity, the only thing exchange effectively determines is membership in a unit. Ties of consanguinity cannot be erased, and continue to connect a married woman with her brother, a child or man to his maternal kin, forming the basis for further claims in the future which must be met by payments. In this way, consanguinity provides the ongoing element in marriage and recruitment exchanges. Consanguinity is the principle by which people are related to each other, and claims are made by virtue of that relationship. Consanguinity is bilateral and relates a person to his paternal and maternal lines through different kinds of substance. Because consanguinity is bilateral, relationship can be traced through ties based on maternal or paternal substance or through cross-substance ties based on both. Consanguinity effectively creates a network of relationships based on substance around each individual, and the relationships which extend between people in different units are based on the same principle as those traced between people within the same unit. In this way consanguinity serves to interrelate units through the consanguineal ties traced between members of different units.

Consanguinity, the principle of relationship, thus connects individual to individual; exchange, by contrast, serves to define units composed of individuals. The two principles can be said to interact by virtue of the fact that the members of a unit are interrelated by consanguinity as well as being defined as a unit by exchange, and a person's consanguineal relatives will include persons who share membership in his own unit as well as persons who belong to other units, and thus will have differential exchange obligations with respect to him. This area of interaction between the two principles, wherein consanguinity operates on the unit level and exchange on the individual level, corresponds to the normative system.

Exchange, as a principle of definition, is restrictive: it draws distinctions among people according to whether they share or exchange wealth; consanguinity is extensive: it relates people through substance regardless of the exchanges that are made. The normative system provides norms of interaction between these principles; the distinctions made in terms of the principle of exchange are associated, respectively, with the two kinds of substance recognized by Daribi, so that relationships traced through paternal substance stipulate the sharing of wealth and those traced through maternal substance require the exchange of wealth. Thus, the idiom of normative patriliny, resulting from the fact that paternal substance ties are "reinforced" by recruitment payments, and hence constitute an idiom of unit membership, is opposed to the pagebidi relationship, in which claims made by virtue of relationship through maternal substance are redeemed by exchanges.

As the normative system imposes the distinctions drawn by exchange onto the realm of consanguinity, giving rise to such "idioms" of intraunit and interunit relationship, so it provides for the extension of exchange functions through ties of consanguinity in the hai' relationship. Cross-cousins are linked by cross-substance ties and treat one another as "brothers," sharing wealth as do members of the same clan, although they belong to different clans. In terms of unit definition, consanguinity is governed by the restrictive principle of exchange, and separate "substance-lines" are distinguished; in terms of unit alliance, exchange is governed by the extensive principle of consanguinity, matrilateral and patrilateral cross-cousins are equated, and exchange functions are extended outside the unit on the basis of consanguineal ties.

The two principles derived from the analysis of Daribi symbolism in the light of our criteria of unit definition and unit alliance, exchange and consanguinity, thus in their application and interaction determine the structure of Daribi society. As they govern distinct and contrasting functions, those of unit definition and alliance, so do they employ contrasting symbolic principles; were this not so, it would be impossible from the native point of view to distinguish unit boundaries symbolically as against the bonds which serve to interconnect units.

Following our discussion of symbol and model in the preceding section, wherein we have demonstrated the derivation of principles of social organization from an analysis of native symbolic categories in terms of the criteria of unit definition and alliance, it can be seen that the contrast in function between unit definition and unit alliance should, therefore, correspond to a contrast in the native symbolizations which apply to these functions. Further, we have seen above that the Daribi principle of exchange, which governs unit definition, is "restrictive": it draws boundaries, distinguishing certain persons as members of a unit in contrast to others, who are not members, while the principle of consanguinity is "extensive," tracing connection among persons, regardless of unit membership.

The model we have derived for Daribi society resembles that proposed by the "alliance theorists," Lévi-Strauss, Dumont, Leach, and Needham, for certain other societies, in that both correspond to the scheme described above; in each case the principles of social organization are derived directly from symboliza-

	Daribi Model	Alliance Theory Model
Unit Definition (restrictive)	exchange	consanguinity (unilineal descent)
Unit Alliance (extensive)	consanguinity	exchange

FIGURE 30.—*The Daribi and alliance-theory models.*

tions of the society analyzed, and in each case we can distinguish a restrictive and a contrasting extensive principle. The models themselves contrast in the ways in which unit definition and alliance are symbolized, respectively, in each, for, in fact, the alliance-theory model is simply the inverse of the Daribi model in this respect; unit definition is effected by substance-ties in the alliance-theory model, whereas the bonds between units are those of exchange (Fig. 30). In the model of the alliance theorists, ". . . the segments are articulated into a logically interrelated system by the descent rule, the mode of classification of kinsmen, and the relationship of perpetual alliance between segments."[2] In this kind of system, the restrictive principle is that of connection through substance. Because such a principle must necessarily draw boundaries and serve to recruit some persons to the unit while excluding others, there must be a factor of selection here, and this is provided by the recognition of *unilineal* descent, in which recruitment is effected by means of a sub-

[2] *Ibid.*, p. 58.

stance bond with only one parent. The term *descent* can, therefore, be used here in Rivers's sense, stressing connection through both substance and recruitment. Unit membership, in such a system, is given by birth.

The extensive principle in the alliance-theory model is that of exchange, which links the units differentially defined by descent by opposing them as "potential affines" in a relationship of "continuing connubium." All members of units thus opposed are involved in such a relationship, whether or not they are actually concerned in a marriage exchange. The principle is extensive, because it embodies links across the boundaries defined by descent. Just as consanguinity, in the Daribi model, relates people across the boundaries defined by exchange, so in the alliance-theory model there is a permanent, ongoing relationship of affinity among units defined by descent. Daribi units define a group of people, in each succeeding generation, against the claims of consanguineals external to the unit; unit membership in the alliance-theory model is defined from birth through unilineal descent, and marriages are made among units, actuating or expressing the permanent exchange relationships existing among them. In social systems based on moieties, non-intermarrying units within each of the moieties may be articulated on the basis of descent, and all of them together exist in opposition to those of the other moiety.

Because exchange and consanguinity play roles in the alliance-theory model which are the inverse of those to which they apply in the Daribi model, the operation of each of these principles changes from one model to the other. Exchange functions as a restrictive principle in the Daribi model, opposing the claims of consanguineals external to the unit, and the pattern of opposition shifts as lines formerly confronted as affines become related through consanguinity, and marriages are contracted with less closely related lines. Exchange, therefore, operates among the Daribi to settle claims and eventually close the exchange relationship. Within the alliance-theory model, however, the oppositions remain stable, for they are maintained by the rule of unilineal descent, and exchange continues as a perpetual mode of relationship among the units so defined. Consanguinity, as an extensive principle in the Daribi model, is bilateral and operates continually to bring into a closer relationship lines which have diverged to the point where marriage between them is permitted. By contrast, consanguinity functions in the alliance-theory model as unilineal descent and operates as a restrictive principle to define units as against the affinal relationship existing between them. In consequence, then, all persons in a society are interrelated by consanguinity in the Daribi model, but relationships of sharing and exchanging wealth, for any given individual, extend only to limited portions of the total society; in the alliance-theory model, every person in the society is in a relationship of either sharing or exchanging wealth with every other person, but those to whom a person is related by consanguinity embrace only a limited portion of the society.

When we turn to the "descent-theory" model of Fortes, Gluckman, Goody, and others, we find that the symbolization of exchange, as such, is not recognized as playing a major role in the social system. Instead, the cultural usages pertaining to wealth are here seen in terms of *property*, emphasizing the holding and inheritance of wealth. The operating distinctions in this model are those of descent and filiation, based on connections between persons and their ancestors or parents, and these notions, in their interaction, regulate the *disposal* of property through the proliferation of various kinds of rights. Wealth and its exchange, apprehended in the form of property, is the subject of regulation in this model and does not form the basis of a principle. Nevertheless, it is obvious that notions such as bridewealth, as well as something very much like the idea of "vital wealth" put forth in the preceding chapters, are extremely important in the African societies for which the descent-theory model was proposed.

The concepts of descent and filiation seem, at first reading, to correspond respectively to our "restrictive" and "extensive" principles, for the former is unilineal and governs recruitment, while filiation is "universally bilateral." Yet, filiation and descent seem to be of the same order of conceptualization, for "a descent rule states which of the two elementary forms of filiation and what serial combination of forms of filiation shall be utilized in establishing pedigrees recognized for social purposes." [3] The functional contrast is between descent and complementary filiation, that aspect of the bilateral factor not sanctioned by the descent rule. According to Fortes,

> . . . filiation—by contrast with descent—is universally bilateral. But we have been taught, perhaps most grapahically by Malinowski, that this does not imply equality of social weighting for the two sides of kin connection. Correctly stated, the rule should read that filiation is always complementary, unless the husband in a matrilineal society (like the Nayar) or the wife in a patrilineal society, as perhaps in ancient Rome, is given no status or is legally severed from his or her kin.[4]

Descent, therefore, does not contrast with filiation as a separate principle, and it is, in fact, a serial extension of one kind of filiation. Filiation is the broader, more general category, corresponding to our principle of consanguinity in some respects, whereas descent is restricted to one of the kinds of filiative tie, resembling the Daribi idiom of patriliny. Descent, for Fortes, represents the more "socially weighted" of the filiative ties; filiation, which is bilateral, may be reckoned through either. Complementary filiation refers to that tie of filiation which happens, through not being "socially weighted," to extend between units. Units, in the descent-theory model, are defined by the more socially weighted of the filiative ties, which Fortes, following Rivers, calls "descent." Members of different units are interrelated by the "universally bilateral" tie of filiation, the complementary aspect of which provides the actual links.

A person is related to a unit other than that of his descent membership through the bilaterality of filiation; in a patrilineal system, a man is related to his mother by matrifiliation and to her unit by a combination of that matrifiliation with her own descent membership in that unit. It is because filiation is bilateral that ties of descent and complementary filiation can be combined in this way. Thus, descent is not solely a principle of definition, for it

[3] Meyer Fortes, "Descent, Filiation and Affinity: A Rejoinder to Dr. Leach: Part II," *Man* 59 (1959), p. 206.
[4] Meyer Fortes, "The Structure of Unilineal Descent Groups," *American Anthropologist* 55 (1953), No. 1, p. 33.

enters into the formation of links between units; nor is filiation solely an extensive principle, for it forms connections which are reckoned partially through descent. A single link between parent and child can participate simultaneously in unilineal descent and bilateral filiation—but it cannot thereby "contrast" with itself. In a word, descent and filiation cannot contrast as principles, respectively, of definition and alliance, because the descent bond enters into both the definition of units and the formation of connections between them.

Fortes, however, does not attempt to contrast them in this way; filiation may play a role in the "politico-jural domain" (i.e., that of the segments and their relationships) in that ". . . filiation originates in the domestic domain, descent in the politico-jural domain, but filiation may confer title to status (which means rights and capacities) in the politico-jural domain," [5] but, by and large, it is descent which governs this domain. In addition to defining units, descent per se also serves to ally them.

A society made up of corporate lineages is in danger of splitting into rival lineage factions. How is this counteracted in the interests of wider political unity? One way is to extend the lineage framework to the widest range within which sanctions exist for preventing conflicts and disputes from ending in feud or warfare. The political unit is thought of then as the most inclusive or maximal, lineage to which a person can belong, and it may be conceptualized as embracing the whole tribal unit.[6]

The contrast here between descent as an idiom of unit definition and as a means of allying units is one of levels of segmentation. Again, as with filiation, the contrast is made here within one conceptual area of two discrete, opposable functions, neither of which has a distinct idiom of expression. Descent and filiation are but two of many ways in which, within this model, units may be interrelated, and ". . . another way . . . is for the common interest of the political community to be asserted periodically, as against the private interests of the component lineages,

[5] Meyer Fortes, "Descent, Filiation and Affinity: A Rejoinder to Dr. Leach: Part II," p. 208.
[6] Meyer Fortes, "The Structure of Unilineal Descent Groups," p. 28.

through religious institutions and sanctions."[7] The word "alliance," even as it has been used here, could scarcely be used to designate the functions proposed by Fortes for descent and religion insofar as interrelating units is concerned, for this interrelationship involves the whole society at once, and a term like "solidarity" or even "integration" might be more suitable. As I have used it, alliance refers to a kind of relationship between units which is in a sense optative, in that it provides for the formation of bonds as opposed to the possibility of hostilities, leading to what Salisbury has called a "distributive opposition" of units.[8]

Indeed, the descent-theory model does not provide clear-cut principles for the definition and alliance of units; to describe its application to these functions at all, it is necessary to consider the plethora of preordained functional categories to which descent theorists address themselves, those which refer, in a manner recalling Malinowski, to property-holding, jural rights, "integration" of the total society, and domestic relations. Our model for Daribi social structure cannot, therefore, be contrasted with that of descent theory, since there is no common basis of contrast or comparison; the analytical points of departure, the functional criteria, of the two models are essentially different. This fundamental difference in approach is enhanced by the fact that the descent-theory model makes no reference to native symbolic categories by way of relating these to the several functions predicated in its analytic scheme.

Thus, where both the alliance-theory model and our own Daribi model can be said to consist of principles derived from a consideration of native symbolic categories in the light of general criteria of analysis, according to the scheme presented in the preceding section, descent theory applies a set of preordained functional categories to the complex of native usages and relationships and proceeds to see the latter as expressions of, or "responses" to, these functional "givens." The concepts such as descent and filiation which characterize descent theory are, there-

---

[7] *Ibid.*

[8] R. F. Salisbury, "New Guinea Highland Models and Descent Theory," *Man* 64 (1964), p. 169. According to Dr. Salisbury (personal communication, 1966) this term was originally used by S. F. Nadel.

fore, not principles in the sense that I have used this term for the contrasting roles of exchange and consanguinity in the alliance theory and the Daribi models. The contrast between descent theory on one hand and the alliance theory and Daribi models on the other is one of approach; it is in terms of the criteria of the latter approach that we can contrast societies, through the models derived for them, with reference to principles manifesting their own symbolizations of unit definition and unit alliance.

It has not been my intention here to present a critique of the various analytic approaches to the study of social structure, although certain obvious differences between two of them have emerged from our discussion in this chapter; nor do I propose to set forth a typology for the classification of social systems. My chief purpose has been to show how, given certain very general criteria, the symbolic principles recognized by societies can interact in a variety of ways to determine social structure.

There are, of course, a great many kinds of social systems in the world, and there are many social systems which are characterized by large, multifunctional segments, only some of which will resemble, in their organization, the models we have discussed. Yet, symbolizations centering around consanguinity and exchange have a widespread distribution in the world of ethnography, and I have also indicated here some of the ways in which these can be fruitfully recombined to generate different kinds of social system.

When a Daribi sigibe' is to be built, a grill-like framework of crossed poles is first laid out on the ground to indicate where the house-posts are to be set, and an elaborate scaffold is erected above this, throughout the space to be occupied by the house, to aid the workers in their construction. The framework and the scaffolding resemble the finished building only very remotely, but they are, nevertheless, necessary if it is to be built true to form. Likewise, the theoretical scaffolding of concepts and principles erected in the course of our analysis may bear little resemblance to Daribi groups and their relationships as these appear "on the ground," but it has been set up as an aid to our understanding of the social system to which they belong.

Appendix

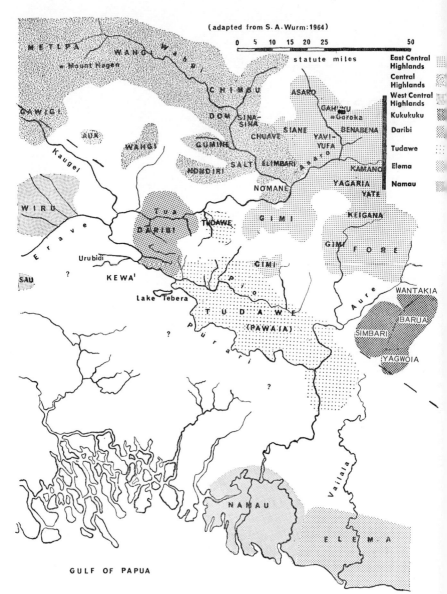

0   5   10   15   20   25   50

statute miles

East Central
Highlands

Central
Highlands

West Central
Highlands

Kukukuku

Daribi

Tudawe

Elema

Namau

METPA   WAHGI   Wahgi

• Mount Hagen

CHIMBU   ASARO

GAWIGI   DOM   SINA-   GAH-KU
SINA   • Goroka

AUX   WAHGI   GUMINE   CHUAVE   SIANE   BENABENA

SALT   ELIMBARI   Asaro

MONDIRI   YAVI-
YUFA

NOMANE   KAMANO

WIRU   YAGARIA
YATE

Tua   TUDAWE   GIMI   KEIGANA
DARIBI

Urubidi   GIMI   GIMI   FORE

SAU   ?   KEWA'   P   r   o
WANTAKIA

Lake Tebera   T U D A W E   BARUA
(PAWAIA)   SIMBARI

?   P   u   r   a   r   i   YAGWOIA
Aure

?

Vailala

N A M A U

E L E M A

GULF OF PAPUA

MAP 5.—*The linguistic environment of Karimui.*

Appendix A

The Daribi Language

The ultimate goal of much of anthropology can be seen as an attempt to translate the categories and concepts of one culture into those of another. Were it possible, therefore, to achieve the ultimate degree of precision in the glossing of native terms, the purpose of anthropology would be in large part obviated. Such precision is, of course, beyond our present abilities, and rather than blunt the very specific significances of the Daribi words quoted in the text by replacing them with English commonplaces, I have chosen to present them to the reader as "blanks," to be filled in as he becomes familiar with the ethnographic details. This practice, as well as the frequent reference to grammatical forms, has made the inclusion of a brief sketch of the Daribi language advisable. I would like to thank Dr. Joel M. Maring for his help in preparing this section, and Mr. George MacDonald, of the Summer Institute of Linguistics, for the material on Daribi which he has provided.

Phonemic System and Orthography

The identification of phonemes in a given system can vary markedly according to what the recorder "hears"; therefore, although my phonemic tables are based on the work of George MacDonald, they differ from his in a few particulars (marked with an asterisk). Allophones are given in brackets.

CONSONANTS			
	Bilabial	Velar	Alveolar
Stops	[p] [b]	[k] [g]	[t] [d]
	b	g	d
Fricatives		[h] [r]*	[s] [z]
Nasals	m		n
Lateral			l (?)
Semivowels	[hw] * [uw]*		y
	w		

SOURCE: Adapted from Mac Donald, 1966.

VOWELS			
	Front	Central	Back
High	i		u
Low	e	a	o

SOURCE: Mac Donald, 1966.

Each vowel has both a nasalized counterpart (indicated in the text by a Polish hook, [nạ], and a high-tone counterpart (indicated in the text by an apostrophe, [na']); thus it is possible to isolate "minimal triplets," as the following:

na' "father's sister"   hai' "cross-cousin"
nạ "shoulder blade, spoon"   hại "edible bamboo"
na "dream"   hai "stinging nettle"

Regarding stress, George Mac Donald, in a personal communication written in 1966, observes that

Stress is characterized by intensity and/or slight length, and occurs on the initial syllable of all words, except on imperative forms of verbs, where stress falls on the first vowel of the imperative ending. Length is sometimes present on a stressed syllable, and in the absence of intensity it denotes the stress. Word-timing is a feature of Mikaru, which causes vowels in one-syllable words to be lengthened and vowels in multi-syllable words to be shortened.

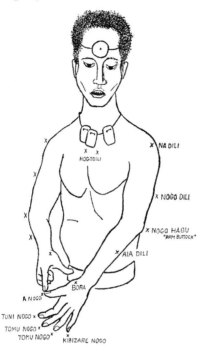

FIGURE 31.—"A dari bora dari si." *Daribi counting* (nerebo) *is binary; body parts or counting sticks* (wabidagi) *are used as tally markers, but cannot function as numbers. The counter enumerates* "me si, me si" ("*and two, and two*"); *when counting on the body, he proceeds up one arm, across the chest, and down the other, marking off two's by naming the parts, as shown. Three two's are always counted on each hand, and another at the* aia dili; *the other points are either grouped into two's or given two counts each, for a sum total of 26 to 30.*

Native words in the text have been transcribed, with some inconsistencies, in a generalized Latin orthography, giving each letter a distinct sound value. The pronunciation of a few of the more important words is indicated here in a kind of folk-English orthography.

pagebidi	PAH-gay-biddy	noma'	NO-ma
kebidibidi	KAY-biddy-biddy	sigibe'	SIGgy-bay
izibidi	EAsy-biddy	zibi	ZIBby
gominaibidi	GO-min-EYE-biddy	kibu	KEE-boo

Syntax

The constituent elements of a Daribi sentence fall ideally into the sequence: subject—object—indirect object—verb, although each element may be expanded into a number of clauses. The sentence may be preceded by sentence-modifiers indicating the speaker in indirect discourse (with the instrumental suffix *–go*), and/or the time at which the action took place, in that order. A sentence-modifier may also follow, in the form *tobo ware*, "(thus) he sent word."

An important principle is that a modifier precedes the modified word, as in English (*eno ware huǫ*, "my fine ax"). This usage is reversed in the case of numerical modification (*bidi si*, "men two"); ellipsis of the verb in a short sentence of the regular subject—object—verb form gives a false impression of such reversal where the situation actually involves a predicate adjective (*te bidi duare-(ebo)*, "that man bad (is)").

e bidigo	*megi*	*eno*	*ama'*	*ware*	*kibu*	*Sogo*	*bidi*	*mane*
this man:	today	my	brother	fine	pig	Sogo	people	gave
indirect discourse	time	modifier	subject	modifier	object	modifier	indirect object	verb
sentence-modifier		subject		direct object		indirect object		verb

tama	*ena*	*tubu*	*kibu*	*bidi me, we me, wai' me*			*mane*	*tobo ware*
then	I	eating -	pig	(to) men, women, children			gave	sent word
time	subject	modifier	object	indirect object			verb	indirect discourse
sentence-modifier	subject	direct object		indirect object			verb	sentence-modifier

te	*bidi*	*kibu dari,*	*ǫ dari, huǫ dari*	*serama*	*Nekapo*	*saburare*
that	man	pig with,	taro with, ax with	taking	Nekapo	arrived
modifier	subject	object		verb	object	verb
subject		verb clause			verb clause	

Pronouns

ena	I, me	da	we, to us
eno	my, by me	dago	our, by us
nage	you, to you	dage	you (pl.), to you (pl.)
nago	your, by you	dagego	your (pl.), by you (pl.)
aga	he, him, she, her, it	augwa	they, them, their
agai	his, hers, by him, her		
		de	"who? whom?"
		dego	"whose?

Noun Qualifiers

-*go*   by, of: *e bidigo kibu enare*, "this man killed a pig"; *eno e bidigo kibu enare*, "I killed this man's pig"

-*ba*   toward: *be'ba pobau*, "leave for the house"

-*de*   at: *be'de bidiba*, "stay at the house"

-*du*   from, via: *be'du azare*, "came from the house"; *balusidu azare*, came by aircraft

-*ma*   place of ——— (action): *bidiboma*, "place of staying"; *paboma*, "direction of leaving"

-*re*   of: *aware we*, "mother's brother's wife" (seldom used possessive form)

-*ai*   adjectival: *bomu*, "strength"; *bomai*, "strong"

-*bi*   plural marker, kinship terms: *ama'bi*, "brothers"

-*zibi*   the descendants of ———

-*soro*   the group of my —— (kin term)

-*buru*   my (singular) ——— (kin term)

-*nami* (*si*)   (two) persons related reciprocally as ———: *aga hai'nami si*, "two people who are cross-cousins"

-*rape*   member(s) of the class ———: *Belezirape*, "Chimbu(s)"

-*digi*   number marker (cf. Pidgin-*pela*): *sidigi*, "two (of them)"

-*ruba'*   ——— by himself: *ena ruba'*, "I myself"

horobo-   our (common) ———: *horobo baze*, "our (common) brothers-in-law"

Verb Qualifiers

Much of the meaning in a Daribi sentence is carried by the verb. As in the case of a Daribi noun, a verb may be modified by prefixing it immediately with one of a number of adjectival/adverbial classifiers, thus: *ena ozogo pobau*, "I temporarily leave," *aga oro*

bidibo, "he stays (there) to no purpose." Otherwise, verb qualification is effected entirely by means of suffixes. The following
account presents an incomplete and somewhat skeletal catalogue
of Daribi verbal suffixes. According to the system adopted here,
the order of occurrence of a given suffix is indicated by the figure
in the third decimal place, the 100 series identifying those which
always follow the stem immediately; lexical content is broadly
indicated by the figure in the second decimal place, with the 10
series identifying temporal qualifiers, the 20 series aspect qualifiers,
and the 30 series modal qualifiers.

The verb-stem *tu-*, used as an example here, is applied abstractly;
in practice it always takes an object.

110 Temporal Qualifiers

111 *-ai-*   past action; when used alone, it indicates action in the recent past: *aga tuai*, "he ate (recently)"

112 *-(w)i-*   future action; when used alone, it indicates near future: *nage tuwio*, "you are about to eat"

120 Aspect Qualifiers

121 *-ru-*   state of being: *aga turubo*, "he is eating"

122 *-aru-*   conditional-positional: *e nai torarubo*, "that thing is in a hand"

130 Modal Qualifiers

131 *-aga-*   immediate intention: *ena tuagawe'*, "should I eat?" *ena tuagazare*, "I came to eat"

132 *-gi-*   remote intention: *ena tugi pobao*, "I leave to eat"; *kegi bidigi pau*, "go hunting" ("to seek, to stay, go")

133 *-ainu-*   volition: *ena tuainubao*, "I want to eat"; *aga tuainu-azibo*, "he comes wanting to eat"

134-*go*   "would": *aga pobazora, azigo*, "if he should go, he would come"

210 Temporal Qualifiers

211 *-ia(i)-*   past action in opposition to present (auxiliary use of stem "he does"): *ena tuainu-iai*, "I would like to have eaten"; *aga tuai-iare*, "it was perceived that he had eaten"

212 *-no*   third person near future (with *-(w)i-*): *aga tuino*, "he is about to eat"

220 Aspect Qualifiers

221 -iza-
(-zia-) negation of action: *ena tuizabazora*, "if I should not eat"; *aga tuziama*, . . . , "he not eating, . . ."; *aga tugizagio*, "he must not go and eat!"

320 Aspect Qualifiers

321 -sogo- fulfilled intention: *ena tuaga-sogobe*, "I did not succeed in eating"; *aga tugisogora*, "if he had eaten, . . ."

322 -digi- unfulfilled intention: *ena tugi-digi-dai*, "I wanted to eat and cannot"; *ena tuainu-iai-digi*, "I would like to have eaten but did not"

323 -guri- nearly fulfilled intention: *aga tugi-guri-dai*, "he wanted to eat and just missed eating"

330 Modal Qualifiers

331 -bazo- simultaneity: *aga nai tubazo, po tagarau*, "when he is eating, do not talk"

332 -badi- possibility of action: *aga tubadibo*, "he could be eating"; *aga tuziabadi*, "if he had not eaten, . . ."

333 -buri- concealed action: *aga tuburiare*, "he ate secretly"; *aga turuburiare*, "he was eating secretly"

420 Aspect Qualifiers

421-(r)a- ligative: can connect (inflected or uninflected) stem to completion-of-action qualifiers, clausal ligatives, or can function as a clausal ligative.

when preceded by 121, initial *r* is dropped, and the combination indicates action carried to its conclusion: *aga nai turua-sareo*, "he ate up the food"

when preceded by 321 and 331, subjunctive forms are produced that can act as clausal ligatives: *nai tubazora, da paibao*, "if we eat, we will leave"; *da tugisogora, duagida*, "if we had eaten, it would be good"

520 Aspect Qualifiers

521 -sa- action (now or formerly) in progress (auxiliary use of the stem "take"), usually follows 421: *torasa-perama*, "carrying-went"; *tora-sareo*, "hold"

522 -siri- action finished (auxiliary use of the stem "finish"), follows 421: *perasiriare*, "went altogether"; *nai turuasiribe*, "not finished consuming food"

523 *-mo-* cessation or avoidance of action, negative imperative, follows 421: *nerudu turuamo*, "cease eating tree fruits!" *nage pierama na eramo*, "sleeping, you should not dream!"

530 Modal Qualifiers

531 *-(stem)-* verb stem inserted to qualify verbal action, follows 111, 131, 132, 133, 322, 323, or 421: *ena tugi pobao*, "I leave to eat"; *paiguri tubeo*, "(he) comes, but does not eat"

620 Aspect Qualifiers

621 *-pa-* action leading to loss or absence (auxiliary use of the stem "leave"), follows 421 or 421–521: *serasa pau*, "take it away!" *gegera-pare*, "lost, forgotten"

622 *-ma-* clausal ligative, first action contemporaneous with or leading into second, follows 421; the following verb-stem constitutes or governs an additional clause, and may be inflected with categories in the series 100–800: *perama da saburare*, "going, we arrived"; *nai tuziama da nazibo*, "not eating, we are hungry"

623 *-iu-* clausal ligative; given first action, the second follows, following stem as in 622: *nago homugo suiu*, "if it suffices you, . . ."; *aga ida tagasaiu, aga aia bidiama soare*, "having left his mother, he goes to stay with his father"

710 Temporal Qualifiers

711 *-bao* non-third person, indicates present unless used with 112: *ena tubao*, "I eat"; *nage sobao*, "you proceed"

when following 112, indicates distant future: *ena tuwibao*, "I will eat (later)"

712 *-bo* third person, indicates present unless used with 112: *aga nai tubo*, "he eats food." When following 112, indicates distant future: *aga tuibo*, "he will eat (later)"

713 *-rau* distant past, follows 111: *ena tuairau*, "I have eaten"
714 *-(d)ai*
　(*-wai*) durative, used with 121 to indicate present, ongoing action: *ena be'de bidu-dai*, "I am living in the house"; *ena piruai*, "I am going"

when following 221 with verb-stems indicating perception, indicates that an action formerly not perceived is now perceived: *suiza-wai*, "I did not see, now I do"

720 Aspect Qualifiers

721 -*are*   perfect, action completed: *ena poro tuare,* "I ate before"; *aga boibidi erare,* "he shot the enemy"

722 -*be*   negative: *ena nai tube,* "I do not eat food"; *aga paidigi tubeo,* "he went (in vain) and did not eat"

730 Modal Qualifiers

731 -*au*   second person present imperative: *nage nai tuau,* "you eat food!"

732 -*mainau*   third person present imperative: *aga nai tumainau,* "let him eat food!" *aga eragazamainau,* "let him come kill!"

733 -*gio*   present negative imperative: *nage nai tugio,* "don't you eat!" *aga pigio,* "he should not go!"

734 -*aganio*   future imperative: *nage nai tuaganio,* "you shall (in future) eat!

735 -*gobeo*   future negative imperative: *nage nai tugobeo,* "you shall not (in future) eat!" *aga pogobeo,* "he shall not (in future) go!"

830 Modal Qualifiers

831 -*we'*   Interrogative: *ena tuagawe',* "should I eat?"

Appendix B

Glossary of Daribi Terms

People

bidi: man, men; person, people

we: woman, women

wai': child

wai'bu: infant

mosogobe'rape ("belly button bunch"): tots

wai'buruba: smaller children

ogomane: boy

wegimane: girl

ona'ogwa ("flute boy"): initiate

ogwabidi ("boy-man"): youth

gezibidi ("new man"): youth, unmarried man

wegi-ogwa-we: unmarried woman

we sai bidi ("woman-taken-man"): married man

monu: old man

mozi: old woman

abagi: friend

hana: follower, subordinate

boibidi ("fight man"): enemy

be'bidi ("house man"): clanmate

genuaibidi: important man

gominaibidi: firstborn, leader

toburubidi ("head man"): eldest son

tomubidi ("inside man"): middle son

sabibidi ("namesake man"): youngest son

nozari wegi ("later girl"): youngest daughter

age ("branch"): agemate

hai'namu: co-natal ("born on the same day")

sogoyezibidi ("tobacco spirit"): shaman

animani-wawi-bidi: sorcerer

bidi-egabo-bidi: surgeon

pagebidi ("base man"): close maternal kinsman

nai-gugu-bidi: (generous) affine

izibidi (~yezibidi): ghost

sezemabidi: tree-dwelling bush spirit

izara-we ("epilepsy woman"): underground spirit woman

takarubidi: sky-person

Yasa: Tudawe (Pawaia) people

Belezi: Chimbu (S. Chimbu dialect) people

Erai: Mengino (Gimi) people

Kewa': Kewa' people
Pobori-Bąria: Wiru (Pangia) people

kanama bidi ("tan people"): Europeans

Exchange-Reciprocity

sizibage ("soot things"): vital wealth
ba' nizi ("bird feathers"): trade feathers
tubu nai ("eating things"): food
tegebo: he exchanges
orowagubo: he betrothes (marks)
hagebo: he gives pay
ponabo: he reciprocates with pay
aberebo: he purchases

wei: reciprocity, reciprocally
wei-mawai ("giving back"): to give in return
(*bidi*) *wei-sai* ("taking back"): to kill in return
wei-ponabo ("he pays back"): he pays in return
nai dabau bidi: generous man
nai yogo bidi: tightwad

Speech

po: information, speech, language
> *po mene*: "I have nothing (more) to say"; spoken in anger or satisfaction
> *po page* ("talk base"): origin myth
> *Daribi po*: the Daribi language
> *kanama po* ("tan talk"): Europeans' language
> *waro po*: angry talk
> *wiegi po*: pleasing talk
> *dwaidwai po*: idle talk
> *tibu po*: lie
> *mu po*: true talk
> *iri po* ("grease talk") flattery
> *hai po*: yodelling cry
> *hai' po*: talk about cross-cousins
> ——— *po*: talk about ———
> *kugumini po*: bad smell
> *denami po*: good smell
> *po mibo*: discussion
> *namu po*: storytelling
>> *namu*: story

> *a namu* ("away story"): string figure

po wabo: he talks, speaks ill
> *turubage wabo*: I warn of rain
> *i wabo*: he sings out
> *i mugibo*: the cry echoes
> *gizi wabo*: he laughs
> *sozogo wabo*: he coughs
> *aziga wabo*: he sneezes
> *kono wabo*: he snores

po pusabo: he tells, narrates
poabo: he names
nogi: name
> -*nugiai*: named for ———
sabi: namesake
abagi: friend (greeting)
nagerau: you (singular) remain (farewell)
nage pau: you (singular) go (farewell)
gera urabo: he weeps
pobi gurubo: he says a spell
gebo wiria: eyebrow gesture "yes"

Religion

izibidi (*~yezibidi*): ghost
sogoyezibidi ("tobacco spirit"): shaman
ho: whistle, ghost
Yazumaru: abode of the dead
noma': soul
mobo: breath
izara-we ("epilepsy women"): underground women
bege buru: bad, dangerous place
amazi buru: bad, dangerous place
gura': two-tailed spirit snake
kebidibidi ("cassowary man"): *sangguma* sorcerer
kebidi ge: implement used in *kebidibidi* sorcery
animani: body-substance sorcery
animani wawi bidi: sorcerer
yei: mourning paraphernalia (clay, beads)
ku: exposure coffin
toburudilibe' ("skull house"): small bone-house used in funerary practice
bidi nia sai: dance to celebrate death of an enemy
habu: ceremony to "bring ghost to the house"
　habu be': bush house used by *habubidi*
　habubidi: participants in *habu* who go to the bush

be' habu: participants who stay in house
　doziano habu: small *habu*
gerua: painted board used at pig-feast ceremony
waianu: former ceremony similar to *gerua*
ona': flute used in initiation
paii: spirit fence
na: dream
na iai bidi: dreamer
hare: shame
homu denebo ("his liver hurts"): sorrow
wabu habo: insanity
izara pabo: epilepsy
noma' tagabo ("his soul is absent"): sickness
gazi: sickness
uyabe: leprosy
sozogo: bronchitis, cough
homulebu: pneumonia
auwahorobo: measles
gezia: scabies
sagaiabo: elephantiasis
kere tobu: swollen gums
orotegaibidi: deaf man
wawi: scratch
keni: ulcer
bagabo: leprosy treatment
pobi: magic spell

Time

si (*~hasi*) ("two"): season
　siburu si: siburu season
　waia si: pandanus season
be' ("house"): spell (weather) condition

be' turubage: rainy spell, season
be' porua: moon (clear) season
mama' be': red sunset
aga be' po wabo: their time to talk (insects at night)

be' *kuruguru:* thunder
be' *ziri':* lightning
be' *huribo:* night
-*sogo:* moment
   tesogo: that time
   mesogo: another time
   paresogo: time of having left
nezu: when?
bobenu: for a long time
sezemani: always
sezabi: always
hazia: first
dua: shortly
megi: now, today
nozari: later
porobadu: before
do: yesterday, tomorrow

duba': day before yesterday, after tomorrow
tegiga: third day from, before to-day
ugwago era: fourth day from, before today
ugwa geremo: fifth day from, before today
kigamu: morning
sia ("fire"): noon
pio: afternoon, evening
mobi: old (thing)
monu: old man
mozi: old woman
gezi: new
poro-: previous ――――
ma: again
   me ma iao: do it again!

Place

buru: place
   burubage (*bage,* "thing"): mountain
   burudu (*du,* "lump"): mountain
   digiburu: distant place
maru: plain, place, shore
   Bosiamaru: plains of the River Bosia

ugwa: up, above
aia: down, below
ibu: down, below
era: here
weri: there
mena: where?
   menaba: whither?
   menade: where (at)
   menadu: whence?

General Classification

moni: large
bobe: long
doziano: small
sege: heavy
koza: difficult
mono: unripe
tau: ripe
duagi: good
duare: bad
duai: of no account

ware: fine, useful
bomai: strong
genuai: important
pusu: tasty, sweet
posogo: hot
kerau: cold
doro: right (hand), correct, short, good
pobaze: left (hand), incorrect, long, bad

waro: angry
wiegi: agreeable
mu: true
ozogo: temporary, temporarily
giri: curly
kopi: straight
uni: striped
sizi: black
huzuku: dusky (dark blue, green, brown, black)
ku: light blue, green
bioi: green
terega: light green
sewa': yellow
tau: orange
mama': red
gezi: pink, buff

kanama (~kunumu): tan
keba' si: grey
ohai: white
nerebo: he counts
wabidagi: counting sticks
mene: none
tedeli: one
si: two
sera': three
hauwa: many
maga: what?
  maga nai: what thing? (what is it?)
  magebazo: what do you have? (what is it?)
  mageare: what have you done?

Subsistence

gi: garden
tomagai: upright stake fence
obo: horizontal pole fence
tagia: horizontal angle-fence
dono: digging stick
kare: sweet potato (about 20 varieties)
tą: banana (about 27 varieties)
waia: pandanus fruit (about 20 varieties)
ǫ: taro (about 10 varieties)
o: sago (about 6 varieties)
awi: pitpit (about 18 varieties)
boru: yam (about 17 varieties)
gabo: sugar cane (about 8 varieties)
dabiza, keba, etc.: leaf plants (about 11 varieties)
sogo: tobacco (about 6 varieties)
burugua: large bean (about 5 varieties)

tegabi: smaller bean (about 2 varieties)
niburu: manioc (1 variety)
yuyu: maize (1 variety)
bobi: cucumber
kiba': gourd
siga: breadfruit tree
enelsigi': blackpalm
busu kare: Pueraria lobata
gagi: ginger
dora': tree, *Gnetum gnemon* (Pidgin "tulip")
genage: bamboo, bamboo tube
hąi: edible bamboo
sili: grove, stand of trees
  o sili: sago patch
  waia sili: pandanus grove
ma: mushrooms
pa: white grubs
nǫ: edible butterfly larvae
temiano: fern in which grubs are kept alive

omono: sago chopper

o sizi: sago-working apparatus

o agau: sago leaching trough

sagabidi: sago strainer

obo: sago basin support

yogo pouw: sago settling basin

o wę: sago water

o maziki: sago magic stone

o be': sago-working house

ba: noose snare for cassowary

ba' pai ("bird spirit-fence"): bird-shooting blind

wę ge ("water egg"—puddle): bird blind at bathing place

morobari: blind near bird bower

kę: falling-stick trap for small animals

bu nobari: set of rat lures patrolled by bowman

bunianobe' (pandanus-leaf house): small shelter used as hunting lodge

koya: broad, bamboo-headed pig-arrow

yaga ("comb"): forked bird-arrow

sobo: needle-like wooden man-arrow

hoyabi: man arrow with tip of *hoyabi* bone

tori: man arrow with tip of cassowary bone

yaga sezemoni ("comb spear"): forked spear for catching eels

hagani: string bag and cane fish net

hogobi'a: bamboo tube fish trap

wę paribo: earthen dam used in fishing

busu: vine used for poisoning fish

wago: vine used for poisoning fish

togozo-ware: tree bark used for poisoning fish

Material Culture

nia: rear-covering (tanget)

hariga-buru ("gut covering"): loincloth net

kerua huguru: cane belt

weria: woven belt

    geru weriai ("eyes fastened"): blind

abe: shoulder strap

togomane: leg band

mo: woven arm band

harape: lake-grass skirt

ugwa: bark cloak

ge ("egg"): crescent pearl shell

kuziki: cowrie shell

yane: cowrie headband

po: shell disk head-ornament

taraba: shell disk head-ornament

wiare: headdress of small shells

dani: shell earring

guni parawe: pig-tusk nosepiece

kagame: linked shell bracelet

huę: ax, knife

    weri huę: round stone club head

    taru hua: round stone club head

    yazare huę: old-style stone ax

    kaia huę: greenstone ax

    kago huę ("cargo ax"): steel ax

    huę di ("ax excrement"): rust

kobe: ax

sinami: chert flake knife

a'wa: full-size bark shield

sezemoni: spear, javelin

ene: arrow
  enelzigi ("arrow stick"): bow
  enebereli: bamboo arrow-sheath
sąburi: wooden chest-shield
  ugwa sąburi: folded bark-cloak "shield"
ozu-ni: tally arrow
bonosezemo: tally rope
pouw: wooden bowl
ną ("shoulder blade"): spoon
genage: bamboo water, cooking, tube
sogonage: bamboo pipe
oboro: stone "mortar" bowl
wa: net bag
  agure wa: basket
o'ro': fiber bag
some: mat
wiru: bark-cloth pounder
uwau: top
mege: tree gum
denema': tree oil used as salve
husare: white, powdery poison
nabi: white poison
kerua: cane, stick
bono: rope
be': house
  sigibe': two-story house
  kerobe': one-story house
  tǫbe': ground-floored house
  bunianobe': pandanus-leaf house
  temianobe': temi-leaf house (for childbirth)
  torianobe': tori-leaf house (for menstruation)

habu-be': house for *habu* ceremonial hunters
sai be': tree-branch nest
  bidigibe': men's quarters
  aribe': women's quarters
mabo: veranda
togobidi: ladder
gezabidibadu ("face place"): front of house
bogobadu ("wing place"): side of house
turibadu ("back place"): back of house
turubu ni: house post
sue: floor
kau: floor
kau ni: floor beam
uru: bark flooring
taka: wall
mename: crosspiece
enesobare: roof beam
warawa: roof stringer
pe'ru: roof
pe'ru ni ("roof tree"): roof centerpole
tǫ: road, door
pagu: fire-making apparatus
ara: fire tongs
sia: fire, firewood
  sia keni: firebox
geba': dugout canoe
sezeba: raft
habasigi: paddle
ta': vine bridge

Body Parts

wai' tabi ("childgut"): womb
be' ("house"): afterbirth

mosogobe: navel cord
ware: skin

dili: bone
    toburudili: skull
    turidili: spine
para: rib cage
punari: rib
mị: muscle tissue
iri: fat
kamine: blood
kawa: semen
ami: milk, female breast
kere: tooth, teeth
    ami kere ("milk teeth"): baby teeth
    kere mu ("true teeth") permanent teeth
gui: vagina, female genitals
kai: penis
sogori (du): testicles
hoburudu: heart
dinihomu: lung
homu: liver
sine: spleen
muahaza: pancreas
moni hamago: stomach
tabi: intestines
hariga: intestines
(en)enawe: kidney
pobi: bladder
poi: urine
di: feces
nizi: hair, fur, feathers
    toburunizi: head hair
    giritoburunizi: curly hair
    kopitoburunizi: straight hair
    gerunizi: eyebrows
    penarenizi: beard
toburu: head
abuai: brains
turuguare: brains
gezabidi: face
gebo: forehead

geru: eye
    geru ge ("eye egg"): eyeball
oro: ear
    oro ge ("ear egg"): earlobe
guni: nose
    guni ge ("nose egg"): nasal septum
    guni tụ ("nose door"): nostril
naboge: cheek
peraware: mouth
hamena: tongue
penare: chin
togoni: throat
    togoni ge: Adam's apple
horo: back of the neck
nạ: shoulder
hagawia: chest
aguriawe: armpit
nogo: arm, hand, finger
    nogo habu ("arm buttock"): elbow
    nogo samare: palm
    nogo ge: knuckles
    nogo dani: fingernail
    a nogo (saga): thumb (large toe)
    tuni nogo (saga): index finger (second toe)
    tomu nogo (saga): middle, ring fingers (third and fourth toes)
    kibizare nogo (saga): little finger (last toe)
kiru: wrist
habu: buttocks
turi: back
sili: hip
teli: thigh
saga: leg, foot, toe
    saga saware: bottom of foot
    saga dani: toenails

pizini: lower leg
kigibidi: leg tendon
po: ankle

bagaware: tattoo
mazaru: scar

Nature

giliga-ge ("sun pearl shell"): sun
sia ("fire"): sun
porua-ge (moon pearl shell): moon
  moni porua ("big moon"): full moon
  kege we ("woman seeking"): crescent moon
ho: star, firefly
takaru: sky
  takarubidi: sky people
ura': light, flame
sia: fire, firewood
sore: torch
hanu: smoke
to: ground, soil
tu: road, door
maziki: stone
aze: limestone
sagara: limestone
sau: cliff
paro: ravine
  sauparo: gorge
ora': (habitable) cave
bogwanu: pothole
turubage: rain
po: cloud, mist
  buru po: cumulus clouds
wari: wind
mazhuku: windstorm
mari: earthquake
we: water
  we gomo ("water head"): source
  wege: puddle

ai: stream, river
  ai sabo ("stream—it takes"): waterfall
  sigi ai ("pitpit stream"): lake
  mama ai ("red river"): Tua River
hawari: Tua River
gibu: the bush
ni: tree
  ni yape: tree leaf
  ni age: tree branch
  ni ware ("tree skin"): bark
perabo: epiphyte
kari: oak
  kari-du: acorn
abo: beech
ge: kunai grass
genage: bamboo
hai: edible bamboo
so: man-trap bamboo
hai: stinging nettle
nizizibi ("hair lineage"): those animals with hair, fur, or feathers
ba': bird
wiliba' ("wild bird"): bird of prey
temiano: harpy eagle
kemurage: crested hawk
bogobobiai: Australian sparrow hawk
temesogo: Indian Hobby
aziba: white hawk
moroli: sooty owl
tagoa: bush owl

kuguri: barn owl, frogmouth, nightjar

węsi: hornbill

hanari: eclectus parrot

pini: Menbeki coucal

buziba: cuckoo

teaburu: pigeon

nara, terawai: white cockatoo

tąri: corvine bird

puri: red bird of paradise

kawari: red and black parrot

wakuare: megadode

wąri: megapode

tori, kebi: cassowary

bogwa: small bat

tumani: large bat

haza: animal

so: female animal

omai: male animal

yowi: dog

pusi yowi: cat

  sebari yowi: dasyurus (marsupial carnivore)

  uni-yowi ("striped dog"): dasyurus (marsupial carnivore)

domu: echidna

hoyo: wallaby

u'gwa': large tree kangaroo

gawaihaza: Doria's tree kangaroo

mubu: ring-tail

hoyabi: cuscus (Phlanger species)

ogio: striped possum

kezebe: bandicoot

boboro: water rats

boro: rat

sidawi: mouse

dononi: flying phalanger

nizimeniaizibi ("hairless lineage"): animals without fur or feathers

aziba: insect

dinai: fly

bunu: bee

nenemo: wasp

horagape: spider

kawabidi: phasmid

manu: katydid

bena: leech

horogi: monitor lizard

tonigi: smaller tree lizard

yogwa: salamander

gereli: frog

hazamoni ("animal-big"): snake

yowa: python

unigibidi: iridescent snake, rainbow

ai haza: stream animals

hawari haza: kind of eel

sugu: fish

obiare: catfish

Verbs of Equation

qwiai (equation of things): *te pusi yowi qwiai,* "that cat is like a dog."; *te tą ni qwiai,* "that banana is like a tree"

tiwai erarubo (equation of qualities): *eno bomu tiwai nago me bomu erarubo,* "my strength is as your strength"

meniraba' (metaphorical equation): *ba' po urubo meniraba',* "it is as though birds were singing"

Verbs

bidibo: (a spontaneous being) is there

    orobidizhu: visit

erabo: it is (fixed) there

pabo: he leaves

    ozogo pabo: he leaves temporarily

    izara pabo: he has an epileptic seizure

    borapabo: he flies

    kega pabo: it foams

soabo: he continues in motion

azibo: he comes

iabo: he does

    kaga-iabo ("knotting"): he transforms himself

sẹ ebo: he works

sabo: he takes

wi-sabo ("he takes in fear"): he steals

    turubage sabo: he causes rain

    bagura sabo: he surrounds

    pobia sabo: he folds

    siazabo: (the fire) is finished

mabo: he gives

    i ora mabo: he curses

ebazo: he has

muabo: he places, puts

tubo: he eats, drinks

    nono tubo: he kisses (puppies and small children)

    sogo tubo: he smokes

nabo: he eats

subo: he sees

orobo: he hears

erebo (~*enebo*): he shoots

eremubo: he kills

torabo: he holds

dorabo: he stands

duguabo: he sits

buribo: he (it) encloses, wears

tagabo: he is absent, has ceased (doing something)

hwebo: he strikes

paibo: he fastens

usuabo: he (it) suffices

    nage usura ("you suffice"): compliment, word of encouragement

dinibo: he removes

tuabo: he holds

perabo: he breaks

abo: he breaks off

tonabo: he looks

turuabo: he makes

suabo: he jumps

saiabo: he throws

denebo: it hurts

segebo: it is heavy

saburabo: he arrives

sewebo: he builds

izibo: he dies

gazibo: he is sick

nazibo: he is hungry

gizibo: he laughs

pibo: he sleeps

wibo: he is afraid, fears

kegebo: he seeks

gerebo: he cuts

    gera: clear out!

horobo: he climbs up

    uguru horobo: he hiccups

durubo: he climbs down

tabo: he excretes

    di tabo: he defecates

    poi tabo: he urinates

turuabo: he plants

warabo: it hangs

durabo: he hides
dɑrabo: (the fire) burns
siribo: he finishes
tɑbo: he copulates
mobo: he shows
segabo: he fetches
begebo: he turns (it) over
pobo: he sharpens
hobo: he ducks, crouches
kagaribo: he plays
oi-bo: he is happy
hagarabo: he dislikes, is tired of
sagobo: he picks up
degebo: it falls
gebo: he turns (it) around
sobo: he sews
degabo: he digs
tobo: he kneads
paribo: he fastens, holds fast
manabo: it balances
waribo: (the wind) blows
maribo: (it) earthquakes
dabo: he kindles (a fire)
piribo: he paints
pororobo: he drills, bores
harubo: he flakes (stone)
sarebo: he straightens
gonabo: he twists off
durobo: he sharpens

togobo: he pokes
perebo: he wedges open
bogubo: he vomits
oramabo: he shows
kegabo: he pushes
pogorabo: he pulls
perabo: he tears
urabo: he cooks
obo: he dries
wabu habo: he is insane
wɛ paubo: he washes
poba gebo: he spins
tabisobo: he removes (the insides)
kaga nigibo: he ties a knot
kaga pesagabo: he unties a knot
  pesage: evidence
wa ebo: he weaves
sizibo: he dyes
tagibo: he shows (something to)
nogabo: he cooks, prepares (food)
wɛ teraio: to wash
tomagobo: he ties up
  tomagobe': Eastern Highlands type "round house"
gera urabo: he cries, weeps
sɛgabo: he wrings out
hoborebo: he mourns

Bibliography

Aufenanger, H., and G. Holtker
  1940   *Die Gende in Zentralneuguinea.* Vienna and Mödling: St.
         Gabriel.
Barnes, J. A.
  1962   "African Models in the New Guinea Highlands," *Man* 62: 5.
Barrau, J.
  1958   *Subsistence Agriculture in Melanesia.* Honolulu: Bernice P.
         Bishop Museum Publication No. 223.
Bateson, G.
  1936   *Naven.* Cambridge: Cambridge University Press.
Berndt, R. M.
  1954-5 "Kamano, Jate, Usurufa and Fore Kinship of the Eastern
         Highlands of New Guinea," *Oceania* 25: 23-53, 156-87.
  1962   *Excess and Restraint: Social Control among a New Guinea
         Mountain People.* Chicago: University of Chicago Press.
Brookfield, H. C., and P. Brown
  1963   *Struggle for Land: Agriculture and Group Territories among
         the Chimbu of the New Guinea Highlands.* Melbourne: Ox-
         ford University Press.
Brown, P.
  1960   "Chimbu Tribes: Political Organization in the Eastern High-
         lands of New Guinea," *Southwestern Journal of Anthropol-
         ogy* 16: 22-35.
  1961   "Chimbu Death Payments," *Journal of the Royal Anthro-
         pological Institute* 91: 77.
  1962   "Non-Agnates among the Patrilineal Chimbu," *Journal of
         the Polynesian Society* 71: 57-69.
Brown, P., and H. C. Brookfield
  1959   "Chimbu Land and Society," *Oceania* 30: 1-75.
Bulmer, R. N. H.

1960 "Political Aspects of the Moka Ceremonial Exchange System among the Kyaka People," *Oceania* 31: 1-13.

Bulmer, S., and R. Bulmer
1964 "The Prehistory of the Australian New Guinea Highlands," *American Anthropologist* 66, No. 4, Part 2 (special publication: *New Guinea, The Central Highlands,* ed. J. B. Watson).

Champion, Ivan
1940 "The Bamu-Purari Patrol," *Geographical Journal* 96, No. 4: 243.

Fortes, Meyer
1953 "The Structure of Unilineal Descent Groups," *American Anthropologist* 55: 17.
1959 "Descent, Filiation and Affinity: A Rejoinder to Dr. Leach: Part II," *Man* 59: 206.

Glasse, R. M.
1959a "Revenge and Redress among the Huli: a Preliminary Account," *Mankind* 5: 273-89.
1959b "The Huli Descent System: A Preliminary Account," *Oceania* 29: 171-83.
1965 "Leprosy at Karamui," *Papua and New Guinea Medical Journal* 8, No. 3: 95-98.

Glick, L. B.
1964 "Categories and Relations in Gimi Natural Science," *American Anthropologist* 66, No. 4, Part 2 (special publication: *New Guinea, The Central Highlands,* ed. J. B. Watson).

Great Britain
1945 Naval Intelligence Division, Geographical Handbook Series, Pacific Islands, Vol. IV.

Held, C. J.
1957 *The Papuas of Waropen.* The Hague: Nijhoff.

Keleny, G. P.
1962 "The Origin and Introduction of the Basic Food Crops of the New Guinea People," *Papua and New Guinea Agricultural Journal* 15, Nos. 1 and 2: 7-13.

Landtman, G.
1917 *The Folk-Tales of the Kiwai Papuans.* Helsingfors: Acta Societas Scientarum Fennicae, Vol. 42.
1927 *The Kiwai Papuans of British New Guinea.* London: MacMillan.

Langness, L.
1964 "Some Problems in the Conceptualization of Highlands Social Structures," *American Anthropologist* 66, No. 4, Part 2 (special publication: *New Guinea, The Central Highlands,* ed. J. B. Watson).

266   Bibliography

Leahy, Michael, and M. Crain
   1937   The Land That Time Forgot: Adventures and Discoveries
           in New Guinea. New York: Funk and Wagnalls.
Mauss, Marcel
   1954   The Gift, trans. Ian Cunnison. Glencoe, Ill.: Free Press.
Meggitt, M. J
   1957   "Enga Political Organization, a Preliminary Description,"
           Mankind 5: 133–37
   1962   "Growth and Decline of Agnatic Descent Groups among the
           Mae Enga," Ethnology 1: 158–65.
   1964   "The Kinship Terminology of the Mae Enga of New
           Guinea," Oceania 34: 191–200.
   1965   The Lineage System of the Mae Enga. Edinburgh: Oliver
           and Boyd.
Meggitt, M. J., and P. Lawrence
   1965   Gods, Ghosts and Men in Melanesia: Some Religions of
           Australian New Guinea and the New Hebrides. Melbourne
           and London: Oxford University Press.
Newman, P. L.
   1964   "Religious Belief and Ritual in a New Guinea Society,"
           American Anthropologist 66, No. 4, Part 2 (special publica-
           tion: New Guinea, The Central Highlands, ed. J. B. Wat-
           son).
   1965   Knowing the Gururumba. New York: Holt, Rinehart and
           Winston.
Pospisil, L.
   1958   Kapauku Papuans and Their Law. New Haven: Yale Publi-
           cations in Anthropology No. 54.
   1960   "The Kapauku Papuans and Their Kinship Organization,"
           Oceania 30: 188–206.
   1963   The Kapauku Papuans of West New Guinea. New York:
           Holt, Rinehart and Winston.
Pouwer, J
   1960   "Loosely Structured Societies in Netherlands New Guinea,"
           Bijdragen tot de Taal-, Land-, en Volkenkunde 116: 109–
           206.
   1964   "A Social System in the Star Mountains: Toward a Re-
           orientation of the Study of Social Systems," American
           Anthropologist 66, No. 4, Part 2 (special publication: New
           Guinea, The Central Highlands, ed. J. B. Watson).
Read, K. E.
   1954a   "Cultures of the Central Highlands, New Guinea," South-
           western Journal of Anthropology 10: 1–43.
   1954b   "Marriage among the Gahuku-Gama of the Eastern Central
           Highlands, New Guinea," South Pacific 7: 864–70.

1959   "Leadership and Consensus in a New Guinea Society," *American Anthropologist* 61: 425–36.
1965   *The High Valley.* New York: Scribners.
Reay, M.
1959   *The Kuma: Freedom and Conformity in the New Guinea Highlands.* Melbourne: Melbourne University Press.
Robbins, R. G.
1961   "The Vegetation of New Guinea," *Australian Territories* 1: 21–32.
Ryan, D'A. J.
1955   "Clan Organization in the Mendi Valley," *Oceania* 26: 79–90.
1959   "Clan Formation in the Mendi Valley," *Oceania* 29: 257–89.
Salisbury, R. F.
1956   "Unilineal Descent Groups in the New Guinea Highlands," *Man* 56: 2–7.
1962   *From Stone to Steel.* Melbourne: Melbourne University Press.
1964   "New Guinea Highland Models and Descent Theory," *Man* 64: 168–171.
Schneider, D. M.
1965   "Some Muddles in the Models: Or, How the System Really Works," in *The Relevance of Models for Social Anthropology,* A.S.A. Monograph No. 1. London: Tavistock Publications; New York: Frederick A. Praeger.
Schneider, D. M., and K. Gough
1962   *Matrilineal Kinship.* Berkeley: University of California Press.
Souter, G.
1966   *New Guinea: The Last Unknown.* New York: Taplinger.
Vicedom, G. F., and H. Tischner
1945   *Die Mbowamb, Die Kultur Der Hagenberg-Stämme im Ostlichen Zentral Neuguinea.* 3 vols. Hamburg: Monographien zur Völkerkunde, Hambürghischen Museum für Völkerkunde.
Watson, J. B.
1964   "A Previously Unreported Root Crop from the New Guinea Highlands," *Ethnology* 3, No. 1.
1965   "From Hunting to Horticulture in the New Guinea Highlands," *Ethnology* 4, No. 3.
Williams, F. E.
1924   *The Natives of the Purari Delta.* Anthropological Report No. 5, issued by the Government of Papua.
1930   *Orokaiva Society.* London: Oxford University Press.
1940a   *The Drama of Orokolo.* Oxford: Clarendon Press.
1940b   *Natives of Lake Kutubu, Papua.* Oceania Monograph No. 6. Sydney: The Australian National Research Council.

Wurm, S. A.
1964   "Australian New Guinea Highlands Languages and the Distribution of Their Typological Features," *American Anthropologist* 66, No. 4, Part 2 (special publication: *New Guinea, The Central Highlands*, ed. J. B. Watson).

Index